T0339816

THROUGH ALIEN EYES

Through Alien Eyes

A View of America and Intercultural Marriages

Elena Popova

Algora Publishing
New York

Library of Congress Cataloging-in-Publication Data —

Popova, Elena, 1963-
    Through alien eyes : a view of America and intercultural marriages / Elena Popova.
        p. cm.
    Includes bibliographical references.
    ISBN 978-0-87586-639-0 (trade paper: alk. paper) — ISBN 978-0-87586-640-6 (case
laminate: alk. paper) — ISBN 978-0-87586-641-3 (ebook) 1. Intercountry marriage—
United States. 2. Popova, Elena, 1963- 3. Men—United States. 4. Women—Russia
(Federation) 5. Women immigrants—United States—Social conditions. 6. Russians—
United States. I. Title.

    HQ1032.P67 2008
    306.84'50973—dc22
                          2008030287

Front Cover:
    Above: Diners Enjoying View of Brooklyn Bridge from the River Cafe. The River
    Cafe in Brooklyn overlooking the Brooklyn Bridge, the East River and lower
    Manhattan. Image: © Mark Peterson/CORBIS
    Below: Stepping Out, 1978 by Roy Lichtenstein (American, 1923–1997) (Metropolitan
    Museum of Art)
Back cover: Photo of the author by Louis Sapienza

Printed in the United States

To my mother

Table of Contents

"How did you get to the United States?"

Upon discovering that I come from Russia, 99.99% of Americans ask the same question, sure as the solstice. "How did you get to the United States?"

I give them the short answer. "By plane!"

"Uh..." The first recipient of my technically accurate reply, a Russian Jewish woman, now a Californian, was momentarily speechless. "Well, you know — we want a story!"

I can promise you a story, for sure, because after vacationing in the United States numerous times, I finally married an American — a Southern boy, just so y'all know — whom I met for the first time in Spain. My marital-Martian-intercultural experience enabled me to modify my answer to the unavoidable question. In the South, the dialog sounded something like this:

"What brought you hyah?" the Southern belles pried, their intuitive antennas almost visibly tuning in. ['Are-you-one-of-them-mail-order-brides?']

"Stupidity." ['I-am-not-and-thank-you-for-not-asking-again!']

"So, was it 'bout a ma-an? Oh, bless your hea-art!"

But in traditional Russian manner foreigners are always allowed to go first, so I will begin with some observations of the American lifestyle. This story is not simply and solely about alien women's issues, but just as much about Americans and America, including things that usually are left unsaid. "One of our greatest needs as a nation is to understand how other people see us."[1]

I definitely am "other people" — I try to keep that fresh eye even though I am a naturalized American now. I trust the recipients of these views are ready, and I hope that I can claim that "special kind of vision afforded to those on the outskirts

---

1 Mary Pipher, *The Middle of Everywhere*

of society. From the vantage point of the outsider, it may be easier to see beyond limited cultural assumptions and analyze American culture more critically."[1]

I realize that Americans are not used to criticism, unfortunately for the nation as a whole, and hence some comments may not be accepted lightly. I was advised to steer in the comforting direction of cute self-irony, making an entertaining memoir about foreigners' laughable adventures in the US instead of stepping on American toes, for "self-doubt is not in style with Americans at the moment," as one literary agent mentioned. But I was aiming for "a truthful book, not the sort of thing that wins friends," as Tom Clancy put it. Let's see if I'll be allowed to do that.

As if to make my vantage point even more intriguing, I was anchored in the South, which is a country inside the country, if I may say so. In the deep South, it feels like the Civil War was lost just yesterday, Yankees are called foreigners (this made me feel better), traveling to the neighboring county for a couple of days awakens homesickness in a true local, and a trip abroad is considered as a dubious and dangerous adventure. Speaking about her first trip to Europe with a church mission, a young blonde, a daughter of a Southern preacher, recalled a dumpster with construction debris that they discovered in the backyard of the Grand Opera in Paris and used as a background for taking their European pictures; the other memorable thing was the unsatisfying French food — she seriously missed the hearty Southern breakfast: you can take a girl out of South but you cannot take the South out of the girl.

The longer you live in the South, the more you become attached to its ever-blooming nature, the ever-shining sun, the picturesque homesteads, and the religiously mown lawns. Stress, the inevitable companion of more dynamic lifestyles, starts looking less and less attractive in comparison with simple, cozy country living.

My broad impressions about the US and Americans, together with a much-treasured discovery of the country, are based on my prenuptial experiences. I was quite a world traveler before I got married. Sometimes I joked that my life "before" was like scenes from National Geographic episodes: I talked to British royalty, teased Yeltsin, chased bears (not beers), videotaped a volcanic eruption from a helicopter in synch with a NASA satellite to create a 3D model, walked on the ocean floor in a hard suit, and so on.

When I first came to America, the story about our arrival was on the first pages of *The Seattle Times* for two consecutive days — we managed to earn a celebrity's measure in the news, and even ten years later the newspaper did not miss a chance to mark the anniversary of our unforgettable advent. All that commotion occurred because the Russians were coming in a special manner — our notorious Aeroflot flight could not find the airport. It is still unknown to the public what

---

1 Jennifer Gillan, *Growing Up Ethnic in America*

happened in the cockpit, but in the cabin we sure were worn out after descending several times very low above the highway — were we going to land there, squeezing our way into the traffic? — and then climbing again. There was no panic, though. Probably the forbearing Russians thought that it was a typical American way of approaching the runway. So when I talked to the immigration officer, I was far more worried about the rebellious situation in my stomach than about the obligatory positive impression one has to make when crossing the US border. The officer was nice, but his questions seemed endless, and when we had finished with the mandatory inquiries about the purpose of my visit, he came to some more piquant ones. "Are you married?"

"No."

"Why not?"

I even forgot momentarily that I was green around the gills. "You know, I'm a journalist — it's usually *my* job to ask questions!" [and I don't let myself intrude so aggressively!]

"Well, it's my job, too!"

At that moment we both were laughing. He understood what I had just rephrased in a polite manner, and I realized that the interrogation was unavoidable, so why not to carry on with some humor?

Little did I know then that the compulsory questionnaire hasn't changed much since the end of the 19th century, when some 5,000–6,000 immigrants were passing every day though the facilities of Ellis Island. I had a shocking flash of déjà vu when I saw those thirty-two obligatory questions on display in the Nordic Heritage Museum in Seattle. Just try any of those for an *American* traveler: "Are you single or married?" "Where is your wife/husband?" "Do you have children? Where are they?" "How do you earn your living in your country of origin?" "Who paid for your passage here?" "How much money do you have? May I see it?" "With whom do you live?" "Where are you going to live in America?" (I wrote: "In a red tent in Yosemite.") But at least modern visitors are spared of health checkups in rustic Ellis Island style — the officers inspected the arrivals for the signs of trachoma, which was an incurable disease then, turning out eyelids with hooks intended for buttoning shoes (this was before the invention of Velcro). It scares me even to think how those hooks were sanitized between the customers — the photos show officials working with towels stuck in their belts.

But my first tryst with an American officer brings up only the best memories. I crossed the border laughing and waving to the official. It was nothing like entering the country of the "former potential enemy." The officer gave me a hint that there are some good men among Americans — in case I did not like my countrymen, for some reason.

The "genuine" American from my welcome group had made, along with his wife, a further positive impression. I call them "my American parents." This couple had visited places in the Soviet Union where even I have not been, so they were familiar with Russian warmth and hospitality and they welcomed Russian visitors in the same style.

During my farther roaming around the US, I was lucky to travel from Alaska to Hawaii and from New York to Florida. Envy me — I have seen many beauties of nature in this land: the scorching thermal fields of Yellowstone, the flaming November sunsets of the Grand Tetons, the outlandish stone sculptures of Utah and Colorado, the mammoth redwoods of California, the sea rocks in Connecticut that were torn off African coast when the continents started sailing apart, as my friend, a Yale University professor, told me... Deep in the country, I might have been the first Russian the locals had ever met. They probably thought I was a crazy Russian, too, so carelessly driving around alone. But I felt safe. I usually do — I visited Central Park in New York for the first time after sunset. I took some good pictures and even contrived to meet a healer there.

"You met who — a killer?" My New Yorkers were horrified.

"No, a *healer*! A Filipino healer." The healer brought to my attention some "Central Park Rules," such as not to walk close to the shrubbery in order to avoid a surprise attack. But generally I was aware of everyday life and the cultural backgrounds of the Americans thanks to a first-hand source — American literature, which was widely available in the Soviet Union.

While the American public was spoon-fed with tidbits about life in the USSR from the US propaganda stock, the "evil Soviets" were amply supplying their public libraries with outstanding translations of modern and classical American literature, excluding pulp fiction. When we were kids, we soaked up scary stories by Edgar Allan Poe and the adventures of noble Indians by James Fennimore Cooper. In snowy Russia, Jack London's Alaskan stories fit right in, and Mark Twain made the Mississippi such a Southern river for us that when I saw it *ice-covered* in Minneapolis it was like witnessing a frozen inferno. Henry Longfellow's *Hiawatha*, I swear, sounds even better in the perfectly rhythmic and alliterative Russian translation produced by the famous Russian Nobelist Ivan Bunin. O. Henry was translated so brilliantly that his aphoristic jokes became proverbs in Russia. Consequently, Americans should share responsibility for injecting Soviet kids with the hopeless romanticism that Russians are already prone to. Later, Soviet teenagers moved on, from Carson McCullers and Francis Scott Fitzgerald to such "heavy artillery" as Henry Miller and Norman Mailer, while mass readers preferred Ken Kizi, Kurt Vonnegut, John Updike...

To some extent, this arm-chair traveling, reading about other cultures, might have been compensation for the lack of opportunity to roam the world freely during the Soviet era, but Russia was always a country of readers — now, just like everywhere else, computers and soap operas glue their cohorts to the screen.

When I was trying to locate Mr. Porter's grave in Asheville, I found out that the university students who took a shortcut through the cemetery had no idea who O. Henry was. I hope that *gloria mundi* incident did not make the great fellow turn in his grave. As I discovered, to my amazement, many Russians of my generation know American writers better than most genuine Americans, and now one in four Americans have reported they read no books at all these days.[1]

No wonder I had that strange sensation during my first visits to the United States: being in a foreign country, I did not really feel that I was abroad. I have felt more estranged visiting some republics in the former Soviet Union, where I couldn't speak or understand the local languages and where the people were on guard and sometimes even rude towards outsiders. But every minus has a plus, indeed — at least it had seasoned me for the amusing Southern affectation of welcome, "with false passion and air of phony kindness."[2] Of course, I do not imply that all Southerners emit phoniness, but the majority is very cliquish — it takes several generations to be accepted in a Southern county. I endorse Grisham's conclusion, "One cannot simply move there and be trusted. A dark cloud of suspicion hangs over any newcomer and I was no exception. The people there are exceedingly warm and gracious and polite, almost to the point of being nosy."[3] I am not that sure about "exceeding warmth," though — from my observation, Northerners socialize much more. I even thought that so-called Southern hospitality was an oxymoron until one Southerner enlightened me: "Southern hospitality is for Southerners only." That made sense.

Though I wasn't one of those wide-eyed, brazenly brave — or blind, if you wish — mail-order brides from the former Soviet Union whose first visit abroad was the trip to America to join their brand-new American husbands, my cosmopolitan experience did not safeguard me from a completely different set of problems related to making a home — and a family — in a foreign country. And I should have known better about the choices and consequences. There is a Russian joke that tells of a recently departed man who was choosing between heaven and hell: heaven seemed a tad too boring to him, but hell was a rattler — fountains with champagne, easy women, casinos.

"Hang on — I'll finish my paperwork and be right back!" the man told his Black Jack partners. But when he came back, he couldn't recognize the place: his card partners were screaming in hellfire.

"Hey, where is the casino, the girls?" the man asked Satan.

The devil flashed his devilish smile, "Dude, don't you mix up tourism with immigration anymore!"

"Every joke has a touch of truth," Ronald Reagan could say, as he liked to quote Russian proverbs during his meetings with the Soviets. He was not my favorite

---

1 Alan Fram, "One in four read no books last year," Associated Press, August 21, 2007
2 Jim Harrison, *True North*
3 John Grisham, *The Last Juror*

American president, though — I doubt he is for any Russian. Our hearts belong to Bill Clinton, but I do not envy his "iron lady" of a wife. I was vacationing in the US, leaving for Russia, coming back again — Mr. Clinton's exploits were the immutable main topic on the mass-media agenda, like a never-ending soap opera. It looked like America, with its blooming economy and superficially smooth political relationships, did not have any other, more serious problems than the Clintons' private business while riding the gravy train. But definitely, the Oval Office philandering did hit a national nerve, and certain alien wives' stories may complement that kind of shame.

On my way to those stories, I'll sketch some insider's impressions of life during the end of the Soviet era and of the sentiments of the period, since Americans knew much less about those living on the other side of the notorious iron curtain than we knew about them.

My criticism of American life should be taken as a study of a fellow-citizen — dividing American-born and American-by-law citizens into first and second class would be so politically incorrect — but I anticipate that setting up bristles is unavoidable, and that would be natural reaction. As the Russian poet Alexander Pushkin said in his widely quoted letter to Vyazemskiy (May 27, 1827), "I may deride my motherland from head to toe, but I would be annoyed if a foreigner shared my opinion."

This kind of righteous anger also shows that a person cares; indifference is a bad sign. No wonder that I earned a string of strong epithets: "My mind revolves around such words as tongue-lashing, scathing, verbal abuse, denunciation, obloquy, vituperation, invective, vehemence, derision," a nice Southern gentleman wrote to me, after reading a chapter with an excerpt from a popular Russian newspaper about American gentlemen touring "Russia for love."

Tongue-lashing was definitely not my goal, although I disagree that a foreigner's self-irony is welcomed while American life is out of bonds for critical assessment. I do not care for the primitive black-and-white picture of the world where everything about America is obligatorily panegyric and the criticism is reserved for others. The outside world has started to show less and less tolerance for such a position, and adopting an antagonistic style is not in American interests — even former national security adviser Zbigniew Brzezinski, known for his hawkish foreign policy, points that out. Some twenty years ago, I would never have guessed that I would quote the renowned Cold War ideologist, yet here I am, respectfully adding Brzezinski's name to my MS Word spell-check vocabulary...

Inarguably, newcomers, especially from the countries with troubled political regimes, appreciate the way of living and the respect for law and order that America bestows on them. But if the idea is to make this country an even better place, resting on one's oars won't do — there is still a lot of room for betterment. We are humans, not angels, and we live in imperfect societies.

I cannot possibly be a good guy to everybody and walk on eggshells speaking of alien spouses — and newcomers in general — in America, nor can I be a glacial researcher, for it is my very life, after all. So expect some candid emotions. And some humor: the world has survived this long because it laughed, and surviving in America is much easier if one prefers to laugh rather than cry.

Laughing helps save on shrinks, too, which is especially handy if you cannot afford them.

Needless to say, the circumstances described and the names of non-public figures have been changed; any similarities to real persons are accidental.

Serious Stuff: Food

"What do you usually have for breakfast?" my future mother-in-law asked me over the phone, fussing about our visit.

"Oh, don't you worry, please," I reassured her. "Just a regular Russian breakfast will be fine."

"And what would that be?"

"Why, vodka and caviar, of course!" (Do I have to stress that I was kidding? Go figure — you will understand my precautions when reading about cow's hooves.)

My mother asked me what I eat in America, too — it's a motherly thing, I guess, though she never wondered what I ate, for example, in Turkey, or in Spain, or anywhere else for that matter. But when my Russian friends started asking me the same questions, What do you eat? What do you cook? I realized that the meal theme is a big one, indeed.

In fact, I did have to search out a healthy and simple breakfast solution. I was craving for my favorite *tvorog* — a sort of cottage cheese, but without that crude salty taste. It resembles ricotta cheese but is lighter and tastes absolutely delicious with blueberries, sour cream, raisins, or fruit preserves. Luckily, it can be easily made from sour milk, but curdling that stubborn antibiotic-preserved deadly-pasteurized milk is a hard task. After a fruitless attempt to make it on the sly in the fridge, adding some sour cream as a booster — equally deadly-pasteurized booster, though — I gave up and put the milk in the kitchen cabinet, tucking the jug behind the bottled water. And there it was found by my husband.

"What on the earth is the milk doing here?"

If I were not the one who'd hid it, I would have asked the same question.

"I'm going to cook something..." I murmured shyly.

"To cook? How can you cook anything from that? This milk is spoiled!"

Technically speaking, all sour milk products, all cheeses and yogurts, are "spoiled" by bacteria, and that doped milk had come to a perfectly curdy condition at last. Still, it was hard to argue because Martin had a point, and he could not believe that I was going to pasteurize, strain, chill, sweeten, and eat the "spoiled" milk.

"There's a dead bird in the kitchen!" Martin startled me another time. My heart sank as I imagined that a songbird had collided with the French doors, but as it turned out, Martin brought me a fryer. A whole bird, still dressed in its skin, was too weird to him — he was definitely a "stickler for breasts," skinless ones. They were the only acceptable edible part of table poultry, along with fast-food chicken. I usually retaliated by asking where the chicken nuggets could possibly drop out from, in his opinion?

To avoid a greater shock, I decided to pass up a homemade sauerkraut project because when cabbage goes through fermentation, it does stink, foams, and looks undoubtedly dead. Such improper things were unpopular in our household. Of course, I could have painlessly satisfied my yearnings at a so-called "Russian store," but there wasn't any in our area.

Russian immigrants, especially newcomers, are obsessed with those stores, which are rarely owned by someone of Russian ethnicity — the proprietors usually are Jews, Ukrainians or Armenians. They sell Russian candies, Ukrainian *kolbasa* (sausage) and *gorchitsa* (very mean mustard), Armenian *basturma* (cured meat), Estonian *shproti* (smoked sardines) and *tvorog*, as well as Georgian teas, sauces, and wines — this illustrates how strong the ties of the former Soviet Union feel abroad.

People need their soul food, especially when they change their surroundings so dramatically. For the sake of simple solace, they have to have the familiar kind of food they were raised on in the country they dared to abandon. Leaving their motherland behind, they still want to have an organoleptic connection with it, and the different flavor of the common products in their new homeland irritates them.

Gastronomical nostalgia is a serious issue, familiar to aliens in America and to Americans abroad alike. One American said that he used to satisfy his gastronomical fancy after long business trips to Russia by devouring huge Caesar salads right at the airport restaurant. Now it's a popular "American salad" in modern Russia, though it actually came from Tijuana, Mexico, where it was created by an Italian, the enterprising chef Caesar Cardini, who happened to be short on supplies in his kitchen when a flock of American tourists suddenly descended.

Although the origins of Caesar salad have been pinpointed, the motherland of the American staple, the hamburger, is debatable. American food historians who support the "pro-European" theory insist that in Hamburg, meat scraps similar to modern ground beef were served on a Brötchen, a round bun-shaped piece of bread, and German immigrants brought the Hamburger to the United States. But New Haven, Connecticut; Athens, Texas; and Seymour, Wisconsin, argue that the hamburger was invented in their districts.

The American South, though, has its own staples: "Do you have hush puppies in Russia?" inquired my mother-in-law.

I assured her that we are out of hush puppies completely. Deep-fried food is not a big item in Russian cuisine, and even fast-food potatoes, Moscow style, are served baked and whole, stuffed with salmon or other delicacies. But seemingly everything can be fried in the South. "Fried Green Tomatoes" made a good movie but a weird, I think, dish. When my Southerner asked me at a Christmas party if I had tried fried pickles, I thought he was pulling my leg. It sounded like an oxymoron. So after "them fried pickles," deep-fried candy bars and deep-fried ice cream (could the Orientals have stolen the idea from the South, by any chance?) will not rattle me. I am prepared. After all, I have eaten unusual foods — Norwegian frog legs, Cuban alligator steaks, Japanese shark rolls, sea urchin eggs from the shell, stewed bear paw, puffin breast....

If the American South astonished me with fried pickles, it baffled me with iced tea. Even in winter this is the dominant beverage, and even in summer I shivered in those arctic air-conditioned restaurants like a wet dog in the cold wind after sipping a couple of glasses. In the beginning I enthusiastically shared the opinion that iced tea is an insult to a decent product — otherwise, why for thousands of years has the classic tea always been served hot in such sunny climes as the Middle East or central China?

"Hot tea? Such a different world!" murmured a server, a big young Southern girl, surprised at my request at a fast food restaurant.

"Hot tea? I'll try it — I've never had it before," my husband's auntie, a lovely lady in her seventies, answered sweetly. I almost dropped a cup — how could she have never experienced proper tea in her life? But ultimately, what did I start to order in Southern restaurants? Obediently, I asked for iced tea. Somehow that iced tea creeps into your interior. So I drank it and shivered, but I truly think that each beverage has a special connection with its place of origin. I discovered that logic when I spent a month in Cuba where I started to understand rum cocktails.

"When I was stationed in the Philippines, at one time I was a Food Service Officer," a proper Carolinian told me. "The guy who was directly under me in authority was also from North Carolina. We spent a lot of time trying to duplicate that Southern 'delicacy,' livermush, even though we lacked the ingredients. Probably livermush would be totally disgusting to anyone but a Southerner who was raised on it."

But I liked it, to Southerners' amusement: "Look what she eats!"

Once we were musing about what could be a conventional healthy dish in the Southern cuisine. "Collard greens are good for you," my friend said. But then he took it back since the poor greens, as well as green beans, are traditionally boiled to full unconsciousness, until all the vitamins are successfully murdered. My favorite pick of American foods used to be cheesecake and clam chowder — I joked that those two could be considered as a rationale for moving to America, and only recently did I discover a milk-based seafood soup recipe that was once popular in northern parts of Russia.

One Russian wife noted that every nation is programmed to eat certain kinds of food: "Russians shouldn't go crazy about bananas but should stick to apples and beets instead. I understood the accuracy of this theory in the US, when all at once a burrito lodged in my throat. I felt a sharp nostalgia for pork soup and Russian-style potatoes. Since that night, we switched to Russian cuisine — luckily, my husband likes it — because one may not have survived much longer on American food. Patriotism calls, you see."

A wealthy Ukrainian Jewish immigrant, author of the aphorism "If to immigrate to America, so as with money only," complained that his Canadian technologist couldn't achieve the proper taste for Russian frankfurters, *sosiski*. No wonder the businessman wanted to start production in the United States — the shelf life for the delicate product is about 12 hours since Russians are not fond of preservatives. But he couldn't specify the technological steps that would produce the desired result; he just wanted the taste to be the same as in his homeland. Easy to say! For example, how to explain that strawberries, ice cream, and even cabbage in Russia taste different (I would dare to say better)? No wonder Russians try to smuggle some of their favorite foods through US customs. Who cares about drugs — we smuggle food instead! I witnessed a customs officer trying to solace a Russian deprived of his goods. "Don't you worry, we do have some food in America!"

But he had no idea what he was talking about. The Russian seaman had tried to sneak some decent salted herring across the border, as his shipmates languished without satisfying grub. That vinegary sweetened Norwegian variety of pickled herring just doesn't meet the Russian standards of decency for bub and grub. I apologize for borrowing the British slang for "drink and snack," but the problem is that Russians, as well as the French and other Europeans, do not drink without food: "What a strange habit!" one practical American commented, "It takes more booze to get soused, then."

I have to admit that Russians show some lapses of logic in the food department. For example, everybody knows that the potato's skin is its vitamin depot, but potatoes are consumed only flawlessly peeled in Russia — eating a potato with its skin is far too pagan for a Russian, and the potato eyes must be convincingly chiseled out — that reminds me of Lewis Grizzard's title *Don't Bend Over in the Garden, Granny, You Know Them Taters Got Eyes.*

In a book by another author, an American who once was married to a Russian, I found a strange Polish dish, "jellied cow's hooves." Hooves? I know an old-style dish "calf's foot jelly," that is galantine, aspic, and that probably was what she meant. But it sure draws a colorful picture of a Slavic family, crunching cow's hooves at the dinner table — of course, if one assumes that such sorts of people use tables at all. But I guess galantine seems somehow creepy to an American soul because when my doctor recommended adding galantine to my diet for fortifying ligaments after a sports trauma, my husband had a fit, "You won't bring such stuff into my house!" (Yes, he said "my," not "our," for he meant it.) Definitely, jellied pork feet don't sound like traditional Southern fried chicken, but why is it worse than the cute-looking pork snouts jelly that you can find in any Southern grocery store? How do they say it — "They eat everything in a pig but the oink"? But from a cross-cultural point of view, aspics have proven a slippery subject. There is an old-time story about an American mayor who was dead sure that he had eaten jellyfish during his visit to the Soviet Union. When it comes to those Soviets, God knows what they might eat, right? Somebody explained to him that the unfamiliar dish, fish aspic, was jellied — or jelly — fish.

Somehow Russian cuisine doesn't seem to strike the average American as a sophisticated one, probably because Russians were pictured for decades as primitive potato eaters and vodka drinkers. Slavicist and culinary historian Joyce Toomre, who translated and introduced the Russian homemaking "bible," Elena Molokhovets' cookbook *A Gift to Young Housewives*, made one of the best vicarious atonements. Originally published in 1861, Molokhovets' book became an instant success — 29 editions appeared during the author's lifetime, and the book is still in print in modern Russia, though during the Soviet era it became a laughing matter: people would quote exquisite, decadent recipes allegedly recommended in case "you don't have any food ready but some unexpected guests show up."

In her extensive preface to the American translation, Toomre included fascinating details about Russian culinary and household traditions. Her research is a captivating narrative of Russian culinary history; it was surprising to discover that delicate asparagus seemed to be an ordinary vegetable in southern regions of Russia in the beginning of the 17th century. In the Crimea, asparagus grew "so thick that you could mow it down." If we correlate the Francophile period in Russian history and Toomre's mention of Russian aristocracy inoculating Russian-style formal dinner service in France — service *à la russe* — the tendencies, amazingly, will be synchronous. Even though Russian aristocrats conversed and corresponded almost exclusively in highly fashionable French, they still preferred having their food served in individual portions, carved and arranged, instead of putting French-style whole meats in the middle of the table.

"The Russians chilled and preserved their food and drink in ice long before their counterparts in Western Europe. The first attested Russian use of the word 'ice house' (*lednik*) in 1482 predates the English by two centuries (1687). [The ice in those cellars was changed in the spring — usually in March — of every year.] By the 1660s when the English king Charles II was building his first ice house, the Russian tsar had fifteen ice cellars for storing meat and fish and more than thirty cellars for storing drinks."[1]

Russian tradition calls for cold vodka drinks, but never on the rocks, for melting ice dilutes alcohol and interferes with the flavor. And flavors they were! The suggested array of pre-prandial aperitifs evokes a smile:

> "The variety is bewildering, but presumably no one was expected to taste them all, nor indeed was it likely that all of them would have been served at any one occasion. Nevertheless, [the food expert Radetskij] suggested offering guests a choice of white orange, red orange, bitter orange, mint, almond, peach, bitter English, clove, raspberry, cherry, ratafia, bitter Spanish, balsamic, Danzig, rose, anise, wormwood, gold, cinnamon, lemon, caraway, and Crimean vodka, plus Holland gin, cognac, and arrack."[2]

Really, one's dear guests should have choices. Even now, some hosts follow the old-style tradition and concoct their signature varieties of homemade flavors with fruit, pine nuts, or tonic herbs. My diploma advisor, a botanist from a research institute, was very knowledgeable about those herbs. Little wonder that I was offered to upgrade my master's thesis into a PhD work — that must be the herbs, considering that I don't like vodkas at all. (Don't assume that Russian professors alcoholize their students — I was a full-fledged ecological journalist by then and could study herbs.)

The accompanying conversation is an important part of the Russian meal, too, perhaps more important than the food or drinks; cocktail-style munchies with their meaningless light-weight conversations are popular only among lovers of mixers-squeezers. In Russia, friends prefer more traditional formal seated dinners so the whole table can join in the conversation. "For them the whole [point] of an evening is that everyone sits around one table, and there is one big conversation. The idea of talking to someone for five minutes over a drink and then moving on to another person runs counter to the ideal of long and soulful conversation."[3]

Many Russians concur in this respect. "I was invited once to the country club for a gentlemen's night out," a Russian artist-immigrant told me. "Those important guys, in their uniforms of club jackets and khaki pants, walked around with their glasses, munching on hors d'oeuvres and asking me the same questions over and over again, 'How's Russia? Is it cold there?' One man of European origin asked me if I was bored to death yet and told me that he feels for me."

---

1 Joyce Toomre, *Classic Russian Cooking, Elena Molokhovets' A Gift to Young Housewives*
2 Radetskij, *Al'manakh gastronimii*, quoted by Joyce Toomre
3 Lynn Visson, *Wedded Strangers*

Some soulful Russian food-related activities would be outright alien for Americans — mushroom gathering, for example, which is so popular among Russians and other European nationalities. There is also huge difference between store-bought odorless and, frankly, tasteless mushrooms and those that are picked in the woods. The hunt for mushrooms is not for the stomach's sake solely — that "quiet hunt," as Russians call it, is a small expedition, family and friends gathering, sport, competition, hobby, and, mainly, a meditation, a possibility of melting into nature. Sometimes its beauty is so overwhelming that Tolstoy's hero in *Anna Karenina* forgets to propose to his love, absorbed as he is by the adventure.

Russian and American table etiquette, as an American colleague noticed, can be quite different also — he pointed out that I use a knife in the European manner. "You didn't put the knife on the table after cutting the meat but used it through the entire meal, holding the fork in your left hand." And to me, it looked strange when my American friend always chopped an entrée with fork.

An American single mother of three inquired if her Russian counterparts cook something simple and inexpensive for their kids, like macaroni and cheese from a box. I explained that, luckily, they would cook from scratch. Partially because they know how to stretch a ruble and cooking that way is less expensive — in Russia as well as in America — and partially because it is more nutritious.

One of the major differences in food intake is the Russian custom to have the most substantial meal of the day at lunchtime. Many European nations share this custom, which is not a bad idea considering that easier to burn those calories during the activities of the day. A late, large supper is more of an exception for health- or weight-concerned Russians — for them supper after 8 o'clock is a sin. As my father used to say when we were late with our evening meal, "In proper households, people don't eat after eight."

"But who told you that ours is a proper one?" I teased him back, being a properly rebellious teenager.

I recall an explanation that one woman gave to her son in the United States, that probably the American tradition of having a big meal at night was started by the early settlers, whose children delivered lunch to their fathers in fields. Only at night could farmers' families gather together over a meal. But Russian farmers had a different approach: "Farming was hard work, and most people ate four and sometimes five meals a day, depending upon the season. The first was *zavtrak* or breakfast, often taken by peasants before dawn; this was followed by *poldnik* — the word means midday, but the meal was a kind of second breakfast; *obed* or dinner was the main meal; and the day finished with *uzhin* or supper."[1]

So it was in the genes, that "Muriel was used to grabbing a sandwich at lunch and having a full meal in the evening, while Sergei expected "dinner" (obed) — at midday — including salad, soup, meat, potatoes or noodles, and a dessert. Soup

---

1 N.I.Kovalev, *Rasskazi o russkoi kukhne*

was a must; Russians cannot understand how people can go for days without soup at lunch."[1] A Russian scientist confirmed the observation: "I thought I would die without having my soup during my business trip to the US, but my hostess spoiled me with wonderful steaks, and I loved it." A Russian teacher who emigrated to the US was very annoyed that her American colleagues found strange that she always brought soup for lunch.

After all, soup had even been a political sign in Russian history: "When Alexander I went to Paris for the peace negotiations in 1815, he chose to make a symbolic gesture by having [his French chef] prepare and serve to the diplomats on several different occasions that most quintessential of all Russian dishes, cabbage soup. That was not a case of not appreciating French cuisine; it was a matter of emphasizing his nationality."[2]

Once, when my Southern colleagues discussed the idea of bringing different ethnic dishes for a common lunch — and we were a motley crew, indeed — a Southern woman, whose name started with "Van" but whose Dutch heritage was long forgotten, asked me with noticeable disdain, "And what could you bring? That *borsht* thing?"

I had to defend my borsht, just as any Southern belle who is worth her magnolias would defend her fried chicken or potato salad. When ignorance meets arrogance, it doesn't even anger me, but the lady was going to get the whole enchilada. I explained that the "t" in the end of that borsht thing is silent, just like in the name of her Chevrolet, or like in "ballet," "depot," "buffet" — the other adopted words in English, and pointed out that the beef stroganoff she just had for lunch was a Russian dish.

"Really? I didn't know that!" Now she sounded different.

"Stroganoff, just like Smirnoff — ya'll know that one, right? — is the Anglicized version of a Russian name. Stroganov was a Russian count whose chef invented the dish." I didn't stress that it should taste quite different — the inequality between a real meal and frozen TV dinners went unmentioned. So don't you dare to attack that "borsht thing" — it has become a symbol of the Russian national cuisine, just like the turkey dinner in America. (But what to do with the Canadian "jester and gadabout" A.J. Axline? He declared that "I'm against eating something called 'borscht.' It sounds like a particularly enthusiastic bowel movement." Now, bon appétit!)

The biggest gastronomical disappointment for Russians in America is sandwich bread. Andy Rooney once mentioned, "We make the worst bread in the world." I concur — I have seen the faces of Russians who tried sandwich bread for the first time in American airplanes. The Soviets loved good bread, and even the ordinary sorts customarily were of top-notch quality. It was not counted as

---

1 Lynn Visson
2 Joyce Toomre

an "evil carbohydrate;" traditional Russian mamas even insisted that children not skip their bread, and they didn't intend to harm their kids. Sting was right: "The Russians love their children, too."

So the best-kept Russian secrets probably are not military or high-technology-related, not the formula of the hard-type rocket fuel but the recipes of dark rye — an owner of an American mill told me that rye flour is very tricky to rise, but if dark rye is dark thanks to added caramel color, not due to rye flower, the taste and texture are very different. Southern apologist Lewis Grizzard complained about those "chewy pieces" that you get at the fancy restaurants, but I was annoyed with his favorite biscuits, which stick to your teeth and would complement your smile from lunch till dinner, given a chance.

Once I tested a sample of a Russian rustic specialty and Ukrainian delicacy — pork back fat cured with salt, pepper, garlic and bay leaf — on a brave citizen of Seattle. He was a great eater and was not afraid to try something new — in Sam's Club he customarily treated food sample stands like a buffet, almost satisfying his perpetual hunger after a couple of rounds.

The brave eater dutifully chewed a piece and spit it out. "That's pure fat — it's not good for you!"

"What's good for a Russian may kill a German!" The proprietor retorted with a Russian proverb, similar to the English, "One man's meat is another man's poison." In the inclement and cool climate of Russia, fatty foods are definitely more agreeable. That American became addicted to another dainty bit, Russian chocolates with the intriguing name Bird's Milk — a heavenly silky soufflé covered with dark chocolate. Ironically, this product is hard to find anymore in its fatherland since private Russian factories have taken the "free market" as an excuse to bypass the strict standards, but luckily, a factory in the US makes an excellent product.

However, Russians traditionally practice some "sweets discrimination" — candies and chocolates are among the forbidden items for babies and young children of conscientious Russian mothers who try to postpone their children's contacts with refined sugar for as long as possible. "If they don't know the taste of candy, they won't crave for it," explained to me one young Russian mother, politely declining my offer of sweets for her child.

Hardly any food in America is unsweetened: bread, salad dressings, smoked salmon — sugar haunts you everywhere. Soft drinks are not really drinks but liquid sweeteners. Sugar — and even worse, high fructose corn syrup — is among the leading ingredients in most cereals, especially in the children's, so American consumers get hooked on sweeteners in early childhood. No wonder that the nation has such a high obesity rate. Once at the local library I was automatically counting children that were not obese — alas, that was the minority, easier to count. That enormous sugar intake, as well as deep-fried and refined food that comes in super-size portions, contributes to the obesity curse. One American traveler bitterly complained to me that Russians don't even make sandwiches properly. She wasn't familiar with small European open-faced sandwiches, and it would take more than a dozen of these traditional sandwiches to build a gigantic American sub. During my first visits to the United States, I was positive that only Gargantuans could consume a casual restaurant's portion. The size seemed so overwhelming that I remember losing my appetite when I saw the huge mass.

"That's for convenience, so people can take home the leftovers and make lunch for tomorrow," my friend explained.

Once I met a well-traveled fried rice that had spent all day napping in a doggie box in a hot car at the next day's supper. My prudent American hostess had doctored it with some freshly cooked ingredients. "Throwing it away would be cheaper," my father-doctor would have advised in such cases. In Russia, taking leftovers from a restaurant in most cases would be considered funny altogether, but the portions there are considerably smaller — just as they are everywhere else in Europe, even in restaurants with Chinese cuisine.

And I have to admit that I don't peck like a bird — I am a very hearty eater. My American mother-in-law always commented on my appetite during our family meals, reminding me that I should watch my waist — though I informed her that I can still fit into my high school clothes, size small or medium. Her behavior would be considered astonishingly loutish in Russia. She reminded me of the hostess in a famous joke, who offered her guest more tea. "Oh, no, thank you — it's my third cup already!" the appreciative guest said. "Actually, it's not your third, but your fourth," the graceful hostess answered, "But who's counting?" Russians specialize in a different style — a mannerly game of "have-some-more," "oh-no-I-couldn't," "just-a-little-bit," "well-just-a-bit" instead. One visiting delegation of Russian scientists was asked if they would like to have breakfast, and their coquettish "oh-thank-you, we-don't-know" was taken by their American host as a sign that they were not breakfast eaters. So the Russians could only slobber when their American colleague fried a pan of tantalizingly-smelling bacon and eggs just for himself.

My cooking in the United States, with a super-conservative Southerner alongside, turned a prosaic act of food preparation into a psychological exercise. Every innovation underwent three classic stages, at best: "No!" — "Maybe..." — "Yes, of course!" For example, adding herbs to plain sautéed vegetables in the beginning qualified as a crime against humanity. Then I was told, "Okay, just add it when I'm not looking." (But won't you taste it, silly?) Then Martin graduated to the request, "Now, sprinkle that stuff you use." Hurrah! It was a grandiose step ahead, compared to Lewis Grizzard's Southern ideology, "I want my chicken fried, my steak with gravy, my green beans cooked, and my tomatoes served raw."[1]

---

1 Lewis Grizzard, *It Wasn't Always Easy, But I Sure Had Fun*

And one thing was definitely unbearable for my poor Southerner: the difference between cooking ground beef in traditional hamburger patties, hockey-puck hard because they were made with beef only, and lean at that, and the European fashion of making cutlets with different kinds of ground meats, bread crumbs, herbs, onion, and garlic. The smell of cooking cutlets, divine to a Russian man's senses, was revolting for the poor Southerner. It reminded me of Elena Molokhovets' advice to place a piece of fresh ginger in the cavity of a roasting turkey to reduce the odor — she said many people find the smell of roasting turkey objectionable. Go figure.

But somehow I liked Martin's orders in European restaurants more than my own selections, and he kindly let me trade dishes. He even started asking me, "So, what will I be eating tonight?" But when, in America, he said that this time he would not let me steal his order, I realized that the honeymoon was over.

"The way to man's heart is through his stomach." Russians agreed on that, but if an American has to stick with "these Russians," a great shock could accompany even such a simple task as purchasing tea. Searching for loose tea, we stopped by a quite exotic Asian store. There my husband set off for the frozen foods section. I detected a scent of trouble — he had no business there, and you know what curiosity has done to a cat. Martin examined the partially thawed compartment in one of the freezers — something lively was dripping there — then opened a glass door and picked up a plastic tray.

"What's that?" he sternly asked a shop assistant.

"I don't know, sir!" The abashed girl was obviously very close to springing into a saving I-don't-understand-English mode. Differences in palates can place people worlds apart, indeed: on the tray, neatly packed in the manner of French twirls, lay four huge beetles, strongly reminiscent of giant cockroaches (as I found out later, those farm-raised insects are used in some specific sauces). That "cockroach story" became one of my husband's favorite topics for dinner entertainment. The episode merged seamlessly with his hilarious description of rustic-style bouillabaisse that had been served for us in Barcelona, with crawfish whiskers sticking out of the bowl and scaring the American customer.

He complained mockingly to his Turkish friend, "I'm even afraid now to come close to my fridge — there is squid and fish eggs in there!"

He would not dare to try that. Even fish has been banned from his menu forever because his mother "didn't cook fish." But somehow he started consuming shrimp and those famous Southern crab cakes along the way, so I answered back with a true story.

A friend of mine who used to live in an aboriginal settlement on the seashore of the Russian Far East decided once to pick up a few succulent Alaskan crabs for dinner. But his hosts didn't seem to share his enthusiasm — moreover, the lady of the house grabbed the pot that he had borrowed and defiantly threw it away.

"What's wrong?" The astonished biologist realized that he had broken some local social customs.

"You mucked my pot with your sea spiders!" the deeply insulted woman said. And guess what? Being a scientist, he couldn't even argue with her definition because crabs are the spiders' relatives, indeed.

So I pulled out this story, reminding my Southerner that his favorite seafood delicacy is nothing but a giant underwater spider, a disgusting food item from some people's point of view.

It seems to be a general rule: if you look down your nose at somebody's customs, you'd better be aware that someone might be looking at you the same way. This holds true regarding religious issues as well; more about that later.

Food is taken so seriously in the United States, sometimes astonishingly seriously — my artist friend calls the trend "American 'foodamentalism.'" He loved this story: in one of the most fashionable Soho art galleries in New York, I saw an amusing commentary to the Mikhail Shemyakin exhibition. It offered a comprehensible image of the "river of time." It went like this: "Think back, what did you have for breakfast today? And for dinner yesterday? For lunch?" And so on and so on. I could not help but burst out laughing — "river of time," indeed, with the soundtrack of a commode flushing!

I named this chapter "serious stuff" because I do not know any other nation that would talk and write about food so much while customarily consuming enormous amounts of junk food and processed food full of preservatives. Being widely discussed but not often practiced, the healthy diet theme could compete with another topic which seems to have the same fate — sex.

LEGENDS OF THE SEX DRIVE

Once, talking to an American friend quite animatedly, I accentuated my point by patting him on the hand.

"That's strange," he said. "You touched me and it feels okay, though I can hardly stand it when my girlfriend touches me."

I couldn't believe that a lover's touch could be unpleasant to the man. I knew that Josh had a string of girlfriends he was chasing after (and then running from) and that he had never been married. That was my first introduction to the touchless environment — it was bizarre enough, but more discoveries were waiting ahead.

Reading a phrase from *Dave Barry Turns 40*, I was already giggling in understanding: "Since 1984, their most intimate moment together was the warm embrace they shared when they found out that their homeowners' insurance covered the unexplained explosion in their septic tank." Dave Barry, as a journalist, certainly knows how the masses live. So does Ray Romano, star of the show "Everybody Loves Raymond," who finds inspiration for comedy in the realities of everyday life. He told *Newsweek*, "After kids, everything changes. We're having sex about every three months. If I have sex, I know my quarterly estimated taxes must be due. And if it's oral sex, I know it's time to renew my driver's license."[1]

Allison Pearson's heroine from the popular in the US novel *I Don't Know How She Does It* skulks in the bathroom, brushing her teeth scrupulously, hoping that her husband will fall asleep and will not bother her with sexual advances, so in the morning she can skip the shower. If we are to judge the sexual life of Americans by one of *The Best American Erotica* almanacs, eroticism appears to be a do-

---

1 Kathleen Deveny, "We Are Not in the Mood." *Newsweek*, June, 30, 2003

main of drug addicts, criminals, and same-sex pairs with a criminal streak — the sexual life of straight non-criminal Americans was not highlighted. Hopefully, not because it was considered hopelessly dull but due to a "pendulum law" that eagerly emphasizes non-traditional content only because it was shunned before. Not that long ago, saying "pregnancy" on American TV was unacceptable.[1] Now, a decent American husband is supposed to witness the vaginal delivery of his child: if he cannot share his wife's pains, he can at least share that special time. But doesn't it make sense to retain some taboos, even if just for the sake of preserving physical attraction? I know a Russian cameraman who declined an invitation to document the use of yet another type of anesthetic in a maternity ward, explaining that otherwise he would never desire a woman again. A father of three, he was excused, and being a Russian, he was not afraid to be "politically incorrect," admitting that the sight of woman in labor was unappealing to him.

The outside world gets its impression of American sexual habits mostly from blockbuster movies where men and women demonstrate that lovemaking is on the top of their agenda — after all, war, sex, and violence make the box offices. So America's promotional sex image is pretty robust. The reality is different.

It reminds me of a solecism that happened right after the end of the Cold War when spacebridges, simulcast talk shows with Russian and American audiences in real time, were very popular. Lynn Visson in her *Wedded Strangers* recalls that occasion too: "A middle-aged Russian woman made the sadly famous public announcement, 'We have no sex here...'" The audience started roaring with laughter, and only years and years later, the TV host Vladimir Pozner explained that the woman wasn't given a chance to finish her thought. She was saying that Russian TV doesn't show "rated" scenes, but she changed the order of words in her sentence, and that inversion had such an effect that nobody was listening to the end. That intelligent and sophisticated woman unintentionally became a notorious national hero.

But some Americans can say we have no sex here — and they mean it. In Mikhail Fainshtein's documentary "The American Tears of Russian Wives" ("Amerikansie slezi russkikh zhen"), Russian-American writer Ludmila Shropsher said that the Russian wives of Americans complain mostly about the absence of sex, about the coldness or clumsiness of their husbands. As one heroine of the documentary put it, "A woman feels ashamed to beg for sex." Another interviewee recalled that her American husband, who was a decade or so her senior, first used the pretext that in the United States, people don't have sex until they are officially married. Then he excused himself because he was tired. When his fatigue became obviously chronic, she asked if he would like to see a doctor. He said that he didn't have time; and she finally realized that he simply didn't care. That woman was no spring chicken, but she hadn't been exposed to such

---

1 Melissa Brewster, "Sex and the Century: A History," *Newsweek*, June 30, 2003

strange behavior before — being from a society where men, allegedly, have sex on their minds dozens of times per day and would be more than happy to accept an invitation.

Another American husband, married to an energetic Ukrainian, disappointed her in the same way, but he had a theory underlying his unwillingness — he said that having sex is not good for a man's health and longevity. Soon, Ludmila found another partner, one with a very different view on the subject. Such cases belie the popular myth that Americans look for Russian wives because of lust. Sex might be not requested — not by the men, at least. As Marilyn French's heroine bitterly noted, "Once he is past thirty, he doesn't give a fig for bed... What he wants is for you to take care of him. Fix his dinner and to do his laundry and tell him he is a good boy. Just like mommy did."[1]

This attitude hardly brings joy and stability to a man's life, though. In her book *The Sex-Starved Marriage*, therapist Michele Weiner Davis states that "many sex experts believe that low sexual desire in men is America's best-kept secret... It's even harder for women when they're the more highly sexed spouse because almost everyone in the world assumes it's not supposed to be that way. Their husbands are supposed to chase them around the dining room table, remember?... Men are taught that real men lust after sex. So to be lustless is to be less than a man." She quotes her female readers-patients:

> "The myth [is] that men are always more interested in sex than women. This is a bunch of hooey! There are many, many women who would love to have a spouse who wants to have sex, touch, or a kiss." — "I have a husband who is a good guy, a great father, a good provider, but I have no lover. I'm angry about the wasted years, the years I could have been loving, but spent agonizing about why I was being deprived." — "I have bought lacy gowns, gone to bed naked, ran around the house in a towel, dressed up, approached him subtly, threw myself at him, and begged, and he almost always rejects me anyway." — "I remember in high school, my girlfriends and I were talking about how we would always be here to satisfy our husbands without them having to go elsewhere for gratification. Ha! If I don't ask for sex or make the first move, he can go for weeks without so much as a kiss."

A writer and filmmaker from New York insisted that she still has a great relationship with her husband, but she said that she had actually asked if they are going to have sex this year or maybe shelve it to the next. "I asked him what he would do if I put on a black negligee, and he said he would laugh."[2]

And supposedly, men fantasize about that "omni-sexual woman" who can't get enough sex? What would they do with her? Better be careful what one wishes for, I guess — she could be outright annoying.

According to the ancient *Kama Sutra*, a frustrated woman has a right to seek her sexual "privileges" actively, and rejecting a woman is almost a sin. But Laura Doyle wrote in *The Surrendered Wife*, "I made a mistake of telling my husband that

1 Melissa Brewster, "Sex and the Century: A History," *Newsweek*, June 30, 2003
2 Kathleen Deveny

I didn't think we were making love enough and that I wanted him to be more intimate. He promised to put it on the list between 'take out the trash' and 'weed the garden.'"

Ouch! So making love is not even in the bedroom duties' department — it is a household chore, next to taking out the trash! What is left for the rejected and sexually deprived women then, only the right to question their attractiveness or their relationships? And what about men with low desire — should they change their partners right and left in order to spike their sexual cravings?

> "When we put our hopes on one person, our dependence soars. So do our frustration and disappointments. The greater our helplessness, the more dangerous the threat of humiliation. The more we need, the angrier we are when we don't get. Kids know this; lovers do, too. No one can bring us to the boiling point as quickly as our partners (except maybe our parents, the original locus of dependent rage). Love is always accompanied by hate."[1]

If a woman is a newcomer to the country of her spouse, that dependence acquires an additional sense, making the dependent person even more vulnerable and the leader even more irritable. In international marriages, the disappointments and frustrations often are augmented.

As anthropologist Helen Fisher explained, the chemistry of desire is designed so that "the hormonal cocktail of romance (dopamine, norepineprine, and PEA) is known to last no more than a few years at best. Oxytocin, the cuddling hormone, outlasts them all. The fruits of this ripening love — companionship, deep respect, mutuality, and care — are considered by many to be a fair trade for erotic heat... Eroticism is conspicuously absent from our idea of marriage."[2]

That sad phenomenon of low desire could not necessarily be just lack of chemistry or a consequence of some health problems — it could be the side effect of protective fortification. In an attempt to avoid vulnerability or shield themselves from hurtful feelings, people turn themselves into emotional oysters — and I mean prehistoric oysters, with protective armors inches thick. These shells indiscriminately block all feelings, effectively rebuffing love and intimacy also. Distance becomes an aphrodisiac: if a partner become too close, one feels threatened; the difference between closeness and clinginess becomes so subtle and so personal that it is seductively easy to use the last as a pretext.

No-strings-attached coupling may feel good physically, but that kind of sex is just a good workout; it doesn't make people happier overall, just as Viagra cannot fix those wistful cravings of the soul. No wonder that America sobbed over the "Titanic" story. To condense it in to exaggerated Cliff's note, a boy meets a girl on a cruise, they have an affair, and then he dies saving her — such commitment in its very extreme. Their modern-age mates since childhood are trained to depend solely on themselves. They prefer not to mix love with sex since that may result in vulnerable dependency on the other person, and who can trust that other per-

1 Esther Perel, *Mating in Captivity*
2 Esther Perel

son nowadays? Better safe than sorry. Better to prevent the pain of abandonment by eliminating closeness.

They rob themselves greatly because the real intimacy cannot happen without openness, which leads to vulnerability, and trust, which implies dependency. But they haven't tried it the other way, so they don't know the taste of what they are missing. Though they suspect that they've been cheated, somehow; that something is missing. But sex and pornography on the Web have become a new realm that gives virtually total freedom, anonymity, and simplistic charm — what else could one wish for? Cyber obscurity dwarfs fears of loss and rejection, and diminishes our burning desire to mean the world for that special person.

One of my Russian colleagues noticed once that among her Instant Messenger web-pals, Western male Net surfers over forty, "single, never married" was a popular marital status. A single woman with a child, she was very wary about the maturity of these men. She had reasonable suspicions that, more than likely, they were so set in their ways that it must be a thankless task to try to train them to family life.

But those who dared to start a family are not necessarily intimately close, either. One of the most discussed periodical publications about the sexual life of Americans was a *Newsweek* article by Kathleen Deveny, "We Are Not in the Mood." She wrote: "Lately, it seems, we're just not in the mood. We're overworked, anxious about the economy — and we have to drive our kids to way too many T-Ball games... It's difficult to say exactly how many of the 113 million married Americans are too exhausted or too grumpy to get it on, but some psychologists estimate that 15 to 20 percent of couples have sex no more than 10 times a year, which is how the experts define a sexless marriage."[1]

It is beyond me how the experts define sexlessness: if spouses manage to throw in a couple more acts of coitus, are they free of stigma, then?

> "The statistical evidence would seem to show everything is fine. But any efforts to quantify our love lives must be taken with a shaker of salt," warns Deveny. "The problem, not surprisingly, is that people aren't very candid about how often they have sex. Who wants to sound like a loser when he's trying to make a contribution to social science? When pressed, nearly everyone defaults to a respectable 'once or twice a week,' a benchmark that probably seeped into our collective consciousness with the 1953 Kinsey Report. 'As a result, we have no idea what's "normal",' says Pepper Schwartz, a sociologist and author of *Everything You Know About Love and Sex Is Wrong*. Her best guess: three times a week during the first year of marriage, much less over time. When people believe they have permission to complain, she says, they often admit to having sex less than once a month: 'And these are couples who like each other!'"

That statistic reminds me of a Russian joke about an elderly gentleman who asks his doctor for Viagra because his buddy brags that he can perform three times per week.

"But you can say that, too!" offers the doctor.

---

1 Kathleen Deveny

Overwork is commonly blamed for the trend. Deveny quotes former US Labor secretary Robert Reich, who joked that the abbreviation DINS stands for "dual income, no sex." But isn't it logical, too, that sexual desire in adults has plummeted as we promote a world of equal partnerships? A sexless environment must have its toll on sexuality.

I found some consonance with my observations in this passage from Esther Perel's *Mating in Captivity*: "If I could hazard one unpolished observation," the psychotherapist wrote after exchanging off-stage opinions with colleagues at an international conference, "I would say that egalitarianism, directness, and pragmatism are entrenched in American culture and inevitably influence the way we think about and experience love and sex. Latin Americans' and Europeans' attitude toward love, on the other hand, tend to reflect other cultural values, and are more likely to embody the dynamics of seduction, the focus on sensuality, and the idea of complementarity (i.e., being different but equal) rather than absolute sameness."

The characteristics that belong to the opposite sex attract a person — a heterosexual person, at least — so sameness couldn't be considered sexual, logically. If people are equal partners, then what is left for separate male–female realms? Where does that female softness and male aggressiveness go if a female has to be just as aggressive in her daily professional life? Maybe for some men that is one of the prime reasons for looking for a wife elsewhere, not in the land of political correctness.

"Some of America's best features," wrote Perel, "the belief in democracy, equality, consensus-building, compromise, fairness, and mutual tolerance — can, when carried too punctiliously into the bedroom, result in very boring sex. Sexual desire and good citizenship don't play by the same rules. And while enlightened egalitarianism represents one of the greatest advances of modern society, it can exact a toll in the erotic realm."

Russian "red revolutionaries," for example, flirted with radical feminism so very briefly maybe because they quickly discovered that egalitarianism in sexual relationships strips sex of pleasure; mating with one's *tovarish* (comrade) is not that much fun. They promptly documented that women were given equal rights and didn't enter those treacherous grounds anymore.

"I do believe that the emphasis on egalitarian and respectful sex — purged of any expression of power, aggression, and transgression — is antithetical to erotic desire for men and women alike," wrote Perel. As a researcher of foreign origin, she could safely afford an opinion that goes against the grain:

> "The poetic of sex, however, are often politically incorrect, thriving on power plays, role reversals, and subtle cruelties. American men and women, shaped by the feminist movement and its egalitarian ideas, often find themselves challenged by these contradictions. We fear that playing with power imbalances in the sexual arena, even in a consensual relationship between mature adults, risks overthrowing the respect that is essential to human relationships."

I always said that democracy is not applicable to symphony orchestras or classical ballet either — maybe this is why Soviets were so advanced in the performing arts. Many Russian couples perceive sexual contact as a means to fortify the union and iron out disputes, not as something to proceed with after all disagreements have been resolved in an egalitarian discussion. For so many Russians, sex is not "only a small part of a good union," as an American psychotherapist put it, but a large and important segment, even a form of expression that can convey feelings or hopes or fears that are not in the realms of sensuality. Sexual contact or a simple touch can get across many messages to a partner without any words. Life seems to be brighter that way, and spouses could be comforted in the cocoons of their families and in the embraces of their loved ones no matter what storms shake the society.

"One Muscovite whose marriage ended in a divorce was repelled by his American's wife behavior," wrote Lynn Visson. "'She was unbelievably aggressive in bed,' he recalled. 'Always telling me what she liked and what she didn't, put my hand here and my tongue there, trying to program me as though I were a computer. And she never shut up. It was like being at a horizontal seminar, not like making love.'"[1] The woman perhaps was trying her best, taking away the burden of uncertainty, instructing how to satisfy her in the best possible manner, but that way may seem too harsh and soulless for a Russian man who would prefer to pick up more subtle signals rather than follow direct orders.

Some Americans may have the same perception, too — an article about kissing school in Seattle was headlined "Did the Teacher Say to Put Your Tongue in My Mouth?" Reuters' author Linda Thomas wrote, "As couples left Saturday's class, hair tousled and in search of lip balm, [the teacher] went home to an empty house. The kissing school teacher is not married and at the moment doesn't have a boyfriend."

Having the proper technique, apparently, cannot fix interpersonal problems. As Lynn Visson wrote, offering some curious opinions about differences in sexual approaches in Russian–American marriages, "Fyodor seemed to know more positions for sexual intercourse than the author of the *Kama Sutra*... as he twisted her into a pretzel or flipped her over like a Russian pancake without a single word...

"'I think the most important part of sex is passion,' said Sergei, expressing a sentiment with which most Russians agree. 'The Americans are all rational, all brain and no heart.'" This idea seems to contradict another author's remark, "Many Russian men don't know, or don't care, what satisfies a woman." But if the majority of those men prefer heartfelt, passionate sex, why should the women not be satisfied with the undissembled sincerity of that approach?

---

1 Lynn Visson

Sometimes even gallantries, Russian-style, have to be clarified for an American: "Carol explained to her girlfriend that Fyodor was not trying to flirt when he took her arm while escorting her to a cab after dinner; he was being a gentleman."

For a Russian, a quite noticeable difference would be the attitude towards female intelligence. A witty woman is not off-putting for a Russian man; winning a smart woman tickles a male's vanity, but Florence King stated that "the most important reason why wit fails in America is sexual insecurity."[1] A Southern gentleman, Tim, said about his not too sharp, but young, Byelorussian wife, "I married her because I'm comfortable with her." He was wary about more sophisticated and mature candidates from the marriage agency's catalog. "A woman who is *sharp, incisive, and surgical* is displeasing to men."[2] In 1993, the term "surgical" became ominous — Melissa Brewster even acknowledged the incident as a milestone in the modern history of American sexuality — "Lorena Bobbitt cut off her husband's penis with a kitchen knife. Men nationwide cross their legs a little tighter."[3]

That was literally incisive, *sans* the wit. Little wonder that after that shocking example of interpersonal aggression, the American media was so charmed by nonviolent bonobos, pygmy chimpanzees — they set a perfect example of sexual relationships. "'They are less obsessed with power and status than their chimpanzee cousins, and more consumed with Eros,' *The Times's* Natalie Angier has written. 'Bonobos use sex to appease, to bond, to make up after a fight, to ease tensions, to cement alliances. . . . Humans generally wait until after a nice meal to make love; bonobos do it beforehand.'"[4]

But how could bonobos set an example for humans — considering all those clerical and political efforts that have been invested in scrubbing off any relation between humans and primates? As a result of such efforts, 25 percent of respondents in the *USA Today*/Gallup poll diplomatically said that both creationism and evolution — conflicting theories! — are definitely or probably true.[5] But when it boils down to sex, the biological laws might be indiscriminative. Take the steroid androstenone: "Farmers spray it on female pigs in heat [sorry to bring in pigs, but that's biology, nondiscriminatory science], and they'll get in position for mating almost instantly — no questions asked. In human females, studies show it may cause arousal, sweating and a surge in stress hormones. Women are also much more sensitive to it near ovulation."[6]

Nancy Etcoff in her book *Survival of the Prettiest* points out that instinct directs a male to pick a younger female in order to be the first to impregnate her

1 Florence King, *Reflections in a Jaundiced Eye*.

2 Florence King

3 Melissa Brewster

4 Maureen Dowd, "The Baby Bust," *New York Times*, April 10, 2002

5 news.yahoo.com/s/afp/20070608/ts_alt_afp/usevolutionreligion

6 "Man's Scent Depends on Woman's Perception," Dave Mosher, LiveScience.com, September 16, 2007

and dominate her productive years, so he can pass on his genes and produce as many offspring as possible — even if consciously a man doesn't have the slightest desire to father a child. She also points out that women's full red lips, when naturally plump, suggest extensive estrogen production — the hormone has the same effect on vaginal lips, heightening woman's readiness for intercourse. Somehow I doubt that the American manufacturers of lip plumping cosmetics would be eager to incorporate that fact into promotional slogans, though human pheromones research did stir up a marketing frenzy: conveniently bottled, sexual attractiveness was available for overnight shipping.

That was very consumerist-friendly — a modern love potion, which promises a relief of doubts, heartaches, guesswork, and other inconveniences associated with the uneasy process of bonding with a strange human being. Sex with strangers has always being among the most popular of erotic fantasies.

> "Sex with strangers is an alternative to language, the code that replaces speech. When you put your body against someone else's body the cells can't help but talk to each other, see where they match up and don't, make billions of calculations as to where your histories and dreams speak a common language, what might be the chance of a happy life for the two of you and your as yet unborn child. It's biological, I think, and more than biological, part of the whole mysterious package..."[1]

And what if, on top of that, the stranger is from a different culture — a total stranger, an alien — does it make the speech-replacing language utterly primordial and thus more tempting? Exotic can be erotic, at least initially.

---

1 Rosemary Daniell, *The Hurricane Season*

Pets, the True Love

I looked at the couple through the bedroom window. They sat on the steps, side by side, my husband's arm on her shoulders, watching and listening, soaking in the freshness of the early morning before the fall of the excruciating heat. Something caught their attention — they looked upward simultaneously and followed a flying bird. The dog's large ears pricked, her pink nose twitched — she heard and smelled things beyond the human senses, but still the Man and the Beast were a perfect pair, one entity. Before getting into his car, Martin bent over and planted his lipless kiss on the top of the dog's head while she bashfully kept quiet. Clearly, she was the most precious creature in the world to him.

When I was a student, I rented rooms in the city, dealing with an array of landladies, usually lonely elderly women with their precious pooches. Typically those small mongrels, lovingly fed to their capacity, were so fat that their flat broad backs reminded me of overstuffed footstools. The bond between a dog and an old lonely woman was a part of what Russians used to call the "old maid syndrome": sadly, the mutts were the women's only soul mates. Later, I heard of a grim incident that disturbed Muscovites: an elderly actress, very popular in her early years, died alone in her apartment and her lap dogs, mad with hunger, gnawed her face. I thought about my landladies hoping that they were okay.

In the US, I discovered that the "old maid syndrome" can affect much younger people too, and not necessarily females. A pet in America is more than just a pet; it is a cut above a human being. Relationships between pets and humans are often more intimate than connections with partners — if there are any partners, of course. Before my American experience, I was an enthusiastic pet lover; now I have became very wary of pet loving extremes.

I generally agree with Andrew Rooney, though, that "the average dog is a nicer person than the average person," making an exception for my former Southern neighbors' dog. That ill-tempered Labrador of an unfortunate shade of brown betrayed her very breed's fame as the all-American sweet pet, though she was friendly to Ana — short for Anastasia (my husband named his dog after the legendary Russian princess). People kept asking what kind of dog Ana was and finally I started answering that she was a bleached German shepherd. One man's face clouded with righteous anger about such cruelty, before he got the joke.

Ana, a pure beauty, had a regal appearance, indeed: imagine a German shepherd, with its noble intelligent face, but without that signature droopy butt — Ana had a straight back, a proud bushy tail, and was as white as a royal ermine mantle, with a slightly brownish hue on her ears, which is called "sable" by breeders. I christened her a "sable and ermine dog." Her habits, though, were far from noble. I was shocked when I saw her trick for the first time: she unloaded a big pile of scat, turned around and gobbled it right up. She ate any kind of droppings she could get her mouth on, licking liquid matter and crunching frozen poopsicles. If she had a suspiciously smug face, satisfactory licking her muzzle after being out of sight for a while, it was enough just to ask her — she couldn't lie about her hanky-panky. Tail tucked between her legs, ears set back, head drooped — she knew that she was in trouble. She was a hereditary fruitcake: her mother ended up tearing apart her breeder's poodle. The breeder, quite an unglued country girl, loaded Snow White in the car — her fur still spattered with dead poodle's blood — and simply dropped the dangerous bitch off on a back road.

Ana also was unsociable with other dogs, and on the top of that had numerous phobias. She was afraid of the dark, loud sounds, wind, birds' feathers. Always eager to jump in the car, even if she wasn't invited, she would freak out once the car started moving. She yelled — it wasn't barking, or whining, or yelping, it was as close to yelling as a canine can muster, and she stunk — her very skin emitted the odor, that chemical of fear. She could sense a thunderstorm brewing thirty miles away; storms triggered her panic attacks and she tried to break into the house. Once I discovered her muddy footprints all around the place, with an especially intricate pattern on the bottom of my bathtub as if she had been dancing inside. I cleaned it all up but the bathtub evidence, leaving it for my husband who habitually went into denial about her break-ins.

"Taa-da!" I sang, withdrawing the curtain.

"What the...?" he said.

When Ana dislocated my finger, jumping on me with joy, I realized that her puppy-like demeanor, combined with her formidable size, had become quite dangerous. Once she tried to nibble a jogger's calf — Martin just laughed artificially, but the woman didn't find it funny. I realized that he was not going to train this white furry knot of uncontrollable energy. Ana was spoiled rotten and knew too well that she could probably pee on top of her master's head if she chose to do so. After all, she was raised in Martin's bed — until one night she turned in her sleep and fell on the floor. Then it became evident that the beautiful sleigh bed, scratched by her claws, had become quite small for the doggie.

However, Ana proved to be quite susceptible to training when I started explaining things to her. Finally, if I caught her chewing on poop, I could just point, mimicking a flight attendant's gesture, in the general direction of the garage door while pushing the door opener button, and inside she went. A real estate appraiser was impressed.

"The dog is on remote control," I explained.

When Martin let her out of the basement in the mornings, she habitually made a beeline to the prospective delicatessen spot outside the kitchen's door. Once she found unfamiliar food there, sautéed cauliflower. She looked at me. I reassured her, "Veggies are good for you."

Martin chuckled. The dog looked down, then looked up at me again — and started crunching the cauliflower, spreading pieces around. Trying to locate the tidbits, she moved in the wrong direction, so I corrected her, "Go right, Ana!"

She looked at me again and turned right. Since she didn't know the words for directions, Martin didn't chuckle anymore but looked at us apprehensively.

"Girls; we understand each other, you know," I explained coyly.

That was as far as I could go in anthropomorphizing a dog. When I hear, "Doggie, wait for Mommy!" I cannot help thinking that if a woman names herself the mommy of a son of a bitch, then what does it make her? The same logic comes to mind when a man, usually a bachelor, identifies himself as a "daddy" of his precious canine. If a dog is his son, then with whom did he conceive it?

When people make their pets the centerpieces of their lives, it leads to many kinds of weird effects. One lawyer bragged about helping his colleague and ex-girlfriend with the veterinary bill — her dog underwent neurosurgery that cost more than five thousand dollars. "In developing countries, a child cannot get this kind of care," said the lawyer with a smug smile. It was horrible, but the lawyer was a solitary pet lover, so what could be expected?

I have met women — one owned fifteen cats, the other five — who loved their whiskered companions so much that they became cattish themselves: they were moody and scratchy with humans but purred with tenderness talking to their fellow felines. I met an elderly man, who had been living alone with his dogs for decades, still considering himself a highly eligible bachelor; he had a made a small shrine to a dog that he inadvertently had run over. Perhaps he also "remembered with inconsolable anger that the Church had decided in the seventeenth century that animals couldn't go to heaven because they were unable to contribute monetarily."[1] On that shrine shelf was a miniature statue of a doggie with a halo

---

1 Jim Harrison, *True North*

around its head. I wondered what more orthodox Christians would say about such a heretical object.

My husband also admitted that losing his dog would be the worst thing imaginable, and I would concur with him in this respect — as far as I can see, his relationship with a dog might very well be his ceiling in the relationship department. But a dog's life is shorter than a human's, so I feel sorry for his unavoidable grief. However, now there are groups and therapists that can help a person to deal with the loss of a pet. A retired doctor showed up at one of those group sessions with photos of his beloved Dalmatian and the doggie's ashes in an urn. "He just curled up and cried like a baby."[1] He had lost that dog 25 years ago. Didn't the doctor need medical help himself? Even pet-loss grief professionals admit that deep mourning for a pet for more than a few weeks may indicate that some bigger issues affect the mourner's psyche.

"The bonds with our beloved pets are in many ways stronger, purer, and far more intimate than with most others of our species," says Wallace Sife, a retired psychologist and author of *The Loss of a Pet*. "We feel loved and secure in sharing our secret souls with them. How often can you do this safely, even with someone who is very close?"

That is exactly the point. Let's face it: communication with a human being is a far more sophisticated task that brings risks and responsibilities. Much easier just to settle for a less disturbing object of adoration that won't threaten you with its intellectual facilities and won't stir your insecurities. The problem is that such companionship, no matter how cozy and peaceful, is not a family. One can mate with his beloved dog only to some extent, I hope. But that pet can become a fanciful anthropomorphized creature, some in-between species, a substitute for a human partner, an idol.

A dog can provide a very soulful and comforting silence indeed, but usually doesn't carry on much of an intellectual conversation. Even Ana, who had a bilingual "passive vocabulary" and made a poster listener with her habit of cocking her huge ears and tilting her head from side to side while listening, couldn't share her opinions on topics outside of food, walk, and, strangely enough, my separation from her master. When Martin and I discussed the latter issue, even if calmly and without raising the tone of our voices, she seemed to pick up the matter somehow and refused her food the next morning — and this is a dog who was always hungry! She repeated the trick three times, though it could have been just a coincidence.

I have to admit that it was easier for me to separate from her master than from her — after all, she wasn't mean and never wrote a single anonymous letter against me. Even now, when I hear a noise downstairs, I catch myself about to call her name. "The more I see of men, the better I like dogs," Mme. Roland said.

---

1 Richard Sine, "Coping with Pet Loss," www.webmd.com/balance/features/coping-with-pet-loss?...

Dogs are undeniably adorable, especially in comparison with some disappointing humans. But it is sad if a man states that "[the dog] had been the only creature in my life that had at least a few aspects of a good wife or lover."[1]

In America, the chance of running into such characters is pretty high. Though it doesn't really matter what nationality the man is — one of the most notorious pet lovers in history was Adolph Hitler, who adored his German shepherd.

So in general being nice to a pet doesn't prove anything, by itself, but it may speak volumes if it goes to extremes. People provide medical treatment for their beloved pets that they wouldn't give to their closest relatives. They can grieve over the loss of their pets more than over the loss of their parents. Professional grief-recovery specialists pop up like mushrooms after the rain — one such specialist owned 16 dogs herself — providing for the pet mourners much needed reassurance that their grief is normal. But the fact that there is an abundance of mourner-extremists doesn't automatically make them normal. A proliferation of bizarre styles often indicated that something is wrong within the society that affects the human psyche — in this case, for example, normal communication between the sexes seems to be vanishing.

But evidently, there is a vast market for pet-loss therapists, just as the production of pet paraphernalia is big business. Dogs and cats will not appreciate the difference between a swanky $5,000 designer pet bed and a cozy, moth-eaten old wrap which carries the comforting smell of their beloved master; but the owners, for reasons of their own, feel better making ritzy purchases for their pets. It reminds me of Ana's experience with our cars: my husband would melt with joy when she stood on her hind legs, greeting him through the van's window — truth to be told, she was habitually checking a human's breath: "What did you eat today?" — but he was unhappy when she scratched the shiny new Mercedes that way.

"You think the dog can recognize a car make?" I laughed, seeing Ana's bewilderment at the inevitable reprimand. "Dogs don't care!"

As John Grogan put it, dogs try "to point humans to the things that really mattered in life... Loyalty. Courage. Devotion. Simplicity. Joy. And the things that did not matter, too. A dog has no use for fancy cars or big homes or designer clothes. Status symbols mean nothing to him... A dog doesn't care if you are rich or poor, educated or illiterate, clever or dull. Give him your heart and he will give you his... we humans, so much wiser and more sophisticated, have always had trouble figuring out what really counts and what does not."[2]

If dogs were meant to teach us these lessons, then we humans are not very receptive students. We've got it all wrong. Instead of simplifying and purifying our lives, we try to sophisticate theirs. Nowadays, pets are taken to therapists.

---

1 Jim Harrison
2 John Grogan, *Marley and Me*

(Imagine what psychological trauma poor pooch Toto must have suffered after his journey to the Emerald City!)

John Grogan's dog Marley joined the family when his masters "grappled with what every couple must eventually confront, the sometimes painful process of forging two distinct pasts into one shared future." The Grogans — and Marley — succeeded, but a huge number of pet lovers don't follow this trend and exclude humans from their master-and-pet all-sufficient families.

Paradoxically, pets, which we might say are supposed to teach people about compassion and understanding, sometimes harm human relationships instead. A new trend is thriving in America: human partners are out, furry ones are in, and everyone is happy. Almost.

Would the divorce rate decline, I wonder, if people started treating their spouses with the same endless indulgence and self-forgetful love as they bestow on their pets?

Isn't That Custom Strange?

Without any discernable reason, my husband pulled over to the side of the road. Most of the cars around us stopped as well. We were on a state road — technically, on a North Carolina state highway, with a divider and a speed limit of 45 miles per hour through the town.

"What's wrong?" I didn't hear any sirens and couldn't see any cause for alarm.

My Southerner pointed across the divider at the incoming traffic lane, partially obscured by trees. "There is a funeral."

Indeed, a hearse with a string of cars was proceeding along.

"So?"

"It's impolite not to stop and show respect."

"On a highway?"

I couldn't get it. I had witnessed the habits of local drivers during the holiday shopping rush hour, when an ambulance, with blazing lights and blaring sirens, was trying to get through — people ignored it. Perhaps that was the idea: if an ambulance arrives too late, then the remains will be accorded undivided attention and respect. Later on, I read a letter from a Yankee in a local paper who said that he was not going to obey the strange custom of stopping for funerals when ambulances are so widely ignored. At least I was not lonely about my opinion.

Sometimes misleading impressions can be formed when observing cultural habits and customs without a certain background knowledge. Judy had the indelible impression that Russians are so poor that they have to make their sandwiches with one slice of bread — she wasn't familiar with open-face sandwiches, which actually express abundance rather than trying to fill you up with cheap starch — and Natalya, evidently, visited only fast-food restaurants during her American visit, so she had the lasting impression that Americans have such bad table manners that they don't use utensils. Should Judy and Natalya meet, they could exchange some interesting comments.

Psychologist Mary Pipher wrote in her book about refugees:

> "Like most Americans, I speak only English fluently... I value freedom and personal space... I am time-conscious. I am comfortable with only certain forms of touch. A certain amount of eye contact and distance between bodies seems right to me. Some things seem much more edible than others. Certain clothes — jeans and T-shirts — feel best to me. I do not cover my head when I go out, and I wear shoes inside my house. I like to talk."

It is interesting to elaborate on those points from the outsider's perspective. Evidently, newcomers to the United States are different in almost all those regards: to begin with, by the nature of their lives they often have to speak several languages. Freedom is a specific issue, and not so much an American privilege, if we compare to European states. Most Americans are enjoyably punctual. As Lynn Visson notes, "that Russian lateness now annoys him [a Russian] more than her [an American]." I admit that it was not my husband but I who was aggravated when my Russian acquaintance, already an hour and a half late, finally called with an update that they are going "to hit the road in a half an hour." But putting an event on my calendar a year in advance still feels weird to me — as it was for that woman from El Salvador who said to the psychologists, "How can we know where we will be in two years and what we will want to be doing?" Of course, family vacations and expensive trips are planned in any country, but Russians take their pleasure in doing things on the spur of the moment.

"Americans resent being captive to a long monologue," writes Visson. But in any culture (the US is no exception), one can meet people who love to talk to the extent of outright logorrhea. "Americans feel that simplicity and brevity are the soul of wit and wisdom. For Russians, a valuable idea is a complex idea." In most cases, I agree. But the form of a talk is a secondary issue — more disappointing is the discovery that a person has very strict boundaries for self-expression in many contexts: "A Southern woman would never correct her boss, especially in an interview," Dorothea Benton Frank wrote. And we don't want to go into the swallow-your-pride rules of the American corporate ladder, or local governmental hierarchy, or chain of command in big or small businesses. There is one other way, mentioned in a book about Cold War drama: "The boy was not afraid to speak his mind. Part of that came from having money and being married to more money."[1]

Money talks, certainly, and the fat purse can afford to speak its mind. But generally, subordination is such a sacred American cow that a frank opinion from the lower echelon is almost nonexistent.

Though even in the latter days of the Soviet Union, officials had to be "open to criticism," even if just to let off steam. I can attest that non-profit organiza-

---

1 Tom Clancy, *The Hunt for Red October*

tions really had a vote in the USSR. I participated in the burials of several grandiose multimillion projects of the century that were environmentally hazardous. One group of project engineers looked down at us, public ecological experts who worked for free, and gathered up their plans and diagrams saying that they shouldn't waste their time since the matter had support in the highest executive and ideological quarters. They just could not see that without this committee's approval and signature their plans would remain just drawings. The project got bad press — I participated by publishing articles in a journal of the Russian Academy of Sciences and in European ecological magazines — and the big plans were shot down. So I can feel that pain when I read an American author writing: "A public hearing is called for the purpose of what's gracefully labeled 'soliciting citizen input.' ...The hearing is just a slick way of getting people to *think* they've had some say, ... *input* has nothing to do with the final *output*."[1]

Freedom of speech has quite specific applications: discussing politics or religion can spoil one's appetite at a cocktail party; friendly neighborhood talk has its neighborly boundaries. "Oh-you-have-such-lovely-flowers! [And your stupid yapping dog drives the entire neighborhood crazy, but all I can do is bitch behind your back.] Have a nice day!"

Anyway, who would sincerely answer the questions, "How do you do? How are you?" Nobody, since the answers are irrelevant. One Hollywood host made a hilarious experiment: while his guests were oozing those hollow greetings, he answered, "I'm okay, yesterday I killed my grandma, I'm just fine, tomorrow I'm planning to kill my grandpa." His oblivious guests patted him on the shoulder, "Good, good!"

"Our front desk secretary, an elderly lady, lost her only son," recalled Peter, an officer with a famous New York philanthropic organization, "I felt for her — she had to answer that she was 'just fine' when her loss was so fresh."

Illinois State University offers interpretations on its website for members of International Studies and Programs: "It is sometimes difficult for foreign students and faculty to understand how Americans form and maintain friendships. In this mobile society, friendships may be transitory and are often established to meet personal needs in a particular situation. The casualness of friendship patterns in the United States allows people to move freely into new social groups."

Russians traditionally valued friendship on an entirely different level. For them, friendship was not about particular needs but about soul needs. Older generations tried to maintain contact *regardless* of a particular need at the moment, even with friends who probably could never be seen again due to relocation, and some prominent people kept up relationships with old friends who knew them before their fame precisely because these friendships were certainly not based on utilitarian needs or reasons of vanity. Now everything has changed, of course.

---

1 Robert James Waller, *High Plains Tango*

"In Russia, friends were there to help you get a job, fix a car, or lend you money... When it comes to really opening up, Russians find Americans quite closed," Visson wrote about her experience in the USSR, noting also, "That a broad smile and a warm handshake may not be an invitation to closeness is something the Russian arrival needs time to learn." Sweetness which consists only of pleasant manners not in lined with real feelings might be hard to digest for neophytes, and political correctness may seem hypocritical.

"I prefer not to ask certain questions," a Southern matron pointedly told me. Her walking on eggshells did not safeguard her from a divorce, even so. "Americans are so uptight, so slow, so biased," noted actress Tatyana Leshchenko-Sukhomlina after traveling through the US almost a century ago.

Comfort space varies in different countries: I felt very uncomfortable back in Russia when someone breathed down my neck in line at the post office. In the US, the person would be two polite steps back. Professor Jan Perkowski noted, "The Russians' lack of personal space at home in their apartments, on public transportation or on the job causes them to erect their personal space boundaries next to their skin. Therefore it is common for Russians to have deadpan or frozen expressions on their faces. We tend to perceive this as unfriendly and it may ruffle our feathers."[1]

I feel like ruffling my feathers too when I meet the eye of a Russian beauty. Their faces are not just frozen — ice age is written over those chiseled features. No wonder Russian men are famous for their reckless bravery; they have to break that ice casually. My beautiful mother somehow was always able to keep a friendly, open expression on her face and she rarely rode in a bus without engaging in a soulful conversation with a complete stranger, or running into somebody who remembered her from thirty years ago, or just getting a marriage proposal on the spot.

My father mentioned once in St. Petersburg how to distinguish a foreign tourist from a Russian. "The foreigners have animated faces." Once I was walking in my Russian city, deep in thought, when I met a stranger's eye and smiled back automatically. In a flash, I realized that this face didn't belong to the environment. And indeed, I was passing a hotel, that man was a foreigner, so his facial expression, neither deadpan serious nor frivolous, was strikingly different.

Some other differences come to mind: a Russian man usually brings flowers/bonbons/wine to the hostess. Coats are always checked in at a theater. Russians dress more formally. I asked my niece if all the girls from her group had fallen for a drop-dead gorgeous young American scholar who gave a couple of presentations at her university, but she just raised her eyebrows, "Why should we? He wears those awful wrinkled tee shirts." I didn't think her American contemporaries would understand such pickiness.

---

1 Jan Perkowski, quoted in Craig Strotti, *The Art of Crossing Cultures*

Russian men habitually open doors for women, and once that custom helped me a great deal. When Boris Yeltsin was visiting a submarine base, I went with his group inside a hangar where a big crowd of dockyard workers and naval officers gathered. On the way out, I was behind and had to squeeze with the crowd through a small door. I was traveling with the security service — how I got into their van was another funny story, Erin Brokovich-like. I knew they wouldn't wait for me, and since the press was not allowed inside that high-security location anyway, I had to get out fast.

I chirped, "Officers, please!" Two tall men looked down at me and my azure dress that contrasted so nicely with their manly black uniforms. They gallantly squared their shoulders for a moment, holding back the crowd — I thanked them and ran out, right on time to jump into the open door of the van that had already started moving.

A ride with the security service in the governmental cortege, speed-wise, was a memorable episode, but now even a regular ride in Russia could frighten me. I have to confess that driving in America has incapacitated me. I am not up to driving in Russia anymore — Russian driving style terrifies me. My friend, who shares some of this disability after living in Seattle, said about his fellow Muscovites, "They drive like it's their last ride, so they don't care." Armed with powerful SUVs and luxury cars, the drivers are a grave danger on the road. There is a joke that only in Russia could you be rear-ended while speeding in the oncoming traffic lane. Driving becomes a survival test, which includes dealing with erratic driving, driving on the shoulder, and making up the rules as you go along. Most importantly, in order to survive, one has to consider that right of way is determined not accordingly to law but to the prestige of the participating vehicles.

Being a pedestrian is a dangerous occupation also — one has to ditch any cherished ideas about pedestrians' privileges and learn to jump on a curb with the agility of an Adelie penguin chased by a killer whale (though the sidewalks are quite drivable as well; I have seen a picture of a car that hit a pedestrian underpass in Moscow. It's best to watch out at all times).

Traveling from Russia to the US, I always enjoyed that delightful feeling of a warm, relaxed environment, almost as if human affability could be a tactile sensation — after the stern faces at Russian airports, the easy American sociability felt as comforting as a warm sea.

"I wasn't quite sure how to talk or touch, and when I might inadvertently offend. Encounters with people very different from me were hard work. Often I was anxious, awkward, and even suspicious," wrote Pipher about her interactions with refugees.

Indeed, patting a Chinese child on the head could be considered as a bad blunder, but on the other hand, tactile issues seem to be a problem in the US —

people are immersed in a sexless, touchless environment, and this routine eventually creeps into more intimate relationships.

"He just couldn't keep his hands off his wife!" Marylyn disapproved of her neighbor's behavior at a backyard party. "He had to hold her hand, or to hug her, or brush her knee..." They were not even newlyweds, that warm-blooded couple of Italian descent. I was happy for them.

I agree that Russians tend to gesture far more than Americans, but less than French or Italians. I joked sometimes that my mother would be not able to talk if her hands were tied.

"Fred had to tell Irina not to 'stare' at his American friends," wrote Lynn Visson. Staring is considered impolite virtually in all countries since in the world of mammals it implies aggression. In Southern towns, I experienced some impolite staring and just stared them down in defense. But once at the Miami airport, as I was walking alone through the empty concourses, I found Latino men from work crews checking me out — and I felt as if I was not in America anymore. I was instantly transformed from "a member of a society" into a "woman." Just as I was taken by surprise at the Amsterdam airport, joking with a good-natured airline clerk, when he patted me on my hand. That felt so unusual after the polite but sterile American environment.

The American habit of wearing shoes inside the house may stem from the relatively clean environment: impossible to indulge in it in Russia with its inclement climate and slushy — or very dirty — streets. But sometimes Americans seem to overdo that relaxed attitude: in public restrooms, ladies put their purses on the floor in the stalls, and kids throw down their coats (a Russian mother would have a cow, seeing that), and even in restrooms at a symphony hall bejeweled ladies make a beeline from stall to door, dodging the wash stations. I was called "germophobe" just for reminding my friend to wash his hands between such different tasks as handling a muddy garden hose and ripping salad into a bowl.

Perhaps the difference in domestic habits is one of the most noticeable things for a Russian newcomer. Bathtubs that haven't been scrubbed for years and rooms that haven't been vacuumed for months greatly surprise Russians; they don't understand this laid-back attitude. Clutter, which supposedly plagues two-thirds of American households, is not a very common problem for Russians, irrespective of their income and social circles, though some elderly people suffer from that disease as well. It is unlikely that a Russian teenager will be allowed to turn his room into a pig sty. Clothing scattered over the floor could be seen maybe only in break-in crime scenes — well, in love scenes, too, but that's a temporary jumble.

Irina recalled that her American fiancé, when visiting her in Russia, wasn't annoyed with the hot water outages that irritated her.

"In America, he didn't shower often either," Irina said. "I found an excuse to move into another bedroom and hinted that in Russia, if a man is going to have a date with his wife at night, he takes a shower and shaves." ("He who shaves at night harbors some hopes," promises a Russian comedian.)

Svetlana also couldn't get her American blue-collar husband to shower more often than once a week — he didn't want "to spoil" his skin with water. Resourceful, she found an antidote to her problem: she started washing the sheets almost every other day, and that waste of electricity, detergent, and water her economical husband just couldn't stand.

In some instances and in some quite impressive American houses, fresh sheets are not always offered for a guest who stays for just one night, but even in rural areas in Russia, where bedclothes are hand-washed and water has to be lugged from a well, it is unquestioned that an overnight guest must have fresh linens.

Generations of Russians were brought up to be very perceptive about the cleanliness of their personal means of transportation; probably the tradition started when personal vehicles were a luxury. My untrained sinuses have been clogged almost instantly in some grungy vehicles' interiors in America. I wonder if banal dust could be one of the main reasons for the endless sinus problems in Americans, especially when fortified with a blasting air conditioner.

Another snapshot: Oprah Winfrey was observing her audience in disbelief: "Who knows what a bidet is?" she asked her guests. "Who has a bidet at home, please, raise your hand!"

Her and her guest's hand went up. The TV queen had to explain that in Europe people use those devices to clean their bottoms. The audience chuckled.

"If you clean your dirty hands, you don't just wipe them with a paper towel — you wash them, right?" said her guest-doctor. "Bidets serve the same purposes."

My Southern colleague was tickled pink when I read aloud an article about the unpopularity of bidets in America — he couldn't believe in the existence of such an exotic thing, "a water fountain for your butt."

I was shocked just as much after the discovery of those traditional family pictures of cute babies being washed in kitchen sinks.

"And you were bathed in the kitchen sink, too?" I asked my Southern husband, incredulously.

"Of course — everybody was!"

Dirty babies' bottoms washed in the kitchen sink — yuck! If someone tried to wash a baby in the kitchen sink in Russia I don't dare to imagine the reaction of a potential audience. Nobody is too poor to afford a baby's plastic tub or too lazy to pour some water into it.

"Children are toilet-trained very early by American standards," noticed Visson. In fact, Russian children are trained before they can even talk. Investing time and patience in early acculturation, mothers save on quite expensive diapers and spare the public from malodorous aromas. American children, who already walk and talk very well but still do their business in their diapers, are quite a shock for a newcomer, but this way is just easier and more convenient for busy American mothers.

Another surprising "baby thing" for a Russian woman is the baby shower. Traditionally superstitious, Russians do not publicize the fact that their family is about to have an addition. Only those American couples who have a history of miscarriages would act like. Of course, Russians make preparations as well, and colleagues and relatives chip in for baby paraphernalia, especially for such expensive items as a stroller and a crib, but they usually do so after the successful delivery, when the happy mother is still at the hospital.

The American habit of taking babies out in public at a very early age and then complaining about their babies' ear infections doesn't seem very logical to a Russian. I felt sorry for young children in the smoking areas of Southern restaurants — I doubt that would be babies' preferences, should they have a vote. But their mommies wanted to be out and about, collecting their share of *ohs* and *ahs* from strangers. Russian mothers go to the other extreme, and some of them superstitiously prefer to shun compliments of their new babies.

"A Spanish man told me, 'Americans invented stress. And with globalization, stress will soon be all over the world,'" wrote Pipher. Americans are doomed to be tense — prompted by their highly regulated lives. As John Irwin wrote, "There is no intolerance in America that compares to the peculiarity of American intolerance for lack of success." In the quest for success, simple happiness is forgone. So no wonder those who are familiar with life abroad consider making it a potential relocation. "Maybe I will retire there," mused a Southerner who traveled to Byelorussia for his supply of foreign brides. "That is one of the poorest countries in Eastern Europe, and yet somehow people manage to have more relaxing and quite happy lives."

In addition, he obviously immensely enjoyed the die-hard Soviet tradition of hospitality, whereby a guest from a faraway land is received like royalty. I always thought that if these two diametrically opposite customs, the Soviet habit of self-sacrificing for the sake of a foreign guest and the American tendency to take care of fellow-Americans first, could be combined and then averaged out, it would make quite a healthy attitude.

Myths and Standards

When I was a child, I had a doll named Sally. Sally was black. When I was older, my mother told me that once, when we were walking at the Red Square in Moscow, a young black tourist expressed his admiration that a little blond girl had a black-skinned doll. But that was just my Sally — I didn't give it a thought.

I remember one of my classmates at elementary school — I think he was Korean — who had such dark eyes that his pupils were indistinguishable from the irises; that was unusual. I had school friends — as I recall now, they were a Ukrainian, a Russian, a Georgian, a half-Georgian, a Tatar, a Jew. We didn't care about nationalities. At high school, almost every girl fell for the tall dark and handsome Moldavian boy.

For the generations that grew up at that time and often started intercultural families, the hot, ugly issues of ethnic conflicts in the post-Soviet space are painful and unnatural. But we have never had a real perspective on American ethnic problems, either.

When I saw a housing project for the first time — the federally subsidized, mainly black neighborhood in the Southern city of Hickory — it sure looked unusual to me. The office had bars on the windows, but the surrounding atmosphere was rather festive: shiny sedans were parked at the curbs, people were sauntering around, shouting to neighbors hanging out the windows. It contrasted with a nearby blue-collar neighborhood that looked deserted during the day, with all its battered trucks gone. At night, the project area was full of activity also: at the intersections, nervous-looking young men were hustling "good stuff" to passing drivers.

When I had to stop at gas stations, driving through the Deep South, I didn't appreciate dirty looks that gas station attendants, usually young black women, shot at me. Sometimes I wanted to say that I'm from a country that has never had black slavery, and our greatest national poet, Pushkin, was a quadroon, come to think of it — though we didn't — so I don't appreciate when a black person looks at me the way Lenin looked at the bourgeoisie. Sometimes I itched to remind them that three quarters of Southern white families, "including the 'poor whites,' those on the lowest rung of Southern society, owned no slaves"[1] — or, making it sound more Southern, "ain't had no slaves." But even Oprah Winfrey has been criticized by some overzealous viewers after she featured a story about a black man who battered his white wife. Oprah as a racist? Now, that is a demonstration of "Crow Jimism."

A teacher from a local community college told me that his student, a 40-some year old immigrant from Japan who relocated to the South in the 70s, recalled a KKK parade in town. To me, it sounded like if she had seen a living dinosaur. But in Charleston, South Carolina, I learned that the crème de la crème of local society boycotted a lawyer who dared to believe that blacks have rights, and that wasn't during the era of *Gone with the Wind* — it was in the second part of the 20th century; my older sister was already born.

This double standard was conceived with the newborn American independence: the young nation, which stated that it was breaking its oath to the Crown because of its craving for liberty, kept slaves but democratically voted on the issue: "In 1784, congress considered a ban on slavery in the west, the measure lost by a single vote."[2] Such a triple twist: liberty — slaves — and democratic vote on slavery.

The book *Uncle Tom's Cabin* bore some oxymoronic subtitles during its long and successful publishing life: "The History of Christian Slave," "An American Slave." "Each of these subtitles constructs a cultural oxymoron by yoking the terms "Christian" and "Slave" or "American" and "Slave" together," pointed Henry Louis Gates Jr. and Hollis Robbins in the annotation, noting that "...a truly rational, intellectually honest human being could not help but oppose slavery, though part of me understood that the issue is far more complex than that, especially given slavery's history in black Africa, and even black-on-black slavery in antebellum South."[3]

After all, slavery is not a black-and-white issue. It is about slaves and owners, not the hides' colors, just as emancipation has more than one aspect. "In 1840, a world anti-slavery meeting in London was split over the 'woman question.' The male delegates banished the females to the balcony."[4] So women were also in the

1 Web-site of International Information Programs, http://usinfo.state.gov
2 Larry Gonick, *The Cartoon History of the United States*
3 Harriet Beecher Stowe, *The Annotated Uncle Tom's Cabin*; edited with an introduction and notes by Henry Louis Gates, Jr. and Hollis Robbins
4 Larry Gonick

lower echelon; no wonder American women had reason "to compare their lot to that of the slaves."[1] Henry Louis Gates, Jr. and Hollis Robbins mentioned a striking moment, mostly unseen in *Uncle Tom's Cabin*: "A topic perhaps as central to the plot as race-based slavery, is marriage, of all things. Stowe's novel is thoroughly preoccupied with marriages — broken-up marriages, failed marriages, fatalistic and tired marriages; bittersweet, evergreen, surprisingly emotional marriages; hasty, postponed, 'if-only' marriages; in-name only, bitter, clinging, and doomed marriages." Stowe's own marriage was happy, loving, and sexually charged, even unorthodox and quite open.

The preoccupation with marriages in the book might have been there for marketing purposes, or it could be a method of unveiling an issue inside an issue — just like the theme of alien wives does, by its nature.

By the 21st century, a new black concern has emerged — a differentiation between American-born black and black from the other countries.

"Among students at 28 top US universities, the representation of black students of first- and second-generation immigrant origin (27 percent) was about twice their representation in the national population of blacks their age (13 percent). Within the Ivy League, immigrant-origin students made up 41 percent of black freshmen... Far more black immigrant students had fathers with college or advanced degrees than did other black students... Some [were] complaining [to a Harvard Black Students Association message board] that African students were getting an admissions boost without having faced the historical suffering of US blacks. But Adjei-Brenyah, the president of the African Students Association at Columbia, argued that drawing an admissions distinction based on suffering under slavery is false. 'If you're going to make a slavery case, people from the Caribbean were also displaced and enslaved. How do you begin to differentiate?' he said."[2]

Really, how?

A young black TV star and former supermodel, Tyra Banks, deviating from the appropriate fashion and makeover topics, made an interesting show about racial stereotypes. In one episode, a psychologist asked a group of very young children who represented all races of the American society to describe what they saw on some photos. Almost all of the kids, even a black boy, decided that the young black man in a street scene must have been breaking a law. Among pictures of people of different colors, the black person was chosen as the potential best athlete, while an Asian was considered the smartest one, and a Caucasian, who did look like a seasoned politician, was picked as a potential president. Even the children's parents were flabbergasted, wondering how that could happen, how and when those stereotypes were absorbed by their very young children.

A black writer wrote, "Each of us, helplessly and forever, contains the other — male in female, white in black, and black in white. We are part of each other."[3]

---

1 http://www.pbs.org/now/politics/womenvote.html
2 "Among black students, many immigrants," by Cara Anna, Associated Press, Apr, 30, 2007
3 James Baldwin, "Freaks and the American ideal of Manhood," from James Baldwin: *Collected Essays*

Indeed, immigrants, women, blacks — all have something in common, all have to fight for equal rights. Explicating the idea further, there is always a chance to be a slave: a classical slave was one whose body was controlled, and a modern slave is one whose time is controlled; that puts even more folks in the same boat. I remember an editorial in a Southern newspaper, supported by local statistics, which stated that there is hardly a way for a minimum-wage Southern worker, black or white, to get out of that trap since the only way to physically survive is to take at least two of those minimum-wage jobs; and then one's time would be controlled totally. Paradoxically, highly-paid corporate professionals from the non-managerial echelon have the same lack of personal freedom: squeezed dry after a productive work week and having a meager annual vacation — forget about that European generosity, a minimal five-week paid holiday! — they often spend their leisure time in mindless relaxation, just resting in order to restore themselves before the next week's marathon. Life is living them, and it is living them in high gear.

Is it a wonder then that Americans have the lowest life expectancy among all developed countries, despite the cheery official drone, "we-are-the-best-country-in-the-world"? Benjamin Spock, M.D., wrote:

> "I don't think America is very happy. Americans cultivate cheerfulness and optimism, but my impression is that quite to the contrary, America is probably the tensest country in the world, with the possible exception of Japan. We have much more violence than any other industrial country and we have very high rates of divorce, wife abuse, child abuse, suicide, and crime."[1]

And we, Russians, were surprised that Doctor Spock, who had guided even Soviet moms in bringing up their children, was not overly popular in the US — I guess it had something to do with him being a doctor who could prescribe bitter pills.

Once I was reading a Russian newspaper on-line, glancing at the same time at the TV screen where a pretty young girl, a mother of cute children, was sniffling away into a TV doctor's handkerchief — this was a charismatic "no-bullshit" American psychologist. The girl's problem was that she thought she was unattractive. Her young, good-looking, loving husband was in the studio, too, feeling sorry for his wife. In the article that I was reading, the Russian mother explained that she didn't have enough money to provide expensive treatment in the only clinic in the world where her teen could be cured, and the journalist mentioned that neither the mother nor the child, who knew that she could die without medical help in a course of a few weeks, was crying. (Luckily, after the publication, they received needed financial support.) Because I was reading and watching at the same time, the difference was especially striking. I wondered if that TV girl should blow her nose and the producers would cut the comedy on a national channel. When imaginary unattractiveness is one's top priority, the per-

---

1 Dennis Wholey, *Are you happy? Some answers to the most important questions in your life*

son should probably find some higher standards and greater purposes to suffer for. A couple months of volunteering in a hospice setting could produce a greater miracle than a plastic surgery, and the experience would be free and beneficial for others.

Of course, feelings of insecurity and low self-esteem are distressing — as the saying goes, a nail in a one's boot feels more important than a world's revolution — and excessive selfishness could hide some real fears. To make matters worse, Americans love psychoanalyzing themselves, and that sorcery can create a problem from nothing — even Jerome K. Jerome's stoic Brit, after reading a medical encyclopedia in the British Museum, discovered that he had symptoms of every disease except for postpartum fever. If one invests enough time and effort in the research, something inevitably will be found.

Money, sex, power, status, success, so well promoted in America, do not necessarily bring happiness. Many American idols have discovered that. Perhaps a more natural approach is to be happy in the moment, not according to the standards of society but in harmony with one's inner sense, understanding happiness as a journey — not the destination, or achievement, or a desirable result: I'll be happy if I only get that plasma TV, if I lose that weight, if I get that job. Kozma Prutkov, a Russian literary figure famous for his aphorisms, quipped: "Want to be happy? Be happy!"

The meditative Asian cultures concentrate on the achieving of inner peace, and that inner peace is not a cookie-cutter matter either; it might have a different meaning for everybody.

These cravings for some mythical "total happiness" are puzzling for newcomers. In other countries people are not expected to be perpetually "excited." "Hysterical happiness," as my friend calls it, seems to be a distinctly American phenomenon, and it comes with the price of not being sincere. Americans must keep smiling — which is not bad in itself — but that ostentation of happiness inevitably slides into a rut when people cannot express their frustration anymore, like in some sci-fi movie about futuristic society where a dictator ties every mouth in a perpetual smile and wires every brain for continuous acclamation. No wonder when people come home, after wearing a tiresome mask of charm and agreeableness all day, they might unleash themselves into "home dictators" — the material that alien wives deal with quite often — or bury their frustration inside, where it eventually will find expression as an ulcer or depression.

> Why are Americans the Newfoundland puppies of the New World? ... There are so many different kinds of people in America, with so many different boiling points, that we don't know how to fight with each other... so we zap each other with friendliness to neutralize potentially dangerous situations.[1]

Of course, it is better to zap with friendliness than fight, but sometimes suppressed frustration boils out in an unattractive manner.

---

1 Florence King, *Reflections in a Jaundiced Eye*

The mask of shallow "niceness" can hide quite malicious feelings — even Americans who one would assume were of above average intelligence, education and exposure, if scratched, may demonstrate quite agitated racial intolerance. In his comment on a bookseller's web-site, some "good Samaritan" fumed over Mary Pipher's book about refugees:

> Muslim brothers who are in tears describing how terribly American men treat American women [are] a sort of "mirror image" of how American men view Muslim men's treatment of Muslim women. Yes, it is undoubtedly painful for immigrants to live in a culture they see as sinful.

> What is completely lost on Pipher is that this is exactly why it has made sense historically for people of drastically different cultures to live in separate nations. [...] A nation is not a costume ball, nor is it a bizarre anthropological experiment. "Globalization will change everything forever." Oh, really? Is China becoming less ethnically Chinese? Mexico less Hispanic? Why is this 'salt and pepper' paradise only thought to be beneficial for traditionally white nations? For those who still believe that the forced — we voted on this when? — conversion of America into a "multicultural," ever-less-European caldron of aggravated grievances and simmering sensibilities...

The description of the "ever-less-European caldron of aggravated grievances and simmering sensibilities" is well-worded, but the idea of American society voting on multicultural issues recalls that century-old voting on slavery. This continent had its own population before the Europeans' arrival, and the author himself, unless he is 100 per cent native American, is "a multicultural arrival," just with lighter skin color.

The situation reminds me the tale of a crowded bus: the bus comes to a stop and those who are still waiting to board beg their fellow standees to squeeze in further, to make some space for them, "We want to go home too!" At the next stop, those new straphangers grouse at those who want to get in, "Don't you see it's overfull?"

That "good Samaritan" wrote, "Different refugees, we read, prefer to live among themselves, since they can help each other cope. Sometimes interviewing refugees can be tricky. There are 'highly charged political and personal questions' and 'religion and politics are danger zones.'" But according to Western etiquette, religion and politics *are always* danger zones, these themes are not appropriate for social conversations.

The Western etiquette did not deter some Americans from firing quite intrusive inquiries at me — if I were one of them, would it be considered polite to pepper me with such personal queries? Sometimes it was almost comical: a friend invited his lesbian acquaintance to grill my date about our relationship, but warned me that interviewing her about the lesbian subculture of San Francisco would be inappropriate, "It's too personal." Why does pushiness seem appropriate in interrogating foreigners? That doesn't seem very democratic to me; rather it recalls a minor international incident: "At the Japanese war trials of 1946 [...]

former propaganda minister, Shumei Okawa, inadvertently made a good pun... screaming in his uncertain English: 'I hate United States! It is democrazy!'"[1]

American democracy doesn't recognize any titles of nobility — upon accepting American citizenship, a foreign aristocrat has to relinquish the title. But "blue blood" has found a substitute in the United States, and the concept is amusing not only from an outsider's perspective. "As surely as Europe we Americans had developed an aristocracy whose merit depended on how long their money had allowed them to largely ignore the rest of the human race."[2] Here, "old money" took the place of good lineage, and just as Europe has noble but poor aristocrats with their imperishable titles, "[Mississippi] was full of insolvent blue bloods who inherited the status of family money. It could not be earned. It had to be handed down at birth."[3]

At least most of the dot-com millionaires earned their money primarily using their own brainpower and enterprise, and the "Old money" standard doesn't really merge with the so well-promoted "self-made man/woman" concept, resulting in yet another paradox.

---

1 Florence King
2 Jim Harrison
3 John Grisham, *The Last Juror*

Several Horror Stories

Whatever could be said about Boris Yeltsin, the man undeniably had that talent so priceless for a politician: the ability to absorb and *epitomize* new information, no matter how alien it was for him. When he delivered a perfect summary of the mission of biological preserves — evidently, having just been briefed on the subject by an expert during our helicopter ride to the preserve — I couldn't resist.

"We thought you were red," I said, "But actually, you are green!"

Silence fell. The chief of protocol glared at me ferociously. Yeltsin, quickly recovering from the surprise, laughed and gave me a squeeze. The officials started to chuckle along.

This episode happened right before *perestroika* eased the social climate and the new Russian political leaders started baby-kissing. Yet I never expected or experienced any persecution for my customary relaxed behavior — after all, I came from a family where the father rarely referred to the Communist Party without using adjective like "crappy," and I had my own history of disagreements with the "party line" on a regular basis.

The censors from the Committee of Guardianship of State Secrets in the Press abhorred my articles, especially when I was on duty as a night editor — I used wording that couldn't legally be axed.

"But it's clear what you mean!" the censors complained, "That's a dig!"

By now, I have even started to appreciate my "old foe": at least the censorship guarded the mass media and literature from a strong measure of scum — though they broke many creative fortunes also. Some of us found ways to deal with them: when comrades–communists pointed out that, as head of the propaganda department, I had turned it into a science and art department, I responded with a deadpan face that I was good at propagandizing these issues, which were very important for the mass education of Soviet citizens. I also disagreed that a certain historical building should be demolished in order to make way for a grandiose addition to the Communist Party's office, musing over what the proposed red-dish shade of light fixtures outside the building were supposed to symbolize and pointing out that at least the nearby historical monument didn't deserve to be in the "red light" district. The smell of thaw was in the air, so I tried to push it as much as I could. I have never been a communist, so I could afford to be "politi-cally incorrect" and even to decline "an invitation" to have a conversation with a communist *apparatchik* about my writing, explaining that I had an interview scheduled. I had been an outspoken *enfante terrible* and wasn't punished for that.

Even in my master's thesis on ecology I mischievously combined quotations from the dispensations of Taoism and a Karl Marx saying on the fragile ecosys-tems of the mountain forests, after discovering how precisely they matched. To make sure that the agreement between the ancient religion and the founder of communism did not go unnoticed, I prefixed it as an epigraph. The result? An honors degree and an offer to explicate the work in a PhD thesis. And have I men-tioned that university education was free in the Soviet Union? I was paid a pre-mium stipend for good grades. As I realize now, for that kind of free fundamental education one can tolerate, now and then, some scientific communism, especially considering that it was balanced with scientific atheism — a course that was, in fact, an amplified analysis of major world religions and their branches.

Our generation of "unwhipped cubs" largely missed the times of political op-pression, and I can justify that for so many sensible Soviet citizens those times still existed mostly in their old fears — if they dared to try, they could have re-belled; they just didn't, remembering old times. Although people lent each other "forbidden" literature and exchanged so-called "political jokes." These jokes, being part of the Soviet folklore, could serve as one of the indicators that illustrate the ambience of the society. Jokes about the Communist Party became commonplace in the Soviet Union; it was hard to invent something new about such a stale and dogmatic theme, but the jokes about the KGB were quite interesting. Somehow, an argosy of 70s and 80s folklore didn't portray the KGB as a monster; it was almost as if the organization itself had planted "promotional jokes."

One quite telling example made fun of foreigners' fixation with the KGB — it reminds me of an old Canadian TV movie about their hockey team in "red Mos-cow": in the frenzy of taking apart their room to search for "bugs," the Canadians unscrewed a huge crystal chandelier from its base in the floor; it crashed in the hall below. In a similar Russian joke, a foreigner calls room service on the sly, then repeats the order into the electrical outlet in front of his countrymen. The order arrives, the tourists are dutifully scared, and their host is puzzled since exquisite cognac accompanies the coffee. The bellboy explains, "Don't worry, cognac's on the house — our major loved your joke!"

I remember a banquet table of KGB curators — we had those, though I had never been introduced to one — dying of laughter at a journalists' party when a famous satiric writer, invited to the gathering, decided to read the risky political repertoire that he hadn't taken to a big stage yet. So no wonder that I could travel abroad — evidently, the KGB didn't object to that — though it was frowned upon when, in Cuba, I decided to go sightseeing instead of paying obligatory tribute to Lenin's monument. I might have gotten some black marks for that since later an elderly, fiery-red haired woman from our professional union declared that I could not join a group for a Scandinavian cruise since I hadn't visited all the places in the Soviet Union yet. I was close to snapping at her for telling me where to go and what to see.

But my small troubles pale beside the obstructions that a fearless young editor of a small newspaper in North Carolina had to brave when she published an article about the earnings of local government officials, showed support to a gay community and to immigrants, and generally tried to blow the cobwebs away. She was intimidated, almost got hit by a truck, and received phone threats.

"I have caller ID — I know who you are; please don't bother me at home," she wrote in her editorial.

Eventually, she was forced to leave. So who was in the worst situation professionally, I asked myself — she, in an allegedly free country, or I in a "communist camp"? Sometimes it seemed to me that the singular brave action an average American citizen can afford is watching "South Park" or "Colbert Report" at night, just the way a Soviet citizen was listening to *Free Europe* or *The Voice of America*. I remember with great respect one editor-in-chief of an old communist newspaper who always took full personal responsibility for the material he published, defending his reporters when officials got upset. "If nobody throws stones through our windows, that means we aren't doing a good job," the man reminded his staff writers. And he belonged to an older generation of communists who had witnessed dark, bloody times. For him it was a conscious act of bravery, while for me talking bluntly was easy since I never felt real oppression.

I guess I still follow the man's encouragement in my writing. So those naïve black-and-white pictures — everything in America is good and everything in the Soviet Union was bad — are not quite the exact reflection of the reality. At least the Soviets were very well aware of their greatest luck and greatest misfortune: the luck was to be born in the USSR, the misfortune was to have that luck.

The realities of American life brought me even closer to that paradox: though I opposed the communist regime while living in the Soviet Union, once in the US I started to appreciate some aspects of life in the USSR that we took for granted.

"I think women should have six months' paid vacation after they have a baby."

"You can run as the Idealist Party Candidate," two women converse in an American novel.[1]

But why an Idealist Party? In the Soviet Union women had much longer paid leave — they could stay home until their children were three years old. Employers had to provide back-to-work mothers with the same positions they had before their maternity leave, otherwise the women would whistle up the law, and that would shame the employer. And of course, should a child get sick, his mother — or father — could get paid leave.

It astonished me that American women deliver children almost on the run, coming back to the workplace still dripping breast milk and worrying about their newborns. It is one thing if a woman chooses going back to work as soon as she can — not all women are not cut from the same cloth, and being trapped at home with a baby must feel dreadful for some — but most simply don't have a choice.

In the USSR, we didn't have mortgages. That was a blessing and a curse in one: the state guaranteed housing for all its citizens, rent-free, and the utility bills were also bearable, but for many people the waiting list for a government apartment was unbearably long, and not everyone could afford a down payment for a condominium.

Another popular misconception is that health care in the US is immeasurably better. Well, the USSR provided the best preventive care in the world, according to the World Health Organization.[2] Diagnostics exams caught the earliest stages of cancer, for example — yearly medicals were mandatory, and every institution, factory, and organization scheduled time at the polyclinics for their work force. We had complete medical examinations, visiting physicians and all (!) specialists. Didn't we hate those visits! Everybody had work to do, and languishing in the waiting rooms was seen as a great nuisance, even though we were paid our regular wages while sitting there. Many Russians long for that "nuisance" now!

That healthcare system was demolished before my eyes, and I read analytical reports beforehand and talked to chief physicians about switching to the proposed models — Swedish or American. None of my interviewees had any illusions about the American health insurance system, but the new Russian "democrats" saw the opportunities of the corporate-controlled healthcare system, and right from the beginning enormous sums of governmental money disappeared without a trace in the "black holes" of the newly-formed medical insurance companies. Just like their counterparts in the US, these companies aimed to benefit themselves, first and foremost.

To say that the traditional Soviet universal healthcare system was poorly funded and the medics were underpaid is to say nothing; but lacking so many

---

1 Roland Merullo, *A Little Love Story*
2 Alexander Bronshtein, RANS, *Argumenti I Facti*, #24, June, 13, 2007

advantages of the well-equipped American medical facilities, Russian doctors had to rely more on their expertise and experience, and sometimes that matters the most. An American confirms, "Under the Soviet regime all...care was free of charge, and what the medical personnel lacked in modern equipment, CAT scans, MRIs and medicines they made up with brains, diagnostic skills, and human warmth."[1]

I don't have anything against American doctors in general — after all, their strategies saved me from unnecessary surgeries after downhill skiing accidents, though one of the surgeons, referred by a Seattle millionaire who had had several joint replacements, was incredibly swift in his decision making.

"Do like this," the doctor ordered. "Does your knee hurt?"

"Yes."

"You need a knee replacement!"

"But doctor, when I do that, even my other knee hurt!"

"So you need two knee replacements!"

It was hard to resist the temptation to tell the doctor what he needed to replace, but I bit my tongue. This kind of "diagnosis on the run" is perhaps commonplace everywhere: Harvard Medical School professor Jerome Groopman, MD, author of *How Doctors Think*, notes that according to some research up to 20 percent of all cases in the US are misdiagnosed, and half of those medical mistakes have serious consequences for the patients.

My longest medical Odyssey happened when I arrived in Seattle suffering nagging headaches after a ferocious flu. A friendly doctor provided me with a new antibiotic for sinusitis; it didn't help, so the corporation that had invited me to the States allowed yet another doctor's visit. This time a person from the corporation escorted me, and the doctor happened to share a passion for sailboats with my companion — still chatting about yachts, he scribbled a prescription. I put in a word that, should I be permitted to have some input, I might point out that I had already tried that drug.

"Really?" said the doc, tossing the prescription into the dustbin, "Then try this one."

Once outside, I tossed his second prescription into the dustbin as well, telling my astonished escort a medical joke. An old man goes to a doctor's office, gets a prescription, goes to a pharmacy, fills it, and then throws the medicine away.

"You see," the man explains, "The doctor needs to make living, so I go to the doctor and pay his bill. The pharmacist needs to make living also, so I fill the prescription. But I want to live, too — and that's why I throw out the medicine."

But when I was shooting video in Alaska, the pain got worse. A local doctor concurred with the diagnosis.

"But I don't feel like I have sinusitis!" I protested again. "I just cannot breathe!"

---

1 Lynn Visson

"You don't know. You need a CAT scan," she said, prescribing an antibiotic.

Back in Seattle, I got to see the best (looking) doctor — ever. Dark and handsome, languid and ox-eyed, he was a cosmetic surgeon too. When the dazzler asked, breathily, "What can I do for you?" I was close to blurting out, "Doctor, forget about the sinuses — let's go to Hawaii!" But his "movie star" quality and the CAT scan didn't change the diagnosis.

By this time, after so many antibiotics, food was running straight through me almost as soon as I swallowed it.

Back home in Russia, I went to my local universal healthcare polyclinic.

"Is our ENT doctor good?" I asked the overworked scheduler.

The tired woman looked at me incredulously, "Yes, see for yourself."

The doctor was probably six feet four inches tall, and young. It didn't discourage him that I was toting an armload of medical records in English. He found something amusing there and sent me for an X-ray, since the polyclinic didn't have a CAT scan. With the pictures in his hands, he said that I couldn't possibly have sinusitis since my frontal sinus cavities were not fully developed — the X-ray confirmed the CAT scan descriptions, which ended, to his amusement, with a confirmation of the frontal sinusitis diagnosis. In other words, I was diagnosed with having a stubborn inflammation of something that didn't really exist.

"It has to be a vascular issue, after the flu," he said, performing an acupressure technique as a demonstration. Instantly, for the first time in several months, I was able to breathe freely.

"You may just wash your face with cold and hot water alternately," the doctor recommended, "It will be good for your skin, too."

I felt stupid. I had seen five American doctors, in two states, had a CAT scan, and for several months was destroying my digestive and immune systems with different antibiotics — what for?

When it comes to invasive treatments performed in the US, the statistics are even scarier. Popular weight-control surgeries often lead to stunning — but disheartening — results. Published in the *Journal of the American College of Surgeons* a 2006 study analyzed the outcome of the surgeries for more than 700 patients: 23 percent of gastric-bypass patients and 9 percent of lap-band patients experienced complications after their operations. In the study of weight-loss operations from 1997 to 2002, almost 5 percent of patients died (!) within a year after surgery. And these are operations that often are sought just as a fortification for weak will power. My father–doctor had much safer weight-loss recommendation; he said that an overweight person should build up very strong arms. When amazed women asked how that could help with weight loss, he explained that strong arms are helpful for pushing away the plate.

But there are other unnecessary operations that don't deal with eating habits. Of the 617,000 hysterectomies performed annually in the US, "from 76 to 85 percent" (!) may be unnecessary. According to usual practice, both the uterus and ovaries are removed so the woman's body loses its natural sources of estrogen and testosterone, though a University of California (UCLA) study proved that this routine "double-whammy" can lead to serious health problems. Ernst Bartsich, MD, a gynecological surgeon at Weill-Cornell Medical Center in New York, stated, "I am not proud of that. It may be an acceptable procedure, but it isn't necessary in so many cases."[1] This surgery poses health-threatening complications for the patients, as well as a severe invasion into the very essence of womanhood; and there are quite well-known alternatives. The Boston University School of Public Health found that 73 percent of women are not even asked if they would like to consider having an episiotomy, which is the procedure when the vaginal opening is cut to make it bigger for a delivery.[2] It would be nice to ask beforehand, really.

I had my own memorable "almost surgical" incident when I was living in North Carolina. My husband and I came home after shopping and discovered on the answering machine a message from a doctor's office: I had to be admitted to the hospital next morning, on an empty stomach, for gall bladder removal. I had previously visited that doctor's office when my stomach reacted to stress, but no one told me I needed such a radical procedure. I felt much better, and rather liked the idea of keeping my internal organs.

The receptionist from the doctor's office rang again.

"Why do you inform me after ten o'clock?" I asked in amazement.

"Sorry, I forgot to call — I have five children, and I had to leave earlier today to drive my son to a baseball game."

I asked the football mom why the surgery is so urgent.

"We hate to leave you in pain."

"But I don't have that pain anymore! And Friday is not the best day for planned surgeries anyway." (Should something go wrong during week-end, only on-call doctor will be available.)

"But the surgeon who usually works with our doctor operates tomorrow," explained the woman, "He is a good doctor, he performed the autopsy on Kennedy!"

I said that I was not exactly ready for an autopsy yet, ditto for an organ removal, especially if the doctor doesn't even care to talk to his patients but sends gall bladders — "gold bladders," really — to his pal right away.

"Now I am in trouble!" wailed the lady, "You are scheduled for the surgery tomorrow!"

Was I supposed to be a nice guy and get my organ removed for her sake — and, of course, for her doctor's referral fee? Infuriated but frightened, I reached

---

1 Quoted from "The Scary Truth About Surgery," by Curt Pesmen, *Health*, July/August 2007
2 Ibid.

my doctor of internal medicine in Russia, a brilliant young beauty. She seemed amused. "Are there any stones in your gall bladder?"

"No."

"Are you in severe pain?"

"Not anymore, and I don't even know where that gall bladder is — it never bothered me!"

She started laughing, "Forget about surgery — come home in one piece, we'll take care of you!"

A Ukrainian woman who was training as an X-ray technician in North Carolina said that they had a patient who didn't want to X-ray her right leg since it was the left that hurt.

But the nurse in charge, after consulting the patient's chart, explained, "The doctor needs to X-ray your right leg, nothing we can do!"

"I can understand now why a wrong extremity could be amputated," said the Ukrainian, "But the scariest thing was that the radiologist doesn't even slow down his conveyer when the films run across the light box, not to speak of taking a closer look at individual ones. He just sips his coffee and dictates the diagnoses."

"It's so strange," my mother said over the phone. "We hear all the time that American medicine is the best."

Just like the horror stories of the Soviet regime that are exaggerated in the American imagination, the glossy pictures of American life, rooted in Russian minds, do not quite agree with the actuality.

The documentary "SiCKO" by Michael Moore unveils that myth on a very comprehensible level, comparing American health care with the universal coverage systems in Canada, France, the United Kingdom, and Cuba. A French worker gets three months of 100-percent-pay leave after his free cancer treatment just because he says he needs some time to recover. The French state provides weekly nanny visits to help and guide families with young children — the nanny may even cook and do laundry. A French woman pays a dollar per day for kindergarten. Health care of any level in England, Canada, and France is free. A drug that costs $120 in the US is only 5¢ in Cuba.

A team from CNN decided to check the facts in the documentary, "As we dug deep to uncover the numbers, we found surprisingly few inaccuracies in the film. In fact, most pundits or health-care experts we spoke to spent more time on errors of omission rather than disputing the actual claims..."[1]

I read about groups of prudent elderly from Seattle who pitched in together to make "drug runs" to Canada — that is, to purchase prescription drugs there. "Those drugs might not be safe; they are not approved by the FDA!" raged US officials. But Canadians have a longer life expectancy than people in the United

---

1 "Analysis: 'Sicko' numbers mostly accurate; more context needed," by A. Chris Gajilan, CNN.

States. And India may supply half of the world with medicine, but somehow, it won't work for an American? Meanwhile the number of artificial additives in popular American candies and junk foods are proven carcinogenic in Europe — who will volunteer to prove that those additives are harmful for an American consumer also?

And Americans with a conscience also "sigh and look uncomfortable, ashamed of our rich country that wouldn't help a sick baby without making sure there was money [in it]." That wasn't even the controversial Michael Moore — that was Mary Pipher.

Searching Where the Grass is Greener

When Rotary Clubs were still a novelty in Russia, a visiting American Rotarian fell in love with a Russian club-mate from our city. He just couldn't leave when the time had come, and extended his stay. Then extended it again. And again. His business, left unattended, started to crumble — unlike that of his *amie*. His lady was a successful merchant and didn't want to consider relocating, knowing that the high profit margin that she could rake in just by reselling goods in Russia would be unachievable in more civilized markets.

"Why I should go?" she reasoned. "I'm better off here, and my American doesn't seem to be suffering either; so I guess we'll stay where we are." And they did just that.

The popular belief that Russian–American couples always reside in America is not misleading — some of them choose to live in Russia. To their surprise, Americans discover that they may be much better off in Russia.

> "In Russia, I can do free-lance work, take on interesting translations, and have plenty of time for myself and my family [said one of Lynn Visson's interviewees]. "If we were living in the US, I'd have to work full-time to have an apartment like this and to pay for child care..." Though this was not their original expectation, some Americans ended up better off economically in Russia than in the US. And during the Soviet era Russian cities were among the safest in the world... Even today, young couples... feel they have better jobs and housing in Moscow than they would in the US.

But "top notch" accommodations in Moscow come with a price: in 2008, Moscow ranked for the third time as the world's most expensive city — thanks to the steadily appreciating ruble and a rising cost of living. The survey by Mercer Human Resource Consulting analyzed living expenses, helping big corporations to determine compensation for their multinational workers:

> The cost of living for expatriates in the Russian capital is nearly 35 percent high-
> er than in New York, which served as the base city for the survey... In Moscow, a
> luxury two-bedroom apartment will cost an expat $4,000 a month; a CD rings
> up at $24.83; one copy of an international daily newspaper is $6.30; and a fast-
> food hamburger meal totals $4.80.[1]

The Russian *nouveaux riches* must be proud. I hinted once to my shopoholic mother-in-law that her image of poor Russians who cannot afford to buy a pair of jeans needs an update, but she was stuck with that old propaganda cliché.

And according to another Western researcher, the Russian *nouveaux riches* have so far managed to slip between the Scylla and Charybdis of mindless consumerism and depression. Researching his book *Affluenza*, British psychologist Oliver James trotted the globe, chronicling how people became sadder while obtaining bigger houses, newer cars, and younger looks. In Singapore, where shopping is a national obsession, he found "sad, unplayful deadness." He respected the Chinese for their "best is good enough" stoicism, but he "most liked the Muscovites as they still have an interest in the life of the mind."

Brits can understand Russian souls, even if they are not trained psychologists like Oliver James. Some of them come to Russia for a visit — and stay.

> "Why did I stay in Russia?" Englishman Mark asked. "My mother asks me the
> same question all the time. Five years ago, she came here with Father to check
> on how I'm doing. The first thing they asked me was: "Where is the closest golf
> course?" When I told them that we don't have any, my father was very upset.
> They soon left. And all of a sudden, I realized that if I decided to come back
> to England one day, more than likely I won't fit in there. The Westerners just
> float down the stream. They care about external decorum in the first place, but
> the Russian soul needs something more than that, and this is what I like about
> Russians."[2]

But a Russian person coming back home after living abroad faces the same dilemma as Mark, it is indeed "impossible to wade twice in the same river." And this saying of Heraclites comes to mind automatically because ancient Greek and Latin proverbs were part of Soviet pop-culture. I always marveled that the Soviet system encouraged curiosity and intelligence in its people — I wonder why, if such individuals are trouble prone; it would have been much safer to cultivate public gossip about pop stars in order to create an easily governed crowd. Now, eagerly aping fashions previously forbidden, Russia adopts not the best American customs but the worst, developing its own Paris Hiltons, just with bigger eyes and shorter noses.

When Tatyana Tolstaya, an excellent Russian writer who now teaches at Skidmore College, mentioned to her students that she was quite amused by the scale of Mickey Mouse's anniversary — Mickey was even invited to the White House — she got a very sharp response, "a kind of hands off our Mickey Mouse!"

---

1 Jackie Farwell, Associated Press business writer, "Moscow ranks as world's priciest city," June 18, 2007

2 "Nachalo," *Argumenti I Facti*, June 17, 2004

She wrote that if a comparable Russian literary and cartoon character was "invited" to the Kremlin, it would just seem utterly bizarre. "You'd have to be a Communist not to love Sponge Bob, that nutty fry-cook from the Crusty Crab," an American novelist has stated. I suppose Bob might look "cute" to an American mom, but I still don't understand why on the green earth should Bob be a cultural icon or a touchstone?

Before, it was easy to complain that Soviet censorship had prevented us from seeing the real Western fun, and now Russia, in accordance with the pendulum law, has plunged into the cheapest fun headfirst, losing its own identity. Though we still hold onto some differences: the British show "Who Wants to Be a Millionaire" demonstrates the same trademark studio set and graphics on Russian TV, but offers quizzes tailored to the Russian audience, with topics on science and culture — not pop-culture. The American quarter-million dollar question, "Which breed of dog won last year [doggie's] cup?" would strike the Russian audience as absurd.

I took it as a national shame when quite few of the orchestra seats remained vacant at the opening of a season at the Bolshoi Theatre in Moscow, but my Muscovite friend brought me back to reality, pointing that it might be just that the tickets were too costly for those who would have liked to go. Indeed, in super-expensive Moscow, ticket prices may soar to extravagant heights. Luckily, the US, in truly egalitarian manner, gives everyone a chance to enjoy the best players in the world — ironically, a Russian has a much better chance of attending a concert by a famous Russian performer in America than in Russia. I heard many top Russian musicians when they were touring the US, and I am very grateful to America for this opportunity.

"While Americans expect that everyone will like the United States, the initial reactions of Russian spouses run the gamut from intense admiration to intense dislike," observes Lynn Visson. When Russians abroad talk about Russia, they may find they love their vanishing country more than they knew. It helps that Soviets were not used to gulping official propaganda blindly — people had a habit of establishing their own ideas of right and wrong and thinking for themselves. So they may demonstrate polar opposite opinions about life, based on their personal quest. A Russian lawyer who often travels to Europe with her husband on business trips said, "To me, the answer to the question where to live is evident. Even if it is regrettable, my motherland is not where I was born but where I could be confident of my future." Another Russian woman agreed. "I am glad that there is a chance that in the future I won't see my parents scraping for a loaf of bread. And those who love to talk about patriotism better not overdo it: who said that changing my country of residence has made me a parricide? Maybe I love my motherland, and love it so much that during my next visit I'll be able to help some helpless elderly people whom I cannot look upon without tears. And I'll help them not in exchange for something but just because I want to help, because I'm more of a patriot than those who will never leave their motherland, living in luxury, but never making a move to help the needy."

Yet another woman had a different approach, "Living in America, we understand very well that this country is not bad, not really good — it is simply different. Many of us put up with the crass earthliness, with shallow and distant relationships between people, with boredom. We realize what we have traded: those deep relationships that one used to have in Russia are nonexistent here, and nothing can change that. Some of us decided to go back to Russia; the others accepted this type of life where money is made on everything. For a person who grew up in a Russian environment, building a new life in this country is not an easy task. Russia has always being famous for its soul, and we got to understand it abroad so well — so cold it is here, so lonely, though this is a warm country. Life in Russia is hard, that's true, but the price of American comfort is too high. I dream of going back to Russia, and I am sure I'll do that."

Everything is weighed in comparison. "If one knows many people from a culture, it is easier to distinguish between individual and cultural characteristics," said Mary Pipher. Her young Russian interviewee "had been taught to help his friends, and...] didn't like the competitiveness of the American kids. Anton was shocked by American kids kissing in the hall and shouting, 'F— you!'"

Being a newcomer, Anton still had Russian personality. Usually, the young are yielding material — children assimilate quickly, though that is not necessarily a fortunate event. Lynn Visson confirms that "the transplanted Americans attest almost uniformly to the powerful emotional hold that [Russia] and its people — to say nothing of their spouses — acquire over them. 'I have never had such a warm and intense relationship, with both men and women,' said one husband of his life. 'It will be very hard to go back to cocktail party conversation after this.'" Visson's interviewee "clearly enjoys the intellectual and emotional intensity that life in Moscow can bestow."

But habitually, an average Westerner condescends to Russia. "That is their misfortune, not Russians'," commented Irina Antonova, the director of the State Museum of Fine Arts in Moscow, the renowned "queen of the museums" at the age of 85:

> "The Westerners rarely demonstrate curiosity, but I often notice that many of them are very full of themselves, and they miss so much because of it. We Russians have more curiosity, and broader views. I don't understand how directors of the largest world's museums can not know foreign languages. They are always very surprised when we converse with them in their native language. About 15 years ago, I asked the director of the Louvre which Russian artists he knows. He said, Rep'in, Vereshag'in, with stresses on the wrong syllables — and that was it. He couldn't even recall any of their paintings."[1]

---

1 Maxim Soverteka, "Asiatchina – zdorovii element!" *Argumenti I Facti*, #12, 2007

The well-known Russian violist Yuri Bashmet was periodically asked why he didn't emigrate or move abroad as many celebrated Russian musicians do. He explained:

> "I would rather prefer our public conscience to one of the other countries where people think that they are the best and the most talented. I feel that it is better to live with balanced self-criticism and self-respect. Besides, we have reasons to be proud of many of our achievements. In the beginning, I tried to explain why I didn't emigrate, but then I understood that the answer must be shorter. Now I simply say, 'My daughter Ksenya studies at the Moscow Conservatoire — name me a better one.' I do not hesitate anymore to state that I am a patriot. During Soviet times, the word was overused."[1]

Lynn Visson has noted the specific attitude of Russians immigrants in America, too: "Even those who hated the Soviet system are deeply attached to their country and highly apprehensive of the outside world. The pain of leaving family and friends is compounded by the loss of a government that took care of everything — housing, education, health, and jobs." The Soviet system tried to supply basics for its citizens, and the guaranteed health care, jobs, housing, and education were not necessarily a bad thing — the assurance and security contributed for people's peace of mind and mental health. I am not sure about apprehension of the outside world, though — as evidence to the contrary, Russians love to travel so much that even tsunami and terrorist threats don't slow them down. I saw a slogan on the tee shirt of a Russian tourist, "It's impossible to divert us because we don't care where we go."

It's hard to consider it a great American achievement that an estimated 15.3 percent of the population, or 44.8 million people, were without health insurance in 2005.[2] No wonder Americans "went to work even when they were really ill," as Visson states, but a Soviet citizen could afford the more prudent behavior of calling for a doctor's visit at home — for free. But things have changed in Russia and now all these guarantees are gone. As one Russian said about this catch-22, "We knew that everything that communists told us about communism was a lie, but we didn't realize that what they told us about capitalism was true."

After the Communist Party rulership was dismantled, the first exhilarating moments gave way to the sober realization that the winners were the politicians and the corrupted bureaucracy, not the nation: "The nation is the country minus the state," one witty Russian quipped. From the early days of the new Russian democracy, the state officials-carpetbaggers have been stealing with impunity.

Enterprising Americans did not miss the chance to pitch right in. The American economic advisers, Harvard professors *Andrei Shleifer* and Jonathan Hay (the Russian press has suggested that Hay worked as a CIA agent on the side) and their better halves, Nancy Zimmerman and Elizabeth Hebert, the official heads

---

1 Olga Shablinskaya, "Y. Bashmet: 'Ya bol'she ne stesnyaius' bit' patriotom," *Argumenti I Facti*, #52, 2004

2 Comparison from 2007 federal Report of the US Centers for Disease Control and Prevention

of the "family businesses," were caught and faced a $120 million lawsuit for using USAID funds to push personal advantages. But that lawsuit was for the Americans — in Russia, Anatoly Chubais, the head of the infamous Russian Privatization Center (which was the instrument of the notorious "shock therapy" that threw Russia into economical turmoil for decades while transforming corrupted officials and their buddies into overnight tycoons), still remains an active Russian political figure.

> In a bout of puzzling honesty, Chubais admitted, in an interview to the Russian business daily *Kommersant*, later published also by the *Los Angeles Times*, to defrauding multilateral lending organizations and their Western masters. He said, "In such situations, the authorities have to [lie]. We ought to. The financial institutions understand, despite the fact that we conned them out of $20 billion, that we had no other way out."

> It is a sad testimony to both Russia's dearth of honest talent and to the murkiness of its public life that Chubais is as strong as ever and manages the giant electricity utility.[1]

A Russian tabloid reported that at an air show in Moscow an unidentified Russian, surrounded by bodyguards, asked the US delegation to sell him a B-52 bomber. The reporter allegedly overheard the conversation. "An astounded member of the US delegation said the bomber was not for sale but that it would cost at least $500 million. "No problem — it's such a cool machine!" the Russian reportedly said.

Even if that particular story is apocryphal, "Russia's new rich, who built fantastic fortunes trading commodities and contacts after the fall of the Soviet Union, have made a name for themselves as ostentatious purchasers of everything from British football clubs [Chelsea is owned by Roman Abramovich, one of the world's 50 wealthiest people;] to Fabergé eggs [by Viktor Vekselberg, Russia's third-richest man, who donated the collection to Russia]."[2]

In the midst of Russia's reforms in the 90s, many well-intended Americans asked me that optimistic question, "Now that you don't have communists ruling in Russia anymore, it's much better, right?"

"Not exactly." I had to disappoint those kind souls.

It was hard to explain to someone who was brought up on Cold War images that at least communists could be kicked out. If a Communist Party member was caught doing something naughty, much less illegal, he didn't stand a chance — the communists had to purge him from the party. If journalists and editors were brave and sharp, a single publication could dislodge a sleazy politician. The new Russian democrats don't seem to be punishable under the law — I was fired for unveiling a shady deal that the regional government lawyer had made. When my colleague aired an interview with a lawyer who had attempted to sue the corrupt local health insurance company, she was dressed down by the TV station

---

1 Dr. Sam Vaknin, "Chubais – Russia's Last Oligarch."
2 "Rich Russian tries to buy US bomber at air show," Reuters, August 24, 2007

boss. He'd received calls from the big cheeses — no grass-roots revolution can win a fight with the health insurance industry, in Russia or in the US. Now, if a high-ranking Russian official is caught red-handed, it doesn't surprise anybody: stealing has become a part of everyday political life.

I worked for a Presidential Bureau for a while and the close contact with our "new democrats" was revolting. Right from the beginning they created for themselves a special bubble, achieving the goal that their predecessors had announced: they succeeded in building some kind of weird communism just for themselves; even the prices in the cafeterias in the Russian White House were artificially low. The only car models that the newly minted democratic representatives could possibly use in the execution of their official duties started in the neighborhood of the well-equipped Audi. Entertainment allowances, "lost" laptops, international trips on governmental funds, added up to lifestyles that somehow were hugely mismatched to their official salaries, and astronomically expensive government real estate that had been neatly privatized, for pennies, became commonplace. Those pleasures seemed to come with the job.

The morals in the society plummeted. Once in the 1990s, coming back from the US, I entered Russia through the notorious Khabarovsk Airport in the Russian Far East. To begin with, some items from my luggage had been stolen by the airport thieves and when I tried to file a report with an airport policeman, the *militsioner*, he said, "Oops!" and literally ran away, holding onto his service hat. I found the airport's manager on duty, but she angrily advised me not to keep her from her work — actually, from her rest, for the airport was closing for the night. Next, at the information bureau, a hand-written sign on the window suggested I knock. A clerk who was already asleep aroused herself to inform me that the tickets were sold out, but for a hundred-dollar bribe the problem could be solved. I decided not to rush and in the morning discovered that a wide selection of tickets was available. Meanwhile, in the dark Khabarovsk Airport square suspicious-looking private taxi drivers offered a night ride to the city for the price of an airplane ticket. That was all in the course of thirty minutes. So far, I know only one other country where travelers can be robbed so shamelessly — that is Italy. I hummed under my breath the lines from a Russian pop song that emerged in my memory:

> Motherland, I go to motherland,
>
> Some may call her a fright
>
> But I like her
>
> Though a beauty she is not.

Luckily my cousin, whom I hadn't seen for ages, came to the airport to meet me; otherwise I don't know how I would survive my motherland's welcome. After the friendly and polite US service, it sure felt like running face first into a concrete wall.

"Couldn't you just stay in the US?" my cousin asked me.

"Yes."

"And why did you decide to go back?"

"Because I wanted to."

He couldn't get it, because he hadn't tried it. "The magnetic attraction pulls them back to Russia, hardships be damned," knowingly writes Visson.

I knew a programmer who studied computer science in Brazil, worked for Amazon.com in Seattle and was thinking about accepting a position with Microsoft. However, he was planning to go back to Russia with his family, though they hadn't lived in Russia for the last fifteen years. But they were closing things up, getting rid of mortgages and payments in preparation for return.

When I asked about his motives, he answered simply, "I don't want our son to grow up as an American. Besides, we never felt that we emigrated — we were just living abroad."

But he emphasized that he wasn't going back to *Russia* — he was going back to Moscow, which is a country inside the country with its own income structure, and he intended to secure a job in Moscow beforehand.

Another young professional, an economist with a diploma from an American university, decided to go back to St. Petersburg with his Russian wife whom he'd found via a marriage agency — she was from the same city, and eagerly supported his decision.

It is a trend now — more and more young Russian professionals abroad are opting to go back home, but the trickle of repatriates won't help the grim Russian demographic situation.

Russia is dying out, literally.

> According to the UN prognosis, by 2050, the population of Russia will be reduced from 143 million to 100 million. In 2080, there could be only 38 million remaining. [...] For simple reproduction of the population, each woman of fertile age is supposed to have 2.15 births.... In Russia, from the 60s to the 80s of last century, the coefficient was around 2.2, and it was higher than in the USA and much higher than in Europe. Now in Europe it is about 1.4; in Japan — 1.3; in India — 3; in China — 1.7; in Iraq — 4.5; in Saudi Arabia — 3.8; in Pakistan — 4; in Turkey — 2.4. As a result, by 2050 the population of India will increase from 1.1 billion to 1.6 billion; of Saudi Arabia — from 25 million to 50 million; of Pakistan — from 158 million to 305 million; of China — from 1.3 billion to 1.4 billion. The population of Japan will decrease from 128 million to 112 million.... Speaking from the viewpoint of national security, for the Japanese, with their small waterlocked state and population almost the same size as that of the Russian Federation, depopulation is not a problem. But what is good for the Japanese could be deadly for the Russians: the depopulation of Russia will leave a vacuum that will be filled by numerous the Chinese. And nobody should be blamed for that — the Chinese are not responsible for the laws of nature. In the near future, due to the demographic structure, some 15% of young Chinese will have trouble finding brides: now, for every 188 male newborns there are only 100 female newborns. But to be single is unacceptable in China. And where will these Chinese go?

Just as America is steadily becoming a country of Hispanics, Russia may see a growing minority of inhabitants of Chinese origin. In his piercing article, Vadim Aliev ties the decrease in Russian birthrates not to economical turbulence but to emotional disturbances. Where Cold Warriors failed, Western culture has succeeded. Imperialism came not on the tips of bayonets, but on Mickey Mouse's ears, indeed.

The sharp decrease of prosperity in Russia in the 90s was not the main reason for the plunging birthrate. I think that was due to the import into our country of so-called "western culture" of pursuit of wealth and success, combined with demolishing the old Soviet system of values and disfiguring Christian values of love. Now, the main god is success, inflicted by the West. That celestial is the catalyst of moral degradation of Russians, increasing the degree of individualism and egoism, while the typical for Russian nation spirit of friendship, kindness of heart is smoked out and substituted by Western values, creating in the bared Russian soul a feeling of anonymity and senseless of life.

That makes Russians die early and not bear children. It brings some people to complete narcissism, and others to psychoses, especially when combined with the lost national identity and the obstinate implantation of an ideal successful person who will draw a line at nothing due to not being burdened with spiritual values.

For those who accepted the new culture, childbirth becomes senseless — just having one child would be more than enough for image-making purposes. For those who couldn't achieve success or who don't care for rat races, the entire life becomes senseless. They become embittered, and hence prone for moral lapse also, and all that affects their quality of life and life expectancy. The substitution of cultural fundaments is a reason why one stops giving birth and the others stop living.

A Russian person's soul cares more about personality than about money; Russian life has always been about giving, not consuming as in the West. That's why a Russian organically cannot accept ill usage and total greed. If the fruits of labor benefit the shameless and ungrateful new rich, then what's the sense? Everything becomes mirthless.

According to the World Health Organization (2003), the average number of daily suicides on the planet is about 14.5 per 100,000. In Russia, this number is three times higher — 43.1. [...] The meaninglessness and emptiness programs a Russian person for self-destruction. No wonder that death rates increased so dramatically, especially in people of working age: in childhood, the purpose in life is not sought yet, and in old age is no longer sought. In other nations, inner conflicts and complexes may transform into revolutions and wars, but Russians are genetically good-natured. Up to a point, Russians prefer to give in, and sacrifice, even if it is a self-sacrifice. And only after all the hardships and self-renunciations are exhausted can that infamous Russian revolutionary riot "suddenly" break out.

In pre-revolution times, charity in Russia had a fundamental value and was widely popular in the various strata of the society. A Russian merchant was a Maecenas, patron of the arts, who voluntarily donated large sums of money for piety. And the birth rates in Russia in the beginning of the 19th century were twice as high as in Europe at that time. We were never egoists, but now, according to the statistics, we have more than 700,000 orphans and children whose parents had to be stripped of parental rights. Now, in the national atmosphere of total egoism, uncharacteristic for Russians, we have lost ourselves, our very love has started to decompose. We don't want to love or don't understand how to love, and we cannot do it in self-absorbing Western style.

We are disappearing from the earth not because of famine, infections, AIDS, or alcohol poisoning. We are dying because of our Russian soul, because its essence doesn't match the surrounding cultural reality with its predatory moral climate. A person puts his head in a noose not because everything around him is terrible but because his soul feels terrible. And alas, that's logical, and even healthcare reform won't help because it is not a somatic issue — it is a commotion of the spirits, in the big picture.[1]

Obviously, Prozac is not popular among Russians. Some Russians might be hopeless idealists who don't need a pill to improve their feelings chemically — they need peace of mind and harmony with the surrounding world instead.

And if some people cannot accept that which they are not able to change, then what? There is an old Soviet-era joke about a Jew who begged and begged the Soviet government for permission to emigrate to Israel. Once in Israel, he started missing his Moscow life so much that he appealed for repatriation. Back in Moscow, he started craving for his new homeland and asked about an emigrant visa again.

"Comrade, could you make up your mind, where are you most comfortable?" the annoyed authorities asked.

"I think in the plane, between the USSR and Israel!" the Jew answered sincerely.

You will not believe how true that is. For somebody who is torn between two countries, "home is the inescapable place, the place to which the heart's compass turns."[2] An immigrant almost always feels that compass within, that nostalgia pacemaker device.

---

1 Vadim Aliev, "Rossia vimiraet," *AiF Dolgoizitel*, March, 24, 2006
2 Joanne Harris, *Coastliners*

"A Nation of Victims"

A strange woman in a Southern store, spotting my accent, addressed to me out of the blue. "My nephew is in Iraq."

"I am sorry," I said, "You must be worrying about him a lot."

"No, I am glad that he is there — we must punish those who attacked us!"

"The Iraqis attacked you? When!?"

"Don't you know?" She looked at me incredulously, "[But what could one expect from those with accents?] On September 11!"

I doubt that the woman would recognize it as a valuable piece of information if I told her that the attackers were reported to be citizens of Saudi Arabia, and that there was no way the US could start a quarrel with that country. The woman wasn't looking for knowledge — she wanted to relish the feeling of revenge, and official propaganda readily pours "stirred *and* shaken" cocktails for citizens like her. "'Kill 'em all, and let God sort it out!' My old platoon sergeant used to say..."[1]

What happened on 9/11 was shocking and terrifying, and the propaganda campaign that followed wasn't always equitable, either. "The war has started!" a popular TV channel ran a slogan soon after the attack. Then the official clarification came that the United States had not actually declared war, and the expression was said to be inappropriately exaggerated. But it sure worked well for testing the waters — in no time the term was vernacularized, and the "evilness" of the 9/11 attackers was soundly linked to the danger of Iraq by tying them together wantonly in politicians' speeches — just in the same manner the idea *delenda est*

---

1 Robert James Waller, *High Plains Tango*

Carthago ("Carthage must be destroyed") was planted and eventually carried out.[1] A simple but effective technique.

Through the media, the government had convinced the public that Iraqi terrorists had attacked, so Iraq had to be punished, and thus the war was justified. Feelings of helplessness and rage found an outlet.

I happened to be a guest at a Seattle TV studio when the station featured in the news a 10-second segment about the explosion of an apartment complex in Moscow — right after a detailed report about a bizarre break-in a local convenience store where nothing was stolen.

After the broadcast, the director came to me and apologized, "If I knew we were having a Russian journalist here tonight, I would have switched the emphasis."

I was grateful for that apology, but even so the American mass media called these people mere "rebels" when they were holding hostage pregnant women, newborns, and doctors at a maternity ward in southern Russia. When apartment buildings in Russian cities were blown up, it was called "an act of rebel forces." Only when Americans were hit did the American mainstream propaganda start calling terrorism — well, terrorism. Were it not for 9/11, would they still have referred to "rebels" in the same "rebellious southern region" of Russia when children, teachers, and parents were killed at a school in Beslan on September 1, 2004?

But why was the US so implausibly vulnerable to the attackers? No wonder so many conspiracy theories are circulating about 9/11 — some things just look strange, if not incredibly stupid. Leaving conspiracy theories aside, along with fishy-looking tales of a car found at the airport parking lot where the "terrorists" left detailed information about the plot — no one bought that story — let's address just a few things regarding the American part of the awful tragedy. Everybody knows, thanks to Hollywood movies, that if a plane suddenly veers off course and starts to fly across several states, without responding to air traffic control (there must be air traffic control, right?), then a couple of fighter jets come to escort the escapee to a forced landing. Why was a plane allowed to perform as a missile?

Only a BBC documentary that was broadcast overseas partially answered another simple question, absent in the "politically correct" American coverage of 9/11. The documentary included an interview with the pilots from Colorado Springs airbase. They said they knew that they couldn't reach Washington in time. They said they saw smoke rising above the horizon when they were still quite far from Washington air space — they had to make quite a ride before reaching it.

---

1 The Roman statesman Cato the Elder would always end his speeches with this reminder, even when he had not been talking about Carthage at all.

Entering American planes, I had never realized that their cockpit doors are just as flimsy as the bathrooms'. If I had known that, I would definitely have had some jitters — in Russia, with its own sad history of hijacking, the planes and even helicopters have bulletproof cockpit doors. And I never thought that knives — cold arms, for God's sake! — were legally allowed onboard US aircrafts until 9/11. By contrast, travelers who pass through the Immigration offices in the US had never been allowed to carry even nail files — once, in Seattle, I was quite rudely forced to leave my "Revlon weapon" in the car, as the policeman diligently dug (yuck!) through my cosmetic bag.

Now, the precautions go overboard sometimes. A British patient with fistula-in-ano, an abnormal condition in which the feces discharge through an opening in the skin, was stopped by immigration officials in New York. The tourist had a long-term seton — a loop made of suture material to control perianal sepsis, which he was obliged to have removed by an airport doctor.[1] This notice from *The Lancet* had an ironical headline "The Long Arm of the Law" — one never knows how deep and into which holes that arm can reach, indeed.

Of course, America's mainland geography makes it quite secure — there is a friendly, decent neighbor to the north, and a non-aggressive state to the south. Nonetheless, the airspace could be quite a special concern. Was the United States really so careless about security before 9/11? Why wasn't anybody held responsible for failing to protect innocent American citizens from such insolent attack — a Hollywood style attack, I might say? There even *was* a movie, starring Arnold Schwarzenegger, which never made it to the screens — it was shelved after the attack — in that movie a plane flies into a skyscraper. Speaking of creating a monster...

"Why has it become impossible to admit a mistake in Washington and accept the consequences?" wrote columnist George Packer. "Addressing the CIA's failure to adequately alert the FBI that a known terrorist, soon to be a 9/11 hijacker, had a visa to the United States, [George] Tenet writes [*At the Center of the Storm: My Years at the CIA*; the book earned four million royalty], 'No excuses. However,' he adds 'overworked men and women who, by their actions, were saving lives around the world all believed the information had been shared with the FBI.'"[2]

That is just hysterical. So, was the information shared by the CIA with its "malignant friend" FBI or not? Or "hard-working guys around the world" just thought that it was? I doubt that in criminal court, for example, such a goof would work. But according to popular political fashion, the enemy who found a weak link — or outright nonchalance — is the only figure to blame. Those who are supposed to be in charge are victims as well. Overworked victims, that is.

---

1 *The Lancet*, February 2007, quoted from *Harper's*, April 2007
2 George Packer, "No Blame, No Shame," *New Yorker*, May, 14, 2007

"Victimism is not idealism. Ultimately, victimism is concerned not with others, but with the self," wrote Charles J. Sykes in *A Nation of Victims: The Decay of the American Character*, a daring book that I named this chapter after. The book had been published before 9/11, so the author didn't have to consider the current sensitivity about the topic, "If previous movements of liberation may have been characterized as Revolution of Rising Expectations, this society is in the grips of a Revolution of Rising Sensitivities... where 'feelings' rather than reason is what count."

"Americans don't appreciate being criticized," I have heard many times from "authentic" US citizens. But that is a dangerous approach; maybe this is why such a horrible tragedy happened in the first place. Just days before the attack, discussing some "red-hot" political topics, I happened to mention that America is so much hated in some parts of the world for its cocky style that in the volatile modern climate this feeling might detonate in some ugly manner. Cassandra I wish I was not. But the answer I received, predictable and obtuse, but "politically correct," was that "They hate us because they envy us." Well, why are there no such dangerous feelings toward any other well-to-do countries — let's say, the dynamic ultra-modern Japan, or bucolic yet high-tech Sweden with their much, much higher quality of life, or the stylish and prosperous France?

After 9/11, the pendulum effect sent America from outright nonchalance into another extremity. "[P]rimary reliance on the unilateral exercise of sovereign power, especially if accompanied by a self-serving definition of the merging threats, could bring self-isolation, growing national paranoia, and increasing vulnerability to a globally spreading anti-American virus," wrote Zbigniew Brzezinski.

> An anxious America, obsessed with its own security, could find itself isolated in a hostile world. If its quest for solitary security were to get out of hand, it could transform the land of free into a garrison state imbued with a siege mentality... President Bush was inclined (probably because of his religious propensities) to treat the threat almost in theological terms, viewing it as a collision between "good and evil." He even embraced the Leninist formula, "he who is not with us is against us," a notion that is always congenial to an aroused public mood, but whose black-and-white view of the world ignores the shades of gray that define most global dilemmas.[1]

Americans are as hypersensitive as some small, belligerent diaspora that is always on alert, checking whether its pride has been compromised. Such behavior is dangerous on the part of a huge and powerful nation. George Packer, referring to the David Rieff book *At the Point of a Gun*, ironically states that "for Rieff... a self-proclaimed realist... America is just like any other empire, acting out of self concern, and its moral fantasies make its power only more dangerous."[2]

---

1 Zbigniew Brzezinski, *The Choice: Global Domination or Global Leadership*.
2 George Packer, "Fighting Faith," *New Yorker*, July 10 &17, 2006

But so many "self-proclaimed," self-taught, and simply sober realists agree with Packer:

> "Right now, our beautiful democracy is eroding before our eyes... As has often been the case historically, power is distributed according to wealth, not wisdom or compassion. Bullies and thugs rule the world. Increasingly, it feels as we are trapped in a medieval crisis — Crusaders versus Jihadists."[1]

When the bullies — from either camp — feel victimized, they can turn into a very dangerous breed. Especially if a "victim" has power and is well-trained in the self-justification field. "This belief in utter blamelessness is of course, the inversion of the Puritan ethos that regarded man as, by nature, depraved. In the new ethos, man is restored to his original innocence. The bad boy becomes the misunderstood child; the brutal killer becomes a sociopath in need of therapy," wrote Sykes.

> "What to do about the victimization of America? Sykes argues that the state has become the vehicle for the politicization of victimization in the form of tax-payer-financed and increasingly state-enforced "politically correct" thinking, actions, and institutions. And if self-responsibility and individual character are to be revived in America again, it can only come through the actions of individuals. "...Recognizing our own responsibility and the need to stop blaming others is the first step toward dismantling the culture of victimization.... It is time to drop the crutch."[2]

Unfortunately, the crutch hasn't been dropped. Now it is hard to demarcate a victim from a bully sometimes. No wonder that the nation becomes "a nation of lawyers" — everybody feels slighted and so everybody has to sue everybody. "In 1991, the US had 281 lawyers per 100,000 population — compared to... a meager 11 per 100, 000 in Japan. In sheer volume, the US had 70 percent of the world's total supply of lawyers."[3]

An ideal society — and ideal humans — are still lurking somewhere behind the horizon. No wonder that the Bible and the founder of communism, describing them, concur in many points. Communism was promised to be "on the horizon," just like a free, egalitarian, democratic society with rights for all. But the horizon has a sneaky habit of receding as one approaches it. There is still a lot of work to do — for all of us.

---

1 Mary Pipher, *Writing to Change the World*
2 Richard M. Ebeling, Book Review, February, 1993 http://www.fff.org/freedom/0293e.asp
3 David Margolick, "Address by Quayle on Justice Proposals Irks Bar Association," *New York Times*, August, 12, 1991

The Globe of America

Coincidentally, the biggest statue of Lenin in the Pacific region is not located in the former Soviet Union: that bronze mastermind of the Great October Socialist Revolution is positioned in front of a fast food restaurant in Fremont, Seattle, as if he were touting the tacos: "Comrades, step right up!" Armed with a video camera, I interviewed passers-by about this giant bronze man. They recognized the monument as a landmark in their free-spirited bohemian neighborhood but had no idea who he was. Nowadays, Russian children of school age also have very vague ideas about the turning point of their national history. In a city across the Pacific from Seattle, the Russians have nicknamed their statue of Lenin, pictured in a windswept cloak, as "Batman."

Surprisingly many Americans are childishly unaware of significant cultural, historical, and even geographical facts about other countries. This phenomenon of extreme self-absorption may be called "the globe of America" — the image of the rest of the world is so indistinct that it sometimes seems to be off the globe.

Ironically, this country sends its soldiers to die in countries that many American citizens wouldn't be able to locate on the map. Matthew Hays from the *Montreal Mirror* interviewed Pulitzer prize winner Seymour Hersh, who became "famous as the American journalist who has exhaustively covered both the Vietnam War and the current Iraq War... He was also the first journalist to state unequivocally that weapons of mass destruction would never be found in Iraq. With his staunch criticism of those in power, Hersh has acquired his share of enemies. Pentagon adviser Richard Perle once called Hersh 'the closest thing we have to a terrorist.'"

In this excerpt, Canadian Hays sets up Hersh's bristles in the same way Hersh himself sets up the American administration's bristles.

M: When Bush was asked about civilian casualties, he responded that he thought it was about 30,000. But he wasn't asked by a journalist, he was asked by a citizen in a town hall meeting. Do you feel the media has been too reluctant to report on civilian casualties in Iraq?

SH: ... I think the American people know the casualties are going up. I can fault the press for a lot of other things, particularly in the first couple of years of the war. But I think they're doing all right on that one. In other words, I disagree with you.

M: But we hear about the military casualties, but rarely hear about the numbers of dead Iraqi civilians. I have found that alarming.

SH: Inevitably in a war, that will happen, and it's depressing. But I'll save the alarm for something else, not to be cynical about it... The discrepancy about casualties is pretty alarming, and if those numbers are true, then the average American is doing a lot more killing in this war than in any other war perhaps. [...] I have no idea, but I would think 300,000–400,000 is probably about right. But it's hard for me to give a rational answer, because I don't have one.

M: Why does so much of the American public often seem willfully ignorant? Much of the populace seems intent on not knowing what is going on in terms of political and foreign affairs.

SH: ... The ignorance may not be willful. The problem with this is, in order to answer your questions, I have to buy into what it is you're saying. I have no ***ing way of knowing whether they're ignorant. I mean, Americans are pretty ***ing ignorant. What we don't know is pretty huge. You could never accuse Americans of learning from history or learning from past mistakes. You're talking about a country that went to war in Vietnam with the theory that we had to bomb North Vietnam in order to keep the hordes of Red China from coming, right? Not knowing that Vietnam and China had fought wars for 2,000 years and would fight one four years after the war was over, in '79. What we don't know is just breathtaking in my country. To call this ignorance willful as opposed to general ignorance, I don't know. On any issue, Americans can display an incredible lack of information. I doubt if there's a society which has paid less attention to the facts than any else."[1]

But history lessons rarely teach politicians, anyhow — just think about the British, Soviet, and American soldiers invading Afghanistan at different times. Or about the fact that Yugoslavia, just as well as Vietnam, has quite a history of civil wars — just try renting the award-winning movie "Before the Rain" by Milcho Manchevski. The movie, awarded with the Golden Lion at the Venice Film Festival, was shot long before Yugoslavia was broken up.

After the media, the next most important cultural brokers are educators, especially primary schoolteachers, who are supposed to guide young minds. "Cultural pluralism is not the issue... The issue is the teaching of bad history," wrote Arthur M. Schlesinger, Jr., in *The Disuniting of America*. "Wicked textbooks and incompetent teachers can do a lot of damage."

I had a memorable incident when a teacher from a Southern elementary school invited me to make a presentation about Russia for her young students. We discussed the topic beforehand, and I had to make a couple of geopolitical

---

1 Matthew Hays, "Digging through a stupid war," *Montreal Mirror*, Thursday, Oct. 26, 2006

corrections. But unfortunately the information didn't stick, since the teacher energetically opened the presentation with a disarming statement.

"As you know, Russia doesn't exist anymore."

I tried to steer in the direction of the undisputed crumbling of the Soviet Union, but the young teacher didn't give up easily.

"Okay, then it is Slovakia that is not part of Russia anymore."

I thought I understood the teacher's logic: since Russians are the Slavs, then Slovakia must be a part of Russia. I showed Slovakia on the map, and it was evidently quite far away for being a part of the former Soviet Union. I decided not to muddle with Slovenia, the other potential candidate for a part of Russia, and just mentioned that the Old World map is quite a quilt, indeed.

After that experience, I'm not so sure that all of those members of the Yahoo community were kidding — on May 30, 2005, the Yahoo forum sparked a controversy discussing hot news: Russian troops in Georgia.

> bonnie_and_clydesdale, 28 year old female from St. Louis, Missouri: "I had no idea Russia had troops in Georgia. Never was a word ever said that communist soldiers were stationed in one of our Southern States. How did they get away with this? Why didn't they tell us?"

> kung_fu_at_you, 21 year old male, Chicago, Illinois, "Next we'll find out Chinese army in NYC."

> jjmartin1275: "Russian troops need to be moved to New Mexico, and Arizona, to protect our borders. We don't need them in Georgia anymore."

> stephphany, 18 year old female, "I'm going to Atlanta. I want to meet some of those hunky Russian troops before they leave!"

> bobwastaken2004, 34 year old male: "Stupid freaking people. Thinking that this article means Russian troops in Georgia, USA? How stupid can you be?"

> jar_il2000, 26 year old male from Israel, "Americans r u dummy or just kidding!?"

> usa_number11111: "We are dummy, you are not dummy, oh great world we are stuped that is why we the great super power."

If news from Georgia were taken to heart, regions "far from home base" evoke a different reaction. A young American celebrity was booed by the press when she unwarily blurted out at a press-conference that she didn't care about publicity in Australia. "Like, where is that Australia?"

A Miss Teen USA 2007 contestant was asked why one-fifth of Americans can't locate the US on a map. Were she from a Russian high school, she could have parried with a quotation from the classic satirical comedy *The Minor*, where Mrs. Simple states that geography is "not a noble science. A noble man has only to say, 'Take me there!' — and cabbies will take him wherever he pleases."[1] As a Russian immigrant ironically noted, "Americans would rather pay than think."

Even sharp American professionals might be surprised with some ordinary facts of overseas life: a lovely, smart lady was amused by the 24-hour display on

---

1 Denis Ivanovich Fonvizin, *The Minor*

my electronic wristwatch: "You mean, two o'clock is fourteen? And then there could be, what — twenty hours, too? That's so funny!"

I guess it must be comforting when foreign artifacts look just like those made for regular people:

> The dailies were as sleek and modern as any in the States, and they were being read by people who had a thirst for the news. Perhaps Brazil wasn't as backward as he thought [John Grisham's hero noted].... A young Brazilian tells him, "Three years ago, my cousin and I rode a big bus, a Greyhound, across the country. We were in every state but six." Jevy was a poor Brazilian boy of twenty-four. Nate was twice his age and during most of his career had had plenty of money. Yet Jevy had seen much more of the United States than Nate.[1]

Not a fictional, but an ordinary, real Texan said in an interview that if he won the lottery he would fulfill his old dream to see the sea. That I couldn't understand: Texas has quite a shoreline, so why not just go there? This was before gasoline prices went skyrocketing, a person didn't have to hit the jackpot if he wanted to go for a drive.

But maybe this is a tourists' privilege: tourists usually visit places where the locals are going to go "someday," places that beckon like Virginia Woolf's lighthouse. I showed my husband the state where he was born, dragged him to cultural events, and I knew many foreign wives who prompted their spouses to move around in the same manner.

"They must be so grateful — we made their lives more interesting!" exclaimed the rapturous Ukrainian Ludmila. "If not for us, they would never experience all those things!"

I was more skeptical, "This is your point of view — they might be just as happy and definitely snugger watching TV all day. Your urge to travel could be irritating."

One witty American, an armchair traveler-droll anthropologist, told me, "We can just wait till other people come to America. Everybody comes here, right? So eventually, we will know how people in the other parts of the world look."

Hard to argue.

---

1 John Grisham, *The Testament*

THE WAR OF THE WORLDS

That TV show reminded me of a conversation between the blind and the deaf-mute. The commentator expressed his astonishment: How could those terrorists who lived in the US and saw how nice everything is in the country, who *went to American stores*, commit such a horrible thing as 9/11 attack?

Why on earth should suicide attackers care about goods and malls? The dead don't need possessions. Many suicide bombers die for ideas; why should they possibly care about the highly promoted American consumerism and life of affluence? They undergo a brainwashing different from the one that American citizens receive — religious extremism preaches asceticism, not consumerism.

That broadcast included interviews with Afghan schoolchildren who had Osama bin Laden's photo as their screensavers. The young Afghans recognized bin Laden as a hero; they assured the reporter that should bin Laden be killed, there would be dozens of others ready to take his place. The journalist didn't ask why the young Afghans dreamt of becoming bin Laden's followers one day — the kids and the reporter conversed freely in English, but their different worlds didn't reach each other. I dare to assume that those children were quite different from American kids, even if they liked computer games as well. Now those teenagers are young adults, and might very well do just what they had promised, shooting their American counterparts and not just on the computer screen — if they were not killed by these counterparts first, of course. It is so utterly sad.

Examples like this TV show made me wonder if dissimilar standards at least could be acknowledged by official American propaganda — I don't mean always accepted, since slaughter couldn't possibly be vindicated — but even such an ultimate tragedy as 9/11 doesn't seem to have affected the standard approach.

"No one, no single center, can today command the world. No single group of countries... can do it. Under the current US president, I don't think we can fundamentally change the situation as it is developing now... It is dangerous. The world is experiencing a period of growing global disarray." That is former Soviet President Mikhail Gorbachev, who won the 1990 Nobel Peace Prize for his role in ending the Cold War. Politicians from opposite sides of the "political fence" agree upon the danger of using state power to satisfy national self-conceit. "Gorbachev echoed President Putin's frequent endorsement of a so-called 'multipolar world,' without the perceived dominance of the United States. 'The Americans want so much to be the winners. The fact that they are sick with this illness, this winners' complex, is the main reason why everything in the world is so confused and so complicated.'"[1]

Brzezinski was more optimistic: "American power and American social dynamics, working together, could promote the gradual emergence of a global community of shared interest."

The European Union — or the United States of Europe, as the popular post-First World War slogan called it — proved that the emergence of a global community is possible, though it is hard to imagine European and American interests merging to the same degree. It is hard to see how the US would ever agree to play as an equal, not a senior, partner.

As an example, when France disagreed with the US about invading Iraq, the American media started slandering France and attacking everything French to a bizarre degree. The hostesses of the TV show "The View" chatted that good Americans should boycott French merchandise. "But what about French butter — it's so good!" moaned one.

National Geographic in its world-in-photos issue gave the "good guy" Spain extensive coverage but France was represented by a photo of a laughing Polynesian carrying an obese Caucasian woman in his arms from a boat to a tropical beach. I wondered if the woman was even of French origin, as I had never seen such abundant flesh in France — she looked like she might have been borrowed from the nearby Sandwich Islands that belong to a country with an obesity curse. That was such a pity: during the Cold War, *National Geographic* provided for those behind the Iron Curtain a view of trends in Western photography and had served as yet another window into the outside world. But by the time I became an American subscriber, I discovered a different *National Geographic* altogether: Mr. George W. Bush had hardly uttered his famous neologism about North Korea being part of an "axis of evil" — and the magazine readily jumped in with a publication about the Koreas. Another issue was annotated with a nostalgic foreword about the editor's military experience in the Far East. That was enough for me — I

---

1 "Gorbachev blasts American 'imperialism'", by Alex Nicholson, Associated Press, July 28, 2007

replied to the reminders to renew my subscription that were coming in the mail that I had intended to subscribe to *National Geographic*, not *Politicians' Geographic*.

Even such events as the Olympic Games, which are supposed to be above politics and wars, according to ideas of ancient Greeks and Pierre de Coubertin, have been turned into political theater. In Salt Lake, jingoism outgunned Olympic regulations: by Olympic rules, the torchbearers were supposed to wear Olympic uniforms — not even the uniform of their national team, much less the particular hockey uniforms. When I read about "competitions with a North American accent" in the national media, it gave me shivers — that was literally a paraphrase of the Third Reich games with an "Aryan accent."

No wonder that the Olympic Games are broadcast in a very peculiar way: in the US, this spectacle is not about the international competition with a very special spirit but about American athletes, or allies with the "right accents" at the very best. When some unpopular nationalities get in their way, not just the unfortunate athletes but the entire nations they represent might be booed. Peggy Fleming emitted such pearls in her reports from Salt Lake that I can attest as an insider: should she be a Soviet commentator — God forbid, of course, but just for the sake of comparison — she would have been reprimanded for exaggerated fomentation of national divisiveness on the air, according to Soviet standards, which results in a permanent ban from a broadcast. The Soviets didn't broadcast the Olympics in that tone, Cold War or not.

There must be a sheer pleasure in breaking IOC policies just in order to demonstrate one's power. Despite the IOC rules, the tattered national American flag from the World Trade Center was brought to the stadium at the opening ceremony. The Olympic Games were meant to be *above* any wars or attacks, precisely. They were meant to unite nations *and* adversaries. Though, who cares about their history and meaning — when Jay Leno interviewed young folks in Salt Lake City, they showed very little knowledge about the Olympic movement. One of his interviewees boiled it down perfectly. Just like the others, he had no idea where the Olympic Games had originally started but he defiantly added that to him, the Games started in Squaw Valley.

That was just brilliant! He already understood the effective political recipe: substitute troublesome facts and other high matters with plentiful exaggerated patriotism — and that will produce perfect cookie-cutter electorate. Modern Russian politicians employ this effective formula also, but the Soviet "brainwashers" were kindergarteners compare to their American counterparts. Besides, they dealt with a nation that knew better than to gulp down official stories. In the Soviet Union as I remember it, the majority of the nation seemed to be in opposition to its government. In contrast to the general American spread-eagle attitude, in communist countries people were used to thinking for themselves and drawing their own conclusions.

This brings us again to the point that it takes an optimist to envision how the quite seasoned differences between the Old World and New World could merge seamlessly in the near future. Europe often holds onto its more refined standards, compared to more practical American, and sometimes deals with more problems because of it. While structured legal immigration benefits the American economy, egalitarian Europe often burdens the social system of the host country. Only recently, many European countries have started to "Americanize" their immigration policies, downsizing immigration from some countries and promoting it from another, introducing a test in the host country's language and encouraging minorities to mix with mainstream society.

"Since the end of the Cold War, the European criticism of America as a global bull in the international china shop has become more pervasive and elaborate," noted Brzezinski. America provides more than enough grounds for that criticism. For example, when a US missile hit the Chinese embassy in Yugoslavia, even the American politicians realized, even if just for a moment, that they might end up breaking more "china" than they had planned. The very idea of bombing a European country at the end of the 20th century could not look normal to the outside world — or to a moral American insider, either.

"We have both an immense innocence and an enormous sense of entitlement. We are spoiled children in a world of hurting people, and we take far too much for granted," writes Pipher. The entitlement to decide what is good for everybody from the viewpoint of American standards runs parallel to the notorious Soviet "best intentions" to force nations into happiness by the iron hand. Why should it work? Hasn't this been proven a military–political dead end?

And every American newcomer has to make that moral choice: to enjoy the sheer pleasure of becoming part of a powerful nation and accept everything without a doubt, or to check every issue that arises against personal moral standards.

American perceptions and common values may become valueless or countercultural when applied to unlike societies. Especially when it comes to such special matters as patriotism and disloyalty, only an approach from a broader perspective can bring a person — or a country — closer to understanding the opponent's values. Even mighty money, for example, is not always a master key. It was interesting to note that Spy Museum in Washington didn't bluntly label Robert Hanssen, a FBI special agent who was spying for Russians, as a primitive "traitor for money." The explanation was that his treason had complicated moral reasons. Such justification was certainly atypical, not CNN-style, but maybe it was due to professional courtesy — the spy museum couldn't automatically tag all spies as evil foes.

On the opposite end, the denial of common human values may be equally astounding. On the eve of an informal meeting between the American and Russian presidents, Georgie Anne Geyer, a dame of American journalism and a columnist for Universal Press syndicate, wrote: "This meeting is based upon the idea that you can woo and win the Russians by inviting them to your home, by cordially embracing them and forgetting for the moment all the socks-in-the-jaw you'd really like to give them. You can show them that, in the end, we all live by the same principles, the same family values. It's just like at home in Nebraska, with a barn raising, or just like in Ohio, when the floods come and everybody pitches in with pails."[1] Sure — it's like inviting a bear to your barbeque party. And who said that Russians belong to a nation where people help each other — it's not Kansas anymore, you know.

Maybe Ms. Geyer was still holding a grudge against President Putin — she said that he "recently compared the United States to Hitler's Germany, and W [George W. Bush] was 'puzzled' by such inopportune remarks." Joking aside, I have heard such a comparison before — from a Stanford-educated Californian, born and raised American. It could be interesting to analyze why such an opinion could possibly emerge and try to find out where the roots of the problem are, since there is no smoke without fire. And if the ultimate journalistic goal is to give people instruments and information for better mutual understanding, this style won't do it: "But the Russians are *not* just like us; they sit upon a history of woe and a memory of pogroms and czars and mountains of skulls."

Holy mackerel! I am dutifully scared, envisioning Russian tsars sitting on mountains of skulls and American presidents sitting on mountains of, let's say, femurs, since America knows a thing or two about racial discrimination and genocide. The KKK was not invented by Kremlin, and many American researchers consider America's Indian wars as the only example of successful genocide in the 19th century. "'By the end of the 19th century,' writes David E. Stannard, a historian at the University of Hawaii, 'native Americans had undergone the 'worst human holocaust the world had ever witnessed, roaring across two continents non-stop for four centuries and consuming the lives of countless tens of millions of people.' In the judgment of Lenore A. Stiffarm and Phil Lane, Jr., 'there can be no more monumental example of sustained genocide — certainly none involving a 'race' of people as broad and complex as this — anywhere in the annals of human history.'"[2]

So it might be risky to attempt to dish up one's own "national virginity." Though Ms. Geyer assures readers that "we can deal with them [Russians], rather easily, if we can tap into their memory, acknowledge their genuine interests and act judgmentally only on the important issues." Good idea, but if it's the results we care about, it might be better to employ Sting's way to evaluate major issues:

On either side of the political fence,

We share the same biology,

---

1 http://www.uexpress.com/georgieannegeyer/
2 http://hnn.us/articles/7302.html

Regardless of ideology.

The British media know that Americans are missing the point. Their quality press announced an "American invasion," intending to cater more broadly to affluent, well-educated young Americans with a cosmopolitan outlook. The Brits are going to provide for the American market a view of the modern world that the biased American media fails to deliver, bringing along targeted advertising for the young with money.

> "I think there has been a bit of a retreat from covering serious global news," said Jeremy Hillman, the editor of BBC World and former New York bureau chief. Hillman cited the aftermath of an earthquake that struck Pakistan in October 2005. The BBC, he said, covered the story for months, reporting over the winter on victims who were left with little shelter and medical aid in the mountains. US television networks covered the quake, "but moved on very, very quickly even as the real crisis really kicked in," he said. US media have also devoted little coverage to investigations into corruption in Kenya, he added."[1]

But no wonder — tragedies in Pakistan and Kenya are nothing like raising a barn in Nebraska or pitching in with sandbags in Ohio.

The British medical journal *Lancet* published a letter that "compared the role of doctors at Guantanamo to the South African doctors involved in the case of anti-apartheid activist Steve Biko, who was beaten and tortured to death in 1977 in police custody. Signed by some 260 people from 16 countries — most of them doctors — accused the US medical establishment of turning a blind eye to the role of military doctors at Guantanamo."[2]

On the other hand, Michael Moore's castigatory documentaries and controversial mockumentary about the imaginary Muslim anti-Semite "Kazakh" Borat were a commercial success. The latter plot, baited with exaggerated "bathroom humor," made the audience react as if accordingly to the famous phrase from the Russian classic farce *Inspector-General* by Nikolai Gogol, "Who are you laughing at? You are laughing at yourself!" "Borat" acted like a medieval jester — he could afford to tease the sovereign because he was droll, a fool, and he packed the uncomfortable truth in a funny wrapper, assailing dullness, pseudo tolerance, pseudo democracy, and pseudo piety. "He does offend some people's sensibilities, but the youth of today are offended if they're not offended," noted *Time* magazine, putting British actor and writer Sacha Cohen on the list of the 100 most influential people who shaped the world in 2007.[3] Vladimir Lenin, the father of the October Revolution, was right when he stated that "of all arts, the cinematography is the most important" for getting a message through to the masses.

Mainstream American fiction reaches the multitude as well, being a medium somewhere between biased journalism and political writers, and it is always interesting to see its opinion on political issues. A Southern author, "weighing the

---

1 "British media seek new readers on US shores," by Robert MacMillan, June 25, 2006, Reuters
2 "Guantanamo detainees tell of abuses," by Andrew O. Selsky, Associated Press, September 11, 2007
3 http://www.time.com/time/

question of our collective national intelligence," wrote, "The political world that had once fascinated me now just left me shaking my head wondering how America, who had fed, sheltered and defended the masses, had arrived at a place of such low esteem to the rest of the world."[1] Those who have much pain in their own genetic memory cannot appreciate military or political bullying either: "There's no good reason to kill as many people as you can, for as long as you can, until the ones who are left surrender their lives, or their resources, or their culture, or their self-respect, or their ancestors, or their spirits, or their oil, until they get strong enough to throw you off their backs and the whole cycle starts again."[2]

Cycles they are, indeed. Once, in an article about Soviet atrocities, I used a quotation without revealing immediately where I had borrowed it from. From the context, it was clear that it referred to the dark times of Stalinism when a citizen could be executed just because some rival or envious neighbor came up with some slander; a person could be killed simply because someone wanted his house or his wife. At the end of the article, I revealed the source: it was an ancient Roman author. Just another confirmation that history repeats itself.

So, what country or regime is modern America reminiscent of?

***

I feel that I need to apologize for ending that last sentence with a preposition. It reminds me of a Southern joke:

"Where are you from?" a Southern belle asked a Yankee lady.

"I am from an area where people know better than to end a sentence with a preposition," answered the Yankee.

"Oh, I see," said the belle sweetly. "Where are you from, bitch?"

---

1 Dorothea Benton Frank, *Pawleys Island*
2 Pearl Cleage, *Babylon Sisters*

Borrowed Lifestyle: American Extravagance

"Sorry, but I just have to tell them." My American started bragging to his friends what an economical wife I am — he saw me saving the water after boiling some potatoes. I had to disappoint him since he quite overestimated my thriftiness — I was simply making vegetable soup.

But conservation — in the big picture — sure was my thing. Yet he didn't find it amusing when I demanded that he exhume from the basement the recycling container, in which some of his old junk was cozily resting. Sadly, my Southerner did not care about recycling since it "doesn't bring in any money." But what can you expect from an individual when even the local nature park, with its motto "to educate and preserve," didn't offer containers for recyclables? Ironically, the everlasting picnic tables in the park were made from recycled plastic. But in Seattle, a woman cited for me by heart the numbers assigned to the types of plastic recyclable in her district. A resident in an Alaskan town explained that ordering take-out food he always inquires about the containers since plastic is not recyclable there — he refuses to support environmentally-unfriendly restaurants.

For Russians, America appears to be a marvel of environmentally-conscious individuals and advanced energy-saving technologies, like super-progressive energy-saving Californian homes with their solar super-batteries. But as the communists used to say, "America is a land of contrasts."

It angered me that Southern belles who only travel between the grocery store and the shopping mall have to drive monstrous trucks or SUVs because "that's a Southern gal's thin'." Indeed, why should they care about the environment if it has nothing to do with shopping? Only rising gasoline prices might alter that custom.

When I asked if it was possible to re-charge a store gift card, a Southern sales associate condescendingly told me, "Honey, plastic is cheap in America." But I would rather go with the Russian slogan: we didn't inherit natural resources — we are borrowing them from future generations.

I remember a remarkable episode from my childhood: a friend from a wealthy Georgian family — I don't mean a Buckhead family, I mean the other Georgia — offered to kiss a piece of bread that I couldn't quite manage to finish during our lunch and so it had to be thrown away. She wasn't exactly kidding me — I guess that Georgian kiss symbolizes respect for bread both as a symbol and as a result of so many people's work.

Surprisingly, in the book *Growing Up Ethnic in America*, I found an episode about the same "bread kiss." "Once, Nadia told her uncle about how Mikhi had imitated the ritual that old people had of kissing a piece of bread that had fallen to the floor. It was so funny, she had to tell somebody... Uncle Eddie didn't laugh."[1] That uncle didn't laugh at all, and the little guy got himself in trouble for mocking an old Oriental ritual.

Wasting food is considered immoral in the Old World. A German immigrant — let me specify: she emigrated to the US from Western Germany — who worked as a substitute teacher, was shocked by an episode at a school picnic. "The kids got huge, juicy apples. Most of them didn't even touch the fruit, some took a bite or two, and in the end all those beautiful apples were thrown away." Nobody else seemed to mind, but for her it was a shocking example of mindless, arrogant waste, and it happens so routinely in the environment that is supposed to educate young Americans. Education and upbringing don't show concern for careless squander — neither of the divorced parents seemed to care about their chubby kid's routine of piling his plate with food, trashing it after a couple of bites, and then coming back for more: "But the kid's entertained, and anyway I have him only 14 days per month," the indulgent father commented on the pre-teen's habit of playing with the shower for hours.

An American psychologist and author collected several similar stories from schoolchildren, kids of emigrants:

> One of the boys said, "Whenever I see someone throw away food, I wish I could give it to my grandmother."

> "Afghanis believe it is a sin to waste food." She was upset when her children made art with macaroni and uncooked pinto beans at school. She said, "I have many relatives who are hungry. It is disrespectful of school to use food so foolishly."[2]

I believe children everywhere in the world make some "food art." But America, with its abundance of cheap food and resources, practically tells newcomers, 'We'll waste as much as we want, because we can.'

---

1 Joseph Gena, "Holy Toledo," from *Growing Up Ethnic in America*
2 Mary Pipher, *The Middle of Everywhere*

I remember an interesting show on public television about the roots of modern American Christmas traditions: how and when the Christmas trees appeared in America and when and why the tradition of wrapping presents started. I admired the narrator's work till he came to the curtain line: addressing the accusations that Christmas has become a mere shopping obsession, he proudly concluded that after all, America is the richest country in the world — so Americans can afford it. To me, his punch line ruined the concept of the show on the spot. But that American sense of extravaganza lures the Americans themselves into a trap. "Plastic money" provides an elusive belief that almost everybody can afford everything. When I came back from a trip to Russia and discovered a new car in our garage, I was more baffled than excited — the car was a brand-new sports Mercedes. I didn't think we could afford it at the moment.

"My friend was going to get one, too, but his bitchy girlfriend talked him out of it," my husband proudly told me. I wish I had known about his plan so I could join ranks with the "mean" girlfriend; but he'd gotten into a lease he couldn't cancel.

When an obnoxious customer asked my friend, a Russian immigrant-artist, why he didn't get a better car, he wasn't prepared for the artist's answer:

"Will it make me a better painter, you think?"

I remember the confession of a Wall Street investment specialist, of all people, who confided that she could not hold back on personal shopping sprees despite being heavily in debt. Among the things she had acquired lately was an unnecessary pair of shoes — and a telescope.

Psychologist Oliver James has named the mean bug that causes the epidemic of mindless consumerism the Affluenza Virus. Infected people, with their compulsive pursuit of money and possessions, become "richer but sadder." He wrote in his book *Affluenza*, "We have become addicted to having rather than being and confusing our needs with our wants.... People in English-speaking nations are twice as likely to be mentally ill as people living in mainland Western European nations."[1] The American stressed state of mind is very noticeable for newcomers. For example, postpartum depression is uncommon in Russian women. New mothers are perpetually tired, sleep-deprived, and upset about the high cost of baby's goods, but somehow they cope even in that harsher environment. None of my Russian friends or acquaintances experienced anxiety attacks or took antidepressants. Mary Pipher says, in her book *Writing to Change the World*, "We are a nation good at consuming and poor at savoring. In my thirty years of being a therapist, I have never seen Americans more stressed." But what can one expect in Consumerland, where "Christmas is on TV from October till January"?

I heard a tearful story about a teenager who went to get her first cell phone and discovered that her own mother had already ruined her credit history. What

---

1 Paul Majendie, "Affluenza: Rampant consumerism erodes us," Reuters, Jan 25, 2007

kind of female in the animal kingdom would hurt her own baby? But the jungle rules pale beside the consumers' reality show, I guess.

"I know a girl who could only show the repossession agents a table that she bought," a very thrifty Seattle citizen told me. "She couldn't explain how all the money from her numerous credit cards was spent."

As one survey showed, "more than 9 in 10 Americans don't know how long it would take to pay off their credit card bill if they made only the minimum payments. Asked how long it would take to wipe out a $1,000 charge, 55 percent underestimated the actual time of 7 to 8 years; 31 percent overestimated; and 7 percent didn't know."[1]

Now Russians have the same "loan traps" and the same troubles. They have a hard time educating themselves since in Russia even such a necessity as a mortgage was an embryonic concept until recently. They learn the hard way: a history teacher from St. Petersburg tried to rob a bank with a plastic pistol, desperate to pay his loan. But surprisingly many can afford to purchase real estate outright in spite of absurd prices. Exorbitant prices for food and essentials always made me wonder about this "Russian miracle" — how did we survive?

My Southern husband also chided me for "maxing out our credit card" — it sounded dramatic, but he had omitted the detail that it only meant I had spent something under $500 on our joint credit card in the course of more than two years. He reminded me of another sly Southerner, from Texas, who assured the world in 2003 that he would have to sanction an intervention into a foreign oil-rich state because that evil state doubtlessly possessed weapons of mass destruction. That happened to be a false claim, and many American lives were lost in Iraq — real lives, not just borrowed extravagant lifestyles. But as George Tenet said during a congressional hearing, "The data do not uniquely comport with policy decisions."

Some justify the excuse for wars in the same "mega-consumerist" manner: "We do it because we can!" A Southern gentleman wrote in the local newspaper, "We had to kick their butt anyway, so who cares about an excuse!"

---

1 Laura Rowley, "Five Credit Card Traps to Avoid" by Yahoo! Inc.

"Moose and Squirrels!" Or Images of Russians

"I know how Russian women are supposed to look! They are burly and they wear dresses made from potato sacks, like it's haute couture!" my friend Josh frolicked.

He was tickled pink, remembering some silly old TV shows — in return, I mocked him that due to his stodgy stereotypes he could no longer pretend to be young. He clearly belonged to the older generation of tube-raised Americans since Cold War-style images dominate his imagination.

Inviting me to the movie "Analyze This," he warned, "There will be no tractors in the movie since it is not a Russian movie." I didn't know that the first scene was a tractor chase.

Josh' s favorites were the Pottsylvanian spies, no-goodnik Boris Badenov and Natasha Fatale from the cartoon about Rocky-the-squirrel and Bullwinkle-the-moose. Once the guy had a laughing fit when I incautiously ordered mousse for dessert. But the satirical jokes about American life went over the head of the "moose and squirrels" lover:

> Rocky: Do you know what an A-bomb is?
> Bullwinkle: Certainly. A bomb is what some people call our show."

Or this one:

> Bullwinkle: You just leave that to my pal. He's the brains of the outfit.
> General: What does that make you?
> Bullwinkle: What else? An executive."

And this:

Bullwinkle: Humble, that's me... Mr. Modesty. When it comes to humility, I'm the greatest![1]

A woman who worked with a sharp-witted Russian girl in a small Southern town told me, "I knew since my childhood that Russian women are short and stocky — I remember pictures in the textbooks — and now I know two young Russian ladies in person, and you are nothing like that."

My Southern aunts by marriage had never met a Russian in flesh and blood before — some of them probably had never traveled beyond the neighboring county — so when they were just about to eagerly "inspect" me for the first time, I was excited even more. "Will they check to see if I have a regular set of toes and fingers?"

But those lovely ladies were so nice, and soon my presence didn't prevent them from chatting in their usual mode, speaking simultaneously about a variety of topics — I felt like I was on the site of the TV show "The View" — so they happened to be more entertaining for me than vice versa.

Discovering what America makes of Russians is quite interesting. Russian women, in particular, have been pictured in a wide range, from sexy women-spies to robust peasants, and now another seductive and confusing type has been added: Russian brides.

I don't know what to make of a small strange book supposedly written by William and Julia Rossedahl, *Russian Wife: Your Greatest Blessing or Biggest Mistake?* I like the title, but the plot is so crude and absurd that it seems to be nothing more than a clumsy attempt to stop all that Russian brides business. But authors' approach is seductively illustrative for critical analysis.

Julia allegedly is a Russian fallen woman who was blissfully converted. William warns, "So, Russian women jumping all over you to marry them. Watch out... The Western World seems to be a 'heaven' of sorts... Life in the West offers many things that the rest of the world does not have: personal freedoms, career opportunities, lifestyle, prestige, financial gains, etc."

Do you feel sorry for the whole big and beautiful "rest of the world" yet? Shady women lurk there, who are "incomplete without husbands" (well, the family is not a bad institution, really), but it is "also possible, ladies, that the [Western] man could pull the same 'con' on you." Thank you for the warning, Willy! Julia — I guess her Russian name must be Yulia — shows no Christian mercy toward a schematic Russian immigrant woman, who is "whining about being homesick," and "even if she does pick up some English, you will still never train her to say 'could you pass the salt, please?'"

But on the other hand, Julia "just couldn't picture a Russian guy" next to one of her friends, some fair Russian lady. And guess what? The lady married a French businessman, as predicted: "She got just what she deserved... The other girl told

---

1 http://bullwinkle.toonzone.net

me once, 'I have spent four years... in University, I have learned two foreign languages, I read a lot, I appreciate art and theater, I love classical music and enjoy
a deep conversation... Why in the world should I settle for a less in a man?' She
wasn't talking about international marriages... but I won't be surprised if she
marries a foreign man, too... I did find it difficult to get interested in a Russian
man..." Can you imagine those Russian universities, where perfect Russian ladies
are trained to the pass salt and to speak foreign languages, but somehow their
male classmates couldn't ascend above the level of the neighborhood jerk? How
could the males of the same species be so pitiful compared to the female population, though they all supposedly have the "personality so much distorted by ten
years in Russian school"?

By the way, here Yulia speaks about the same school system that prepared
her fine ladies for university entrance. Children of Soviet immigrants could usually afford to be lazy in America once they overcame the language problems: the
more demanding Soviet school program had given them a head start, especially in
mathematics and other exact sciences.

Julia "generally hates people asking her about Russia" (maybe the questions
are too crude?), but she obediently "does patiently answer [her husband's] questions." No wonder that her husband concludes, "Yes, there are fine Christian
ladies there, but so few of them that chances are very slim for you to find one."
Evidently, he must feel lucky — the only other fine lady had been fetched already
by that French businessman.

I vote that the best portrait of a Slavic — Ukrainian — woman can be found
in the novel *A Short History of Tractors in Ukraine*. Though the author of the novel,
Marina Lewycka, is British, you can probably tell that she is not an Anglo-Saxon
herself. This is the description of her heroine's new in-law, her father's mail-order
bride from Ukraine.

> A large blond woman is sauntering down the garden towards us on high-heel
> peep-toe mules. Her gait is lazy, contemptuous, as though she can barely be
> bothered to stir herself to greet us. A denim mini-skirt rides high above her
> knees; a pink sleeveless top stretches around voluptuous breasts that bob up
> and down as she walks. I stare. Such a wanton expanse of dimpled, creamy flesh.
> Plump bordering on fat... A broad, handsome face. High cheekbones. Flared nos-
> trils. Eyes wide set, and outlined in black Cleopatra lines that flick up at the
> corners. The mouth curls into a pout that is almost a sneer, drawn in pale peach-
> pink lipstick that extends beyond the line of the lips, as though to exaggerate
> their fullness.
>
> Tart. Bitch. Cheap slut. This woman who has taken the place of my mother. I
> stretch out my hand and bare my teeth in a smile.
>
> "Hallo, Valentina. How nice to meet you at last."
>
> ...I see myself through her eyes — small, skinny, dark, no bust. Not a real woman.
> She smiles at Mike — a slow, wicked smile...
>
> My father's eyes are fixed on her as she moves about the room.

When I was sixteen, my father forbade me to wear makeup. He made me go upstairs and wash it off before I could go out... Now look at him drooling over this painted Russian tart. Or maybe he is so shortsighted he can't see that she is wearing makeup. He probably thinks she was born with pale peach pearlised lips and black Cleopatra flick-ups at the corner of her eyes."

"Weren't you boiling, reading this?" an American asked me, laughing. But I enjoyed the sincerely crafted portrait. Even the narrator's progress was pictured credibly through the course of the novel — from initial hatred for the "painted Russian tart" to longing and almost love. So Slavic!

My Oscar for the best Russian mail order bride-villainess on screen goes to the beautiful Aussie Nicole Kidman for her role in "Birthday Girl." The director Jez Butterworth — sorry, here is another Brit — created "a funky little bauble" that dyed her red hair black and wore clothes and nail polish befitting Dracula's niece.

> A [British] bank teller in a small town...is a lonely guy who clicks forlornly on the photos of Russian mail order brides [his co-worker-teller is always making eyes at him, but evidently she isn't on his radar] and finally orders Nadia, who says she is tall, speaks English, and is a non-smoker. When at the airport Nadia turns out to look exactly like Nicole Kidman, you would think John might be satisfied. But no: She is tall, all right, but she is a chain-smoker, speaks no English, and throws up out the car window. He tests her language skills in a brief conversation: "Are you a giraffe?" — "Yes."
>
> John calls the marriage agency to complain. He wants to return Nadia and get himself a non-smoking English-speaker. Nadia keeps smiling, discovers his secret horde of porn magazines and videos, and cheerfully reenacts some of the scenarios she finds there. Soon John is beginning to reevaluate his consumer complaint.[1]

Actually, Nadia does speak English. Kidman even managed a convincing Russian accent — the reviewer must have gone to refill his popcorn at that moment or decided that he had already had enough. The lovely actress easily upstaged her partners, who had to perform like textbook Russian banditos: leather trench coats, sweat pants, and tired faces. I watched this movie with the American ex-husband of a mail order bride, so when Nadia found a shortcut to the guy's heart — somewhere south of the proverbial stomach — he leaned over and whispered dramatically into my ear, "I've been through that!" I felt sorry for his ex-wife.

Craig Nova, author of ten novels and recipient of a Guggenheim fellowship, in *Cruisers* invented quite dark cardboard Russian characters. The set is simple standard depiction — two couples, the "good guys" are Americans, the "bad guys" are Russians. He named his Russian mail order bride Katrina (the Russian version of that name would be Katerina) Kolymov. Now, a Southern belle and dear friend of mine knew, from reading *Anna Karenina* at the beach (now, that's a choice for relaxing beach reading!), that if a Russian man's surname ends on "ov", then for the women in his family the name takes the flexion "-ova", and the ending "-sky" becomes "-skaya," in the same manner. So my dear friend, who is not a recipient

1 Lawrence Toppman, "'Birthday Girl' a piece of cake," *The Charlotte Observer*, February 1, 2002

of a Guggenheim fellowship but who does read Leo Tolstoy, spotted immediately that the heroine's name should have been Kolymova.

Mr. Nova's victim/villain was much more realistically portrayed as an American loner, who "was tempted. He was willing to admit that. How could he try to do otherwise when he looked at the maddeningly suggestive passport photos, that had a quality that was at once clinical and yet sultry."

"Maddeningly suggestive passport photos" sounds like an oxymoron to me: like most passport photos until recently, Russian ones were black-and-white, and the person wasn't supposed to smile, so they could have seemed sultry only for a recluse. "But he was worried that one of these women, or all of them, might be up to something, and while he was uncertain what this might be precisely, he suspected that it would have something to do with trying to get money from him." Good — the poor thing is trying to sort through the mail-order bulk:

> She said she was from Ukraine. She spoke directly to the camera. She had a lovely smile, beautiful white teeth, but Kohler kept thinking, Why is she sitting there in front of this cheap video camera? Why does she need to find somebody this way? Then he thought that these judgments about how people met were impossibly provincial and what he was seeing in this dignified and beautiful woman was just how desperate things were in the former Soviet Union.

> There was something else she wanted to mention. Russia couldn't even take care of the women whose husbands had died in the Second World War. You saw them sitting in the subway, begging. That incapacity and the desperation that went with it were precisely what she wanted to get away from.

There have been a few portrayals of Russian characters as human beings with universal problems, joys, and sorrows, like in *The Madonnas of Leningrad* by Seattle author Debra Dean. The novel's background is the dramatic siege of Leningrad during the Second World War. Tom Clancy's *The Hunt for Red October* also portraits humans, not cartoon images. The Cold War material seems authentic and accurate enough in its Soviet part. How exact — even if with the help of a small elision — is this observation: "Everything he did was to serve the *Rodina* [Motherland], a word that had mystical connotations to a Russian, and ... was a substitute for a godhead."

But Stephen King has yet another pitch in his *Dreamcatcher*. The book shows some scary philosophy: his hero is reluctant to kill, but it seems that only because "those poor shmucks... are Americans. Folks who drive Chevies, shop at Kmart, and never miss ER. The thought of shooting Americans... that turns my stomach."

Does he mean that if the folks were of some other nationality, it would be easier to kill them? The author scares his readers with aliens from outer space, but looks down his nose at the other kind of aliens, with their strange letters "that have to be Russian, or Cyrillic, or whatever they call it."

That's nice to hear from a writer — "whatever they call it"! They call it a language, and that language is probably one of the most eloquent instruments for a skilful writer.

Typical of the knee-jerk Cold War depictions is this bit from Lewis Grizzard's father, in *It Wasn't Always Easy, But I Sure Had Fun,* "And George Patton was right. We are going to have to fight the Rooshans [his word for Russians] sooner or later, and I don't know why we didn't do it while we were still over there! Lord, please keep us safe from the Rooshans!"

Boo!

The other Southerner, Haywood Smith, referred to frightening eye surgery, using the clincher, "It was invented by some Russian, for heaven's sake!" Indeed, what can one expect if it was a Russian invention? But how many Americans know that the radio, for example, was invented by a Russian? Popov and Marconi did it simultaneously and independently.

And the periodical table of chemical elements didn't appear by itself; it has the name of the great Russian chemist Dmitry Mendeleev. I recall a short story where a child of Russian immigrants had an issue with his chemistry teacher who refused to admit that the table was indeed developed by a Russian chemist. The student stubbornly stood his ground and was punished for it. Finally, the truth prevailed, but the fact that the periodical table is anonymous in America angers me — how can non-American (or non-Western) achievements be so easily omitted by educational institutions? How could bigotry, masquerading as patriotism, be a decent substitution for knowledge? Can you imagine that the principle of universal gravitation could be stripped of the name of Newton?

Some tearful stories, heard from Russian immigrants, may have been a little distorted in translation: one Russian guy "laughed sadly" to Mary Pipher in *The Middle of Everywhere,* "At that time, except for the Mafia, no one in Russia ever had hot water." I have difficulty imagining this huge, unwashed country. On the other hand, I do remember some Russian "religious refugees" in Seattle, and heaven knows how those thick-set, bull-necked guys with crew cuts, square jaws and more than likely a murky past, were able to convince American authorities that they were desperate victims of religious persecution. But I guess if the government asserts that there are persecutable religious victims in Russia then government officials simply have to be logical and grant asylum for the victims, no matter what.

Another young immigrant, a woman, after "she had talked on the phone to her family in Ukraine," told Pipher, "They were crying. They were so hungry they were going into the fields and eating grass." I agree that Ukraine has had some difficulties from time to time, but again, I think that something was lost in translation.

An Alaskan cab driver showed me a local newspaper with a picture of plump Russian ladies with rosy cheeks who were greeting a plane with humanitarian help from Alaska, "Could you tell me," the cabbie asked, "why we have to help people who can afford this?" The ladies, Siberian Red Cross representatives, definitely didn't look like "grass-eaters" and they sported exquisite Siberian sable furs. They were not mafia, they were officials (which sometimes can be worse than mafia) but I think that that humanitarian aid reached its addressees, the really and truly deprived elderly and poor. For a foreigner, it would be hard to understand how poverty in Russia co-exists with the criminal fortunes made overnight by state officials and those who stick around them. Russia now harbors the third biggest population of rich people [according to *Forbes*, now it has moved to the second place], after the US and Germany, and Moscow is the most expensive city in the world in terms of living expenses.[1]

Those facts are outright ugly since many of the fortunes were not earned by business talent or brains. Western media made an outcry, saying that democracy was in danger when one of the Russian tycoons was accused of tax fraud, but nobody tried to draw a parallel with Martha Stewart, for example.

"The Soviet government and press lied to the people, bosses lied to their subordinates, who paid them back in kind, and husbands lied to their wives about everything from infidelities to drinking up the household money," writes Lynn Visson in *Wedded Strangers*, "And when most Russians sincerely believe that honesty with a spouse about extra-marital affairs is hurtful and destructive of the marriage, the atmosphere in the Soviet Union encouraged a general attitude of sidestepping the truth, which included sexual relations, along with nearly every other aspect of life."

I sympathize with the author, feeling some true pain here, but American politicians themselves seem to keep score in extra-marital affairs, and I suppose every government is prone to lying, by definition — politics was never fair play — though Russians are in better shape to size up what their leaders say, being habitually skeptical about propaganda. I cannot picture the Russian public swallowing Mr. Bush's allegations about WMD, for example.

If I were to distinguish the differences between Russian and American style of lying, I would say that Russians tend to lie with a bellicose air, as if challenging one to try and catch them, but Americans lie with very open and trustworthy faces. My American husband never hesitated to lie, but he couldn't stand that I called his lies — well, lies. It was "too Russian" of me, too harshly straight.

So I may agree with Lynn Visson's observation of Slavic nature. "'There are no shades of gray for Irina and her Russian friends,' Fred commented. 'Everything is right or wrong, good or bad. They know everything about everything, from politics to art.'" I do suspect they could be more passionate and opinionated than a

---

1 Mercer Human Resource Consulting, Global-Cost-of-Living Survey 2006

Westerner would allow himself to be. But one has to wonder what is the writer's intention when she goes on to describe a Russian wife in industrial tones: "She did produce a boy and a girl, and imported her mother... to baby-sit while she taught Russian in a local junior college." That "producer" and "importer" of a family "proved an excellent teacher, popular with the students, and was equally strict with them and Fred, who was not quite sure how his dewy-eyed pussy-cat had turned into such a sharp-clawed tiger. 'I never expected such honesty and fidelity,' she confided to her mother. 'That really makes me love him more than I ever thought I would.' They are still together, one case where a calculated seduction led to a marriage likely to last."

I understand that if a cold-hearted calculation took place, the author is entitled to a categorical Russian-style opinion. Visson wrote, "Though the future Russian spouses of Americans may well be free from the paranoia, passivity and blind dogmatism born of the worst aspects of the Soviet system, they will still be Russians — the proud and patriotic products of centuries of Russian history and culture — and not Westerners."

But wouldn't it be sad — in fact a betrayal — if people eagerly renounced their precious national heritage, of any origin?

Though in the course of time, biology might indeed perform the part of the melting pot: if current demographic trends continue, Americans will become a race of the descendants of Hispanic and Oriental immigrants, and in Russia, the Russian Caucasians will disappear also. Survival of the fittest, all labels and political images aside.

Meanwhile, we have to agree that the decades of the Cold War deeply influenced our concepts and stuck us with stubborn labels, and we have to broaden our horizons and improve our attitudes.

DEMONS SHE FIGHTS: ADJUSTMENT PERIOD

I grope in the dark for the lamp on my nightstand, finding none. Slowly, my sleepy mind develops the realization: that nightstand is at my own house, and my own house lies across an ocean and a continent. Then a subliminal, unpolished, "politically incorrect" thought surfaces: What on earth am I doing here?

***

In a story written by a writer-immigrant, the heroine — a girl from a sunny Caribbean island who worked as an *au pair* in New York — had not been opening letters from home for several years. I found that idea strange: to deliberately deprive yourself of such a delicious thing as a letter from home in fear that your heart may burst? Could it possibly be real?

I was a new arrival at that time. Few months later, I found myself explaining to an American friend that in order to maintain sanity and to cope in a foreign country, far from family and friends, a newcomer has to shut some of the soul's floodgates.

That sensation is eerie — it almost feels as if you are becoming less of a human and your soul palpably chars and shrivels into some strange leathery substance while you are hardening, surviving in this new life. Just like that girl, for the sake of self-protection, the newcomers have to deprive themselves of natural emotions consciously, as if deliberately plunging into some sort of autism. Connections with family, friends, relatives, colleagues, acquaintances, neighbors, people one shared hobbies with — all these roots and nerve-endings are severed by relocation, and their stumps have to be anaesthetized.

"I call my friends and family more than I did before I moved to Florida. I keep telling them that it's part of the adjustment process. It's jarring to move to a strange place and live with a strange person."[1] I am pulling your leg here — this passage was written by a young Jew who left New York for Florida for a temporary assignment, and he wasn't even among aliens — he lived among Jewish retirees from Brooklyn.

The best escape is work, of course, or studying — the routine is comforting, it brings sense and makes the brain deal with the realms of everyday life, shielding it from deeper thoughts. "She had learned early to make her mind float off elsewhere... filling her brain with a myriad of things, languages and facts and rationales... She had developed a steel, or, at the very least, polyurethane coating, shielding herself in numbness."[2] This is a sad trend of the modern world: Maids of Orléans, in polyurethane armor, escaping into themselves.

A Russian woman-newcomer must have a very appreciative and kind American husband in order to retain her natural softness. Otherwise she is forced to toughen up, since she feels vulnerable and dependent, sometimes even childlike if she is unable to express herself properly. All newcomers go through the same routine, trying to find their own voices, their own ways, and their possible destinations.

"The English word *wretched* comes from the Middle English world *wrecche*, which means "without kin nearby."[3] A foreign wife doesn't have her relatives nearby to support her during two major adjustments — to the new country and the new family — and people she knew and loved are left behind, thousands of miles away, for who knows how long? Many Americans — and especially Southerners — feel uncomfortable about the idea of traveling abroad, to "another world," even if for a short trip. But what if a trip is one way? This apprehension is very unnerving.

Once, an American friend and I were looking at the display of immigrants' plunder in a Nordic heritage museum in Seattle. "Can you imagine that these few trunks are all the earthly belongings that someone had?" asked my friend, who had recently survived the vexatious business of moving to a new house. Yes, I could imagine that — definitely. Many newcomers have to adopt that light step of an adventurer, traveling light and having no idea what the new life might bring tomorrow, and sometimes dealing with that barren feeling of not being at home in either country.

Natasha, the hostess of a popular web-site "Russian women abroad" warns, "After the marriage takes place, the first year will be crucial for your Russian wife's adjustment. During this period, I will be happy to provide assistance for your new international family in making this adjustment."

Natasha quotes a letter from a client. "By the third month, Val was so homesick that she [decided to] return home, so we did not marry. She wants me to

1 Rodney Rotman, *Early Bird*
2 Rosemary Daniell, *The Hurricane Season*
3 Mary Pipher, *The Middle of Everywhere*

[relocate to] Russia, but I could not earn a living there. I still call and write Julia because she is like my true daughter and loves me. I will continue to travel and search for someone to love, but, I guess, not everyone wants to leave Russia."

A relocated woman has to change her habits and lifestyle according to her new surroundings. In that way, she is no different from refugees who "have lost their routines, their institutions, their language, their families and friends, their homes, their work and incomes."[1]

Of course, in an ideal situation her American husband alters his way of living for the sake of her comfort, but how many American bachelors are willing to do that? My husband reacted like a seasoned drama queen to any changes in his encrusted habits, with the punch line that he "didn't have his life anymore!" When he was a child, he had attempted to move to California with his "runaway" mother, but failed to adjust to the new surroundings and had to return to the South to live with his father. It puzzled me why he couldn't relate that joyless experience to my substantial change of scene nor sympathize with me, even though I left behind, yielding to his entreaties, my friends, family, job, career, and lifestyle as well as my hometown and everything in it.

It seems significant that in the English language foreigners and extraterrestrial invaders should share this cold, outer space name — alien. So it is a big mistake to consider nostalgia primitive "homesick whining." The immigration procedure itself is hardly the joy of one's life, but from a psychological standpoint, all life-altering events are stressful and marriage is one of the greatest, comparable only with the death of a loved one. That makes an intercultural marriage with relocation to another country triple-stressful — for sure, a pleasant overseas tour it is not.

A woman might experience ferocious homesickness blended with a fear of leaving behind a more or less successful life to risk potential failure in another. "Every day in a foreign country is like final exam week."[2] Giving up, going back and pretending that nothing happened simply won't work — the ruins of her old life cannot be restored easily. After moving into an alien land, she eventually pays the price of almost turning into an alien herself: not for the citizens of the new homeland — for them, she will likely remain an alien forever — but for her own nationals.

A foreign wife might feel, deep in her heart, that she made a losing bargain, and her only dubious compensation is the envy of those who are left behind since some of them still believe that it must, no doubt, be better over there. But a sickening feeling might haunt her from the very beginning of her American venture: what if she picked the hopelessly wrong partner — and not for a brief dance, but for an attempt to build a life? In that new life, she might feel always in limbo,

---

1 Ibid.
2 Ibid.

waiting for something, always waiting — trying to establish a desirable relation-ship, then mending and clipping her hopes when they don't sprout the way she hoped, then waiting for an endless string of documents to establish her status in her new homeland. As Nabokov's hero said, "The sense of this émigré life of ours, this perpetual waiting."[1]

Even when the immigration official procedure finally goes through it might bring, instead of satisfaction, a strange feeling of emptiness: what if she spent all those years running from her true loves and real friendships, exchanging them for casual, meaningless small talks in a foreign land? One newly minted American citizen, an immigrant from the Soviet Union, confessed, "And then you think — what were you waiting and fighting for? It feels almost like waiting in the Soviet Union for the promised Communism to come." Another Russian wrote, "Because of the hidden anxiety, time goes slower there. The transition into the other space demands adjustment to the energy of strain... Death also demands from the soul the maximum of recollection."[2]

Probably the association would seem too theatrical or too dramatic for a per-son who hasn't experienced that transition on his or her own hide, but for those who have gone through the ordeal it sounds reasonable.

The changes one undergoes are so deep that even the unconscious alters. Once, riding a bus back in Russia, I automatically answered a stranger's question in English. Luckily, I spoke softly and the passenger decided that she had misheard. In my dreams my Russian friends started conversing in English. By coincidence, my girlfriend was struggling with her English courses at that time. "Well, at least in your dream I could speak fluently!" she laughed.

But some immigrants take it more seriously. "It got so I even began to dream in English and that made me feel very uncomfortable, as if I were betraying some-thing very deep and ancient and basic."[3]

In the light of all that, the opacity of the most arrogant American husbands looks especially boorish — I mean that primitive belief that just the very fact of living in America must fill their foreign wives with endless joy and happiness. Perhaps these men believe that "huge strangeness, America, luring... despite the threat it seemed to hold of loss and vicious homesickness"[4] — the country itself, not the men — should automatically and so conveniently provide eternal happi-ness for their wives. On the other hand, a man might feel too much pressure when he realizes he is the only source of the love and support. That burden is not easy to bear.

American slogans push one to believe that "life can be no better than in the richest country in the world," but political bias is no substitute for human hap-

1 Vladimir Nabokov, *Mary*
2 Aleksey Prin, "Zagranitsa kak lichnyi opyt," *Znamya,#*2 1999
3 Nash Candelaria, "The Day the Cisco Kid Shot John Wayne," from *Growing Up Ethnic in America*
4 Joseph Gena, "Holy Toledo," ibid.

piness. Surprisingly, "according to research conducted by the London School of Economics, Bangladesh is the happiest nation in the world. The United States ranks only 46th, way behind India. The link between personal spending power and the perceived quality of life has conclusively proved that money can buy everything but happiness."[1]

The turning point in my communication with my sister-in-law occurred when she bluntly told me that I should be more than happy simply because I had relocated from Russia to that sleepy Southern town, which she had to call her hometown and yet could hardly tolerate while growing up and was never eager to visit again. She omitted from her consideration that Russians somehow received an enviable education and were able to travel extensively, so that maybe a cozy and mind-numbing place, from an outsider's opinion, was not exactly Canaan.

Traveling is so very important: as my countrywoman and fellow immigrant wrote, "Travel does away with national vainglory, which is one of the greatest stupidities on Earth."[2] My American sister-in-law's only traveling experiences had been camping in some not so prosperous outer regions of Mexico, and she was probably sure, as many American homebodies are, that the rest of the world just suffers and envies Americans.

As Joanne Harris wrote, "[We were] a race apart, we the travelers. We have seen, experienced, so much more than they — content to run out their sad lives in an endless round of sleep-work-sleep, to tend their neat gardens, their identical suburban houses, their small dreams. We hold them a little in contempt."[3] I guess we might. I relocated to a small Southern town, most of whose residents rarely travel anywhere, and my husband resided for most of his life in the same house where he was brought up. Even the hospital where he was born was on the same block. "Then, after a while, comes envy. The first time it is almost funny: a sudden sharp sting that subsides nearly right away. A woman in the park, bending over a child in a pushchair, both faces lit but by something that is not the sun..."[4]

My sister-in-law undeniably beat me in the family department. Her husband was nothing like her brother, and she gave me a distinctive hint that "for the rest of my life I would be merely a guest in my husband's home — not the kind you treat with special meals, gifts or affection, but the kind who is forever viewed as a foreigner, alien and suspect."[5] This passage about a Chinese woman yet again proves that anywhere in the world — in rural China in the beginning of 20th century or in modern America — human nature was, is, and will be just the same.

Families are like countries too: they have their own rules, codes, language, territories, economical crises, even customs. A happy international family suc-

---

1 http://www.nriol.com
2 Marya Pavlova-Sylvanskaya, "Zagranitsa kak lichnyi opyt," *Znamya,*#2 1999
3 Joanne Harris, *Chocolat*
4 Ibid.
5 Lisa See, *Snow Flower and the Secret Fan*

cessfully blends cultures, making a refreshingly different new state. Knowledge and respect for the diversity makes the task easier; but national arrogance or narcissism, rooted in the minds, ends in "international marital wars" when the "countries" don't join but warily watch their borders.

"In the rush to embrace America, people often fail to appreciate their own cultural riches... many other writers wonder how much of their own cultural difference they sacrifice as they plunged headfirst into murky American culture waters."[1] Sometimes immigrants do go to the extreme — I ran across an unbelievable essay written by a self-proclaimed "Russian-American writer"; referring to some disputed results at those notorious Olympic Games in Salt Lake City, he choked with obsequiousness. "How could they [the Russians] challenge the North Americans — it is as if a slave would challenge his master!" That was an ugly example of the immorality of his new immigration life. But undoubtedly, the adjustment period for such people will go much smoother since they will readily embrace everything, without distinction. One of the most daring Russian editors of the *perestroika* period, Vitaly Korotich, wrote about wormy ex-patriots, "Reading the *oeuvres* of writers-immigrants, I couldn't get rid of the thought that these people, with a few exceptions, are very uncomfortable in their relationships with their new homeland, and usually humble themselves before it."[2]

His own example is illustrative: he was very close to getting his full professor's pension from an American university but his wife couldn't leave Moscow, for family reasons, so he decided to go back instead. He wrote about the main dilemma of his immigrant life: "It was a poor choice — you have to blend in with the immigrants' ambience, which is horrible, or stick out in American surroundings as a cute oddball."[3] Was he sorry that he could not continue to live in two countries, or was he relieved to go back to the surroundings where he wasn't considered an oddity? Evidently, the Russian journalist would agree with a Southern writer: "Living where you don't belong can be the saddest mistake you can make. But maybe I needed the suffering and the loneliness to appreciate being home again."[4]

In one of Paulo Coelho's bestsellers, the hero travels through strange lands only to discover finally that the sought-for treasure lies in his homeland. But he didn't recognize the endeavor to follow his dream to see foreign countries as a vain struggle. He saw the desert and pyramids. He saw the world. He lived life.

It is important to realize when — or if — one should turn around and go back. A person who has been exposed to a different lifestyle for a long period of time may become an alien in his own country, "Once they cross over to mainstream culture, they have to decide how often to go back or whether such a return is

1 Jennifer Gillan, *Growing Up Ethnic in America*
2 Vitaly Korotich, "Zagranitsa kak lichnyi opyt," *Znamya*,#2 1999
3 Ibid.
4 Dorothea Benton Frank, *Shem Creek*

even possible. Caught between cultures, they have to sacrifice some of one in order to gain part of the other."[1]

It can be even worse: "Intimate involvement with two cultures can result in a richly bicultural life. It can also create a person who feels homeless in both countries."[2] A person can become a detached watcher who doesn't really belong to any place and just observes life floating by. If you know that you have to leave soon, the detachment becomes a kind of protective practice. In the worst case scenario, one can become "an outcast from two societies, belonging to both but welcome to neither."[3]

Emotional health and balance for a newcomer is a special matter — too much thinking and analyzing can be hazardous, but letting things follow their own course can be outright dangerous also. Though Scarlett O'Hara's principle, "I'll think about that tomorrow," could be useful for keeping one's good complexion. All advisors, veteran immigrants as well as psychologists, recommend new foreign wives get busy with something else besides their new families — to plunge into language study or find a job.

Finding a job, which integrates you better than anything else into your new life, might be an ordeal in America, especially if the newcomer possesses skills that cannot be applied easily in the US environment. A Ukrainian television reporter might end up as a housekeeper, and a Russian doctor might become a cleaning lady — such compromises are hard to call "career advances." The dignity-robbing experience cannot be appended to a résumé, but such is the gloomy reality of the new American life for many novices. In many instances, the employment conundrum parallels the joke, "The only jobs that would take me are the jobs I do not wish to take. It's exactly like sex."[4] Those who have succeeded usually keep away from their ex-compatriots who have not yet found their footing — those with stupid jobs lead dull lives.

> The United States is a series of paradoxes for newcomers. Every plus is married to a minus. It is the land of opportunity and yet the opportunity is often to work in a meatpacking plant... A man who had been an engineer in Africa for years... now was pulling out turkey guts... A distinguished writer fries doughnuts for a fast-food chain. He can speak no English and is treated in a demanding way by some staff and customers.[5]

Easy to imagine how repugnantly the writer's unhappiness smelled of rancid fast-food grease. In cases like this, foreign wives are supposed to accept the Zen of humiliation gracefully, dealing with the paralyzing emotion of feeling helpless and stupid, and just dig in, ignoring — or despising — the small-minded, and chanting affirmations under their breath — they "can do anything if they only

1 Jennifer Gillan, *Growing Up Ethnic in America*
2 Lynn Visson, *Wedded Strangers*
3 Beena Kamlani, Brandy Cake, from *Growing Up Ethnic in America*
4 William Nicholson, *Society of Others*
5 Mary Pipher, op. cit.

believe in themselves." That "one day the resurrection will occur and they will emerge from the cocoon." Maybe. Penelope Trunk stated that one of five biggest workplace myths is the one that says a person will be rewarded for doing a good job. "You'll actually be rewarded only if you're likable."[1] "Those who are "different" are less likable, and that makes their career advance more difficult."

Newcomers may try to get help from such institutions as the Employment Security Commission, but after familiarizing myself with the ESC in a small Southern town I got the impression that its main goal was to provide as less trouble as possible for its employees. The ESC facility offered job hunters computers with the ports and slots sealed with paper ribbons, the explanation was simple: "We haven't installed any antivirus yet. What do you expect — we are a governmental agency, so everything moves slowly!" I monitored that slow pace for three years, periodically checking their always empty computer lab where employees enjoyed conversations with their friends in a quiet air-conditioned space.

Then it became even more interesting: I asked a young black woman who managed the Joblink Career Center to edit my resume. It had two very conspicuous grammatical mistakes right on the first page. It took her about two months "to study" a few pages — I was insistent since I was staging an experiment; anybody else would have given up. All she finally came up with was an offer to change the font in one paragraph. It was ridiculous but so typical: usually those who complain about the slow movement of those proverbial "wheels of governmental" are the ones who are supposed to do the rolling. In Russia or in America, the main agenda for an ordinary low level bureaucrat is to get in and relax, mission accomplished. And those are the institutions that newcomers are likely to face in America — hopefully, somewhere else they might fare better.

The loss of status is one of the most painful aspects of life for educated newcomers. There will always be so-proud, even if not so-smart natives who treat "those with accents" as mildly retarded and firmly believe that "those damned furriners should be kept under."[2] Julia Chang Bloch, a native of China, recalled her coming to America: "My first summer here, I was put in a class for the mentally retarded because, in those days, some educators didn't distinguish between the fact that you didn't speak English because you are a foreigner, and the lack of mental facility. My father told me 'do better than the Americans so that you can compete.'"[3]

Other things could be tricked out to look like "we don't understand those furriners" — intercultural collisions could serve as a Petri dish to show how incomprehension can be misshaped into guesswork and then grown into indisputable facts, or how a misunderstanding can sprout into horrendous gossip. In an educated group these problems are unlikely, but what a perfect breeding ground

1 http://finance.yahoo.com/expert/article/careerist/35700
2 Joseph Conrad, *The Nigger of the Narcissus*
3 Dennis Wholey, *Are you happy?*

I saw, for example, at the local division of a popular European cosmetic line. *Sans* the sophisticated naughtiness of high fashion spheres, the dull malevolence against anything "different" was tailored to the level of a former Southern beauty pageant contestant, flanked by a brassy Texan manager nicknamed "Cruella." Ironically, the environment, which was inherently meant to be international by definition, was poorly assimilated in the South.

"Automatically labeling strangers as savages, weird and inhuman creatures (thus explaining the difference by exaggerating difference) not infrequently justifies mistreatment, enslavement, or even extermination of the Different Ones."[1] Among many American employers, this practical attitude is common: immigrants' labor is cheaper, they are more grateful to get the job, and they don't make waves.

For educated foreigners, the best possibilities to obtain decent professional positions right from the start occur if they are invited to the US by American companies. Specialists of foreign origin who are trying to find jobs by themselves are unlikely to get the same earnings and positions as their peers discovered by American "head hunters" abroad. The latter way saves a lot of stress and scars: "Today, the Tepordeis [a Romanian couple invited to the US by a Microsoft recruiter] fit in well. They see their new country through thin Versace eyeglasses, the windshields of their SUV and sports car and from a comfortable suburban home."[2] The Tepordeis were happy newcomers, all settled, perfect candidates for the newspaper's Independence Day feature about new US citizens.

Though in some professions, such a move is hardly possible: can you imagine an American TV host with a foreign accent? There are quite a few in Europe, but not in the US. And doctors with foreign diplomas have to prove their expertise and pass several grueling exams in the United States. Some have built quite successful practices but one physician of Russian origin admitted, "It helped that we were relatively fresh from school and could easily brush up on the theoretical matter. For experienced doctors and brilliant practitioners it is harder, almost impossible."

I knew a good surgeon turned small entrepreneur — he couldn't tolerate the treatment that he got at the hospital where he had started to work as a nurse. In Seattle, I met a waiter who used to be a gynecologist, a gardener who used to be an emergency room doctor, and a cleaning man who used to be a dentist. Their type of education in Russia claims the longest study — six years at school, plus two years of residency — before they can start practicing. I can only hope that medicine was not really their calling and they realized that obtaining a medical degree was a mistake. Though it would be not a costly mistake for them, money-wise, since higher education in the Soviet Union used to be free. No wonder that

1 William Ryan, *Blaming the Victim*
2 Paul Nyhan, "US companies sometimes bring America home," *Seattle Post-Intelligencer,* July 4, 2006

a foreign doctor has to go through hardship on the way to practicing in the US — those positions are meant for American doctors with their hefty educational loans.

A Ukrainian engineer who tried to have his diploma recognized in America was asked how many American credit hours he had taken on one subject. He explained that he had published a book on that subject in the Ukraine. That didn't matter. He played by the rules, attained the required credits, and started teaching himself at the community college, turning into a stern adversary of foreign degrees: "Why should I help somebody to achieve their goals at my expense? It would be better for me if they attend my classes." Really, what doesn't kill us makes us stronger, sometimes — wiser, sometimes — bitter, but not necessarily more empathetic. However, the man felt sorry for his coed students who nodded off in his algebra lectures after working hard at a factory all day.

Turning bad luck into good, making lemonade from a lemon with a strong determination not to be beaten — that is typical American style. The attitude is very useful for immigrants and may even help some of them to find deep meaning in the unavoidable suffering. After all, that is a typical Russian attribute, Dostoyevsky style — finding meaning in suffering.

The Show Must Go On

Although I believe that the top prize among optimistic sufferers has to go not to immigrants but to the brave Brits, Sir Ernest Shackleton and his men. The story of his expedition should be a crash course for those who think that they have put themselves in a strange land in the worst situation possible.

Advertising vacancies for his Antarctic expedition, Sir Shackleton explained that he could not guarantee survival but suffering was certainly a part of the contract (making it similar, in that respect, to the immigration ordeal). Applicants swarmed the office, just as wannabe-immigrants swarm American consulates abroad.

Amazingly, Sir Shackleton did not lose a single man though the expedition went through a series of misfortunes that make popular American "survival shows" look like a banal trip to a grocery store. Their journey reminds me of a Russian joke where the pessimist drones, "It couldn't be worse," and the optimist gleefully chirps, "It can be worse — and it will be!"

"Optimism is true moral courage," Sir Shackleton said. Just as a reminder: his expedition was icebound, and then was cast away. The explorers had to organize a voyage in lifeboats, and though they navigated precisely and did not miss tiny Elephant Island in the vast, inhospitable icy seas, it was just deserted land, so they fitted out a boat with a messenger group to the Antarctic village of whale catchers. In order to reach it, the group had to cross a frozen mountain range. Nobody from the outside world believed they could possibly survive, but those Englishmen kept their optimism and British humor — Shackleton organized goofy contests in order not to let his men sink into despair and then into languor. Against all odds, those British were determined to hang on and see if things would get better. The same works for the newcomers in America.

The worst and very common psychological condition occurs when immigrants give up and go into torpor. As Mary Pipher wrote:

> Depression is certainly one of the most common reactions to trauma. Paradoxically, torpor and lassitude are common reactions to severe stress. People just don't see any reason to get out of bed in the morning. They don't have the energy to cope with the complex new situations they are in. They don't have the energy to brush their teeth.[1]

The ability to step back and observe the situation helps in those situations; even a change of scene, out of the urban environments into nature, can help. As Wallace Sterner noticed, "We simply need that wild country available to us, even if we never do more than drive to its edge and look in. It can be a means of reassuring us of our sanity as creatures, a part of the geography of hope."[2]

"Look how small your problems with your husband appear from here!" I called to the Ukrainian woman when we reached the mountain top. From this colossal, steep granite cupola, the landscape around us called for celebrating the beauty of the earth, not for self-torment. A human being is an extremely elastic creature, not like a panda that won't mate in captivity and will die without a supply of bamboo leaves of just the right kind — a human can get used to anything, and even in the most pitiful situation can find reasons to be almost happy. One just has to look at the simple pleasures of life. Sometimes it makes sense to focus on the small things, like the beauty of the birds' songs or the unexpected warmth of the winter sun.

That Ukrainian woman was a true survivor, though — not like the noble Brit, but in her particular, practical manner. Since she had difficulty observing her problems calmly or putting things into perspective, she readily verbalized them, sharing her problems with her countrywomen and getting the support she needed. She was very well focused on achieving results in America, and did not consider going back home, probably because she realized that without education she would not be able to compete in the labor market there. For the sake of financial support, she tried every trick to keep her American husband nearby, even after the separation, while she was finishing her education at a local community college. She clawed her way up and adjusted well.

Even comfortably situated natives, after some unfortunate event, can suddenly see things in a different perspective: "Many Americans experience this change of priorities after a cancer scare or heart attack. They stop worrying about unfinished housework or job promotions. They spend more time with their grandchildren, travel, and watch sunsets... One of the great ironies is that stressful life often provokes positive emotions, while easier lives can induce laziness and apathy. Who is happier, a mountain climber or a person who sits around and watches television all weekend?"[3] Here I would afford myself a doubt: a couch potato might be happier just because he simply does not realize that he is unhappy. But

---

1 Mary Pipher, op. cit.
2 Quoted from Brian Keenan, *Four Quarters of Light*
3 Mary Pipher, op. cit.

the next fact newcomers usually discover, sooner or later, to their proud surprise: "We tend to underestimate our own resilience. To live is to suffer. To survive is to find meaning in suffering."[1]

That is a perfect description of the meaning of an immigrant's life. Simply getting through life takes a lot of courage. For an immigrant, a primeval curiosity to see what happens next is a life saver, and even small achievements help to boost self-esteem.

Many foreign wives say that they suffer for the sake of their children who have better chances in the US, in these women's opinion. Children, for the most part, naturally are more suitable objects for pinning hopes on than often-disappointing husbands. A woman solaces herself that she suffers for a noble goal, giving up her own life and not living in full, just hanging on and bearing her disappointments. But shouldn't life to be about joy and happiness? "A man is born for happiness as a bird is born for flight,"[2] said Maxim Gorky, yet another famous Russian expert on human misfortunes. Due to his poor health, he often wrote about Russian sufferers from his retreat on the cozy, sunny Italian island of Capri.

The lack of joy, at least joy in the way it used to be in the "previous life," hurts severely, especially if a person used to dance through life and then had to become a freestyle climber, an equilibrist, a someone who faces the abyss at all times.

In order to adjust more easily, people instinctively seek their compatriots, gravitating towards areas where other people from their homeland live. "Russian spouses often encounter other Russians from completely different backgrounds, with whom they would never have chosen to associate at home, and a musician may find himself socializing with a mechanic,"[3] noted an American wife of a Russian husband.

Though these "motley crews" are rarely stable, the intensity of connections with compatriots often hurts the relationships between spouses in the Russian–American families. The typical close affinity between Russian friends looks strange for an American, but generally, those connections are reliable, even if those friendships have been forged only due to circumstances. Especially during their first year abroad, Russian women are drawn together as if by a powerful magnet because they face like problems and challenges. Later, when language barrier has been overcome, it becomes obvious that as individuals they may have more in common with some of their American acquaintances than with associates of their own nationality.

There is another Russian quirk that may be puzzling for those rational Americans who believe that the Russian soul must be eternally happy once overseas: "Once in America, Russians who had desperately wanted to leave their country became equally desperate to see it again."[4] How can one logically explain that?

---

1 Mary Pipher, op. cit.
2 Maxim Gorky, *The Lower Depths*
3 Lynn Visson
4 Ibid

But another American author wrote, "I had a jolt of insufferable homesickness that was followed ironically by not wanting to go home and resume my normal life."[1] So the feeling is familiar not only to immigrants but to many uprooted people, even to Americans who usually are light on their feet when it comes to relocation for rational reasons.

Irina Selezneva published her essay "Nostalgia is Treatable, or Why the Short Trips to the Homeland Are so Useful" on the web-site "Russian Women Abroad."

> Before my trip home, I lost sleep and my appetite. I was walking around the house like a somnambular, counting not the hours before my departure — even the minutes. Jack understood my condition and did not bother me. He grew very quiet, periodically asking, "Are you coming back?" Somehow he got the strange idea that I was leaving forever, but I was not going back to the Ukraine — I was quivering because I just wanted so badly to see my son, my friends, my city.

On her way back to the US, Irina tried to analyze her trip home.

> I came to the conclusion that I had visited a feast in a time of plague: luxurious restaurants with exorbitant prices — and indigent, scruffy hospitals; luxuriating *nouveaux riches* — and starving retirees; battered pavements — and posh cars with twerps behind the wheels. It is insulting that educated people, who are valued so highly around the world, in my homeland are just trash. That our women — really the best-looking women in the world! — don't even have a clue how poorly they live. The political atmosphere in the country affected the mentality, psychology, and human relationships; everything was turned upside down. Humanity has always moved towards progress, but in the Ukraine, the process went in reverse. How many generations will have to deal with it? During my lifetime, I will not be able to see any positive changes, that's for sure, so I had made the right decision. Why are the people so afraid to make significant changes in their lives, to break the stereotypes and routines that they created? Why are they so frightened of changes if those changes are for the better, usually?
>
> The Russian poet Alexander Blok was right when he said that there is no happiness but peace and freedom, and America gave me exactly that. America helped me understand a simple truth: though we were born in different places, we all live on the same planet, so we are all its citizens. For a woman, the homeland is where her home and a good husband are, and nostalgia is cured by short trips back. I don't mind that my heart now is divided in two: one is in the Ukraine, and the other is in America. A person has to have some problem, after all. But why do I want so badly to walk the dusty streets of my hometown again, to attend a goofy party? I'm so confused.

The feeling that Irina had is not that new, though: "How shall we sing the Lord's song in a strange land?"[2] from time immemorial people have asked. And they almost always found their voices, because the show must go on.

For some, there will be a reward: "We bitch about our difficulties along the rough surface of our path, we curse every sharp stone underneath, until at some point in our maturation we finally look down to see that they are diamonds."[3]

---

1 Jim Harrison
2 Psalm 137
3 Frank Jude Boccio, *Mindfulness Yoga*

Watch Your Language

Adventitious and hence innocent, linguistic imperfections are perhaps the most delightful of all cultural collisions.

What a nice break the Seattle laboratory scientists had when a Russian researcher asked a male colleague to turn on a device for her.

"Please, turn me on!" the woman insisted impatiently.

The laboratory grew silent in anticipation of amusement.

Trying his best to keep a straight face, the male colleague suavely offered, "Well, since your husband so conveniently works at the same building, don't you think it would be more appropriate to ask him?"

She didn't disappoint the audience and delivered the punch line, "No, it's none of his business — you turn me on!"

And wasn't it a memorable service when a pastor of German origin announced that two members of his flock were getting married and everybody was invited to the wedding and "to the parish hall afterward for the conception"?[1]

My friend Ludmila recalled attempting to talk her American friend into going to a dance club party. The girl was hesitant and asked about the dress code.

"Oh, don't you worry — we dress there occasionally!"

"That's why you like it so much!" shrieked the girlfriend with glee.

My own favorite *lapsus* happened at the end of a tiresome quest for a nice hamper (I hate shopping!).

"I need more airtight hamster!" I blurted out.

---

1 Jerome Lossner, from "All in a Day's Work," Reader's Digest, January 2007

Natasha, a Ukrainian native, has being tripped by inversion and words that were almost homophones: she ordered "raw salmon sushi" instead of "salmon roe sushi" and was genuinely surprised when she got raw fish instead of caviar.

Psychologist Mary Pipher recalls about her work with refugees, "At first, I was clumsy with people who didn't look and talk like me. I worried I wouldn't be able to understand people for whom English was a second, third, or fourth language. I wondered if I would be accepted and understood. I was embarrassed that I was fluent only in English."

But fluency in written English is a huge achievement for the average American: I was surprised when an American woman named Carla showed me how to write "properly" the letter "r" — she was not aware of the cursive of "r." Once I saw a manager's reminder, pasted on a sticky-note on a monitor: "Print shits." My eyes popped. But that "sheet" word is treacherous, indeed — native English speakers often mention that foreigners have a tendency to pronounce the double "e" as an "i."

A Japanese woman ordered halibut cheeks at a restaurant, but the Japanese language lacks the sound "l," so the order sounded like "hairybut cheeks." Her dinner party was ecstatic.

"Speak English!" my cute, surgically youthened Southern mother-in-law would demand; but sometimes I couldn't find a reason for her complaint. Finally, the mystery was solved. "She just doesn't hear well and doesn't want to show it," divulged her wise sister, who accepted the unavoidable event of aging without a fuss. At the same time, redeeming a native speaker's right to talk as she pleases, my mother-in-law could say, "I did good," or "I wish you and Martin will have a life" when we were heading to divorce. I was astonished but as it turned out, she meant "lives," not a shared "life" for us.

In Hickory, "the furniture capital of America," I witnessed quite a rude pre-concert welcome speech for a delegation of Russian businessmen: the representative of the hosts got a hand with the remark, "Some of them [Russians] even speak English!"

I wish I could find that smarty and ask him in several languages if he speaks any of those, since he could not possibly have any idea which languages his guests might have been studying: in Soviet schools, from middle to high school levels, a foreign language is mandatory, and usually there is a choice of English, German, French or Italian, and in some areas of Russia, even Chinese. As the joke goes, a person who speaks two languages is called bilingual, a person who speaks several languages is a polyglot, and a person who speaks just one is American. Even a newcomer might start "to believe like the rest of people around you that English is either the only language spoken on this earth or that is the only language worth knowing."[1] In European trains, restaurant staff routinely speaks French, English,

---

1 Roshni Rustomji, "Thanksgiving in a Monsoonless Land" from *Growing Up Ethnic in America*

Italian, and German, and nobody is impressed by such multilingual abilities since this is just the way multicultural Europe lives.

Of course, some Americans take this attitude farther and expect people in foreign countries to speak English. Once in Italy, we entered a wrong toll road and had to communicate with an Italian operator.

"*Inserire il biglietto,*" the speaker on a post came to life.

Obviously, we were being asked to stick the ticket into the slot — anyway, what choice do you have facing a toll bar? It doesn't take a linguist to identify that *inserire*, evidently, is a cognate with "insert," just as the Russian word *bilet* — ticket — obviously derived from the same Latin root as Italian *biglietto*.

But Martin was enraged that he could not get the instructions in "proper" English.

"Can you believe that?" he complained to his friends in North Carolina, "I couldn't find a subway station attendant or a toll road cashier who spoke English!"

"If there were turnpikes in North Carolina, I doubt that a foreigner would expect Southern ladies from the tollbooths to speak Italian, come on!" I teased him. "You were in a foreign country — why do you expect people to accommodate you? They are at home — you are visiting, so who has to adjust?" Newcomers to the US, who have to go through the official procedure of adjustment of status, are pretty clear on that.

A friendly immigrant from Laos who tended the produce stand at the local Wal-Mart asked about my nationality. "You don't have an accent," he said. That was the first time I'd heard that. I'd been mistaken for Irish, been called "my little friend with the British accent" when I was still a tourist, relatively fresh from Russian school where we were taught British English, but I had never ever been told in an English-speaking environment that I did not have an accent.

"You don't speak like the people here," the Laotian explained.

The man was right: when a true Southerner makes fun of somebody's accent I consider that a good joke. The first time I heard the drawl of those serious dudes at local Home Depot I thought that they couldn't possibly be serious — I thought people could only talk like that onstage. I had never been fond of the limping Southern accent, swooping up and down through a phrase like a swimming penguin, with that inevitable drawl at the end; but I absolutely enjoy the Southern lingo. My favorites are "ain't," especially when combined with "them double negatives": "It ain't gonna help you none." Lewis Grizzard, a writer and a Southerner, relished that famous word "fixing" in place of "going to," or "it is my intention to" ("I'm fixin' to do my homework"). "I still say "fixing," and anybody who doesn't like it can stay in Boston and freeze," he wrote. Lovely!

That Laotian from Wal-Mart inquired about some common expressions in Russian, jotting them down right on his rubber glove, and to my astonishment, next time I saw him he fired off the entire list. Definitely, he picked up more Russian while I was choosing my cilantro and cucumbers than my husband cared to master during the entire duration of our marriage. Though our dog was adaptive, she knew the Russian equivalents for the most important words in a canine's life — "dog," "treat," and "walk." Her earnest German shepherd's face looked so poster-perfect smart, she tilted her head left and right while listening, pricking up her huge "piggy" ears.

Once back in Russia, a colleague asked me to name a five-letter American state that starts with "A" for a crossword puzzle. I was negotiating the unlike numbers of letters in Alaska, Alabama, Arkansas, and Arizona when she said, "Iowa, of course!" I realized that I wasn't thinking of Russian spelling in translation — I saw the English words in my mind's eye.

Some transmogrifications happen too: when I mentioned that "I was fixing" to bake some pirogi (end-stress), Craig said, "You mean, to boil pirogi?" (secondary stress). I was lost: the shift of accent was, of course, inevitable, but why boil something that has to be baked or fried? As it turned out, the transformation of the name came with the transformation of an object: for that type of stuffed pasta, a different Russian word, *vareniki*, is applicable. The word "pirogi" was derived, supposedly, from a proto-Slavic word, so Polish, Romanians, Russians, and Slovaks fill that "pasta word" with their own meanings.

When a native English speaker cannot come up with a name for a thing or an abstract concept, those noetic gaps seem very strange for me. If something exists or if something is implied, it has a name. If the name exists in one's native language, one knows it. Fallen trees in the woods after a storm — is it a windbreak or a windfall? The cavity in the tree — is it a hollow or a hole? My husband's frequent "I don't know" was a disappointing answer.

Some colloquialisms are agreeably similar — both in the US and in Russia, a distracted driver will be told that the "light's not going to get any greener." But some English idioms sound strange to an outsider's ear — why is one supposed to be "happy as a clam"? Just think of that clam, in some dark ooze, bound tightly down... "Merry as a lark" is okay, though. The grass *Phleum pratense* shares the same "biblical" name, timothy, in English and in Russian. The polysemous word "comb," in both languages, could name a rooster's crown and a hair rake — the likes of shapes were evident to the creators of both languages. But how come the noun "baby" is neuter? A baby is "it," as if it were inanimate, but a car, for example, may be referred to in the feminine. Of course, there is a historical explanation why boats and cars are feminine nouns, but still... Interesting, that the word "galley" could mean a slave boat ("to drudge and slave") and a book proof, as if hinting what a "glamorous" life writer has.

For some reasons, Americans often change the stress in the pronunciation of Russian first and last names, so the classic Russian name Boris, with end-stress

(Bu-REES), turns into a familiar cartoon villain's name with the stress on the first syllable. Somehow, my last name usually gets the right stress on the second syllable, but many names of Russian athletes and public persons are pronounced with the wrong syllable accented. The Russian tennis stars Sharap'ova and Kurnik'ova are actually Sha'rapova and 'Kurnikova. Imagine what a warm American welcome we could get should foreign announcers rearrange in a similar way names of Serena Williams or Lindsay Davenport — or even, God forbid, John Madden or Ronald Reagan.

But Mr. Bush habitually called Mr. Putin 'Vladimir, with the traditional wrong stress on the first syllable (and as Russian magazine *Ogoniok* stated, invented even a nickname for his 'Vladimir — Puty-Poo).

The New York Times called Hillary Clinton's effort to name the successor of Mr. Putin a "presidential primary spelling bee": "Um, Medved —," Mrs. Clinton began. "Medvedova, whatever."

"Whatever" indeed — the former first lady contrived to turn Mr. Medvedev's name into a female's, using the flexion "ova."

"Fyodor was offended when people he had just met addressed him by his first name," wrote Lynn Visson. "So were Boris's Russian friends when Mary C. addressed them by their first names instead of by first name and patronymic. 'I can't remember everybody's father name!' she wailed. 'It's hard enough remembering all the first names in this impossible language!'" At first, it looked and sounded unusual when the Russian media switched to the Western pattern of first name-last name, and I remember that some Soviet *shishki* — big cheeses — complained bitterly about such familiarities, but now it has become a routine practice. And of course, it is easier not to memorize everybody's father name — even for a Russian.

Sadly, in Russia native speakers seem to become more and more negligent with spelling and grammar, and since the grammatical rules are complicated, that drift of affairs may lead to very sad results. With hilarious examples, though: just one wrong letter on a hand-written label turned tiny Dime cookies into Heels cookies. I couldn't help but ask if those small feet were washed, at least. A single misspelling transformed smoked salmon fillets into "smoked salmon's mother-in-law." When I regained my ability to talk I begged for that label as a souvenir. "I can't give it to you, our manager wrote it," the sales person explained.

Yet in Pueblo, Colorado, I was treated to the purest Russian: an amazing couple, Evgenyi and Elena, had emigrated to the United States right after the Second World War. On their living-room walls were portraits of the Russian royal family and White Army officers. The couple spoke sterling Russian, which is almost lost in its motherland where the language has in recent years been fashionably bastardized in the mass media with coinages taken from English marketing terms. But Evgenyi and Elena, polyglots by necessity, had preserved their native language after more than a half of a century in exile — first in China, then in Yugoslavia, Germany, and, at last, in the United States. In San Francisco, a whole generation of 40-some-year-olds speaks the purest Russian as well — ironically, these descendants of the so-called Russian White emigration, which fled the country after the October Revolution, have never lived in Russia.

"Russian pours from their lips like honey," my Russian friend said, "One of them told me that in his childhood, they spoke only Russian at home, English was banned, and if children casually broke the rule, they had to memorize and recite a classic Russian poem."

But those people are of a special breed, mostly descendants of highly educated émigrés. Most of the modern immigrants usually speak fractured Russian stuffed with English words. I call it Ruglish. It sounds so ugly that usually I beg to choose either language and stick to it. Many of those grammar wizards attach Russian flexions to English words. In that peculiar performance, the noun "farm," for example, becomes "farmah," "cookies" — "cookisy," and so on. Native English speakers don't have a clue that the nouns "pound" or "inch" could be declined: "pounda," "poundov, or "inchei," "inchah," "inchu," and so on. Advertisements in Russian immigrants' newspapers offer to clean "carpeti." Interesting.

Grigory Kruzkov mentioned an adopted habit of conversing in "breaking-in language," using it "without too much of remorse." But using a "breaking-in language" due to the necessity of communication is one thing, and bastardizing one's native language is the other. Of course, languages change over time, though Alexander Pushkin, the founder of contemporary literary Russian language, wrote in such a clear, brilliant style that it still sounds modern almost two centuries later.

Electronic communications bring new economical lingo; even spelling "night" as "nite" has become almost a norm for advertising signs. The phonetic "I c u" or "I h8 it 2" have become quite legitimate in TM, IMHO (in text messages, to my humble opinion). Even in Russia those who speak English actively use in their messages that economical lingo.

Lynn Visson writes,

> After spending two years in America, Pyotr's Russian was so full of English words that his cousin, who came to visit, kept interrupting him to ask what he meant. When Carol returned from a month-long trip to Russia with Fyodor she caught herself saying to an American friend "let's sit in taxi," instead of "let's take a taxi," because she was translating the Russian expression literally into English. Evidently, in adapting to the spouse's culture, one can sometimes go too far!

Too far, indeed: "I don't care that my son forgot Russian." Natasha from Salt Lake City enlightened me. "What for he needs it? To read Chekhov? But who cares about classic literature and Russian life? It's not applicable here; our American life is different."

Luckily, I know other Russian mothers who raise their children in America in a different manner. Svetlana and Marina brought to the US heavy loads of well-known Russian children's books. They obtained delightful Russian cartoons, real gems of animated cinematography, in which violence and cruelty are absent, but whose lines are known by everybody. These mothers have done their best to cultivate a love of their national heritage and native language in their kids.

I had the same warm feelings watching a TV documentary from the North Carolina Language and Life Project series — "Mountain Talk" by Neal Hutcheson. The stars of his film, "them mountain folks," are descendants of Scottish-Irish immigrants who settled in the Appalachian Mountains in the second half of the 17th century. Life in isolated diasporas produced specific mountain dialects that could be understood perhaps only in neighboring counties.

Mountain people translated their routine expressions for the filmmaker. I checked my newly obtained pearls with a colleague whose grandmother was from the mountains, and he passed with flying colors recalling correctly that "poke" means a sack, "dope" — soda water, "airish" — chilly, breezy. "Si-gogglin" is something that is not lined up correctly — a meandering road, for example. "Plumb" means an extreme level — "the copper vein went plumb over the county line." And how welcoming is that cheerful "you'uns come go with us"! I felt some strange deep connection with those mountain folks, almost as if they could be my own great-grandparents who had preserved, despite the hardships of life, the same admirable decency, intelligence, and earthy humor.

Definitely, language can speak volumes.

To Execute or to Pardon?

For a Russian outsider, the relationship between sexes in the US seems to be in a tangle. Should he help her in order to show that he cares or would she take it as a sign of condescension? Will he be executed or pardoned if he tries?

That's just one nuance — there are hundreds of others.

I found in a Southern novel something that struck me as an honest confession from the very bottom of a very confused female heart: "In the process of figuring out what we wanted, needed, and had a right to, women had talked men into and out of their paternity rights so many times, nobody knew who had the right to do what, or when, much less why."[1] I would say that's applicable to more than just paternity rights — that heroine snapped at her lover for patronizing her, demanding at the same time that he help her. Poor guy — what should he do?

Well, maybe guys are not that poor, after all — in the process of trying to figure out what, how, and why, they found out that if women don't show the desire to be protected and pursued, spoiled and adored, then what the heck — life is much easier that way. They won't bother to check whether you want to be treated as a buddy or not — sorry, the section "gallantry" is closed for an indefinite time, at the demand of your very gender.

> American men have very few masculine stances left. If they want to show they can take it, they go without a coat on bitterly cold winter days, like... Ronald Reagan shivering in Geneva while Gorbachev, who is used to much colder weather, bundled up in coat, scarf, and hat and regarded him with undisguised bemusement. "Where is your coat?" asked the translator. "Oh, I left it inside," the other translator replied manfully.[2]

---

1 Pearl Cleage, *Babylon Sisters*
2 Florence King, *Reflections in a Jaundiced Eye.*

It is interesting to see how relationships are described in the modern mass literature that reflects down-to-earth recognizable and self-associable opinions. Relationships seem to be very tiresome:

> Love is for young people... I know I've got mileage and that should be okay, but it's not... You get to a certain age and your own world gets so orchestrated, there's almost no room for somebody else and their whole load of stuff. I'm just tired of the whole mental exercise of sifting though other's people minds and struggling to see myself with them... There were too many people in unsatisfying relationships and too many people with no relationships at all... If I didn't expect anything I could not be disappointed."[1]

Another author had a name for it — the "menacing tedium of female soulsearching."[2]

Having a family is scary. "The waiting family is the source of pleasure and the source of all dread. Desire to see his family conflicting with a kind of terror that they exist at all."[3] Relationships are even compared to natural Christmas trees — "the real thing is certainly more beautiful, but it's just too much fuss, too much mess."[4]

A male writer agrees with his female colleague:

> You could start out with someone who had already been through such horror and misery in other relationships that the hope and eagerness in her had been kicked to death before you even had your first kiss. You could see it in women's eyes, in their postures. You could hear it in the way they talked: their pain quota had been filled, for life; there was only so far out into that naked middle ground they were ever going let themselves go again, and who can blame them?[5]

Indeed, if they were hurt and burned so many times, why try again? No wonder an average American man might decide to go hunting abroad, in the hope that there he will be greeted with primordial excitement and some attractive woman will be willing to give up everything and come to live with him on his terms and his turf — even if foolishly.

Intimacy between partners in America seems to have a double meaning and should be managed with great caution: "She had pushed him away and run, because the man's embrace and kiss overpowered her, made her feel smothered, small and powerless. She did not recognize that his behavior showed he cared only about his own desire, not hers, or that this was a sign of his evil nature.... She felt that, having failed him, she owed him something."[6]

American women definitely try too hard sometimes, not letting their hair down, and here is another description, "She had become watchful of herself, careful at all times to be the kind of woman she thought he wanted... True inti-

1 Dorothea Benton Frank, *Shem Creek*
2 Anita Brookner, *The Rules of Engagement*
3 Fay Weldon, *She May Not Leave*
4 Tony Parsons, *One for My Baby*
5 Roland Merullo, *A Little Love Story*
6 Marilyn French, *My Summer with George*

macy was only possible when two people were simply themselves, not constantly monitoring."[1]

One American friend, being involved in a complex relationship also, explained that the reason for the intricate pattern of interaction between the sexes in America happened to be that way "because, unlike Russians, we ask ourselves many questions."

But why not just relax and go with the flow, indulging yourself? It may save some energy for more pleasant things. An American author of Italian descent, Diane di Prima, describes the comforting simplicities of the traditional culture in *Growing up Ethnic in America*:

> Babies are born and raised, the food is cooked. The world is cleaned and mended and kept in order. Kept sane. That one could live with dignity and joy even in poverty. That even tragedy and shock and loss require that basic of loving attendance. And then men were peripheral to all this. They were dear, they brought excitement, they sought to bring change. Printed newspapers, made speeches, tried to bring that taste of sanity and order into the larger world. But they were fragile somehow. In their excitement they would forget to watch the clock and turn the oven off. I grew up thinking of them as a luxury.[2]

Another American author brings Russian males on stage: "American women see Russian men as handsome, romantic, strong and, despite a good dose of male chauvinism, extremely charming," writes Lynn Visson.

> They tend to be more sexually, intellectually, and emotionally self-confident. "He knows he's a man," said Leslie, a thirty-year-old American teacher, about her Muscovite husband. "He doesn't spend time worrying about who he is. Dmitri doesn't analyze our relationship all the time. My American boyfriend had been to so many shrinks he treated me as if I were one, too."

> Anne was impressed by her husband's love of literature and poetry. "In California the only men I knew who recited poetry were gay."[3]

Just like that American joke: Would you like to have a boyfriend who likes poetry and music, who is sensitive and charming? Of course, you would! But unfortunately, he has a boyfriend already.

When a Russian man says, "Well, they're only women, what do you expect?" they mean that "a very special gender" must be indulged. I like the French saying even more: "If a woman is wrong — apologize." But if the French would only do as they say!

The forbearance of a Russian male isn't seen as deprecation, and a man preserves his dignity while indulging a woman without needing to have everything done his way — after all, men have other vast fields in which to practice their self-affirmation; to a traditional Russian man, the idea of fighting with a woman over minor issues would be beneath him.

---

1 Nicolas Evans, *The Loop*

2 Diane di Prima, from "Recollection of My Life as a Woman," quoted from *Growing Up Ethnic in America*

3 Lynn Visson, *Wedded Strangers*

"The stronger one yields; let a girl have her way" — this is what a Russian boy is told at a young age. "Don't argue with a woman — you are a man!" a young Russian man may expect to hear. Constantly bickering with a woman over domestic issues more likely would be taken as a sign of his weakness.

Maybe such an attitude breeds a healthier psychological environment, where the participants are men and women, not genderless partners fighting for supremacy. When the Bolshevik Revolution catapulted Russia into an agonizing social experience, it also declared that men and women had equal rights. That was the good part — every minus has a plus, indeed — so at least Russian women didn't have to traumatize themselves fighting for co-equality. Since that time, offering different wages for men and women was unthinkable for Soviet workers. Not to Americans, though: the Federal Reserve Bank of San Francisco published a piece of economic research that noted, "...the difference in wages between men and women, the so-called 'male-female wage gap' (MFWG), has shrunk substantially... Unfortunately, ascertaining whether the MFWG has shrunk because of lessening discrimination against women is difficult, because measuring discrimination itself, let alone changes in discrimination, is difficult."[1] Now the gap is "only" about 20 percent. And that is called "progress"?

The Russian corporate world is undoubtedly a male domain as well, just as it is everywhere else. Lewis Grizzard did a parody on "a big-time Texas oilman: 'Now, you ladyfolks just run along 'cause us menfolks got to talk about bidness.'"[2] I can't recall "oil-women" doing "bidness" in Russia, but in the Ukraine, they did have a "gas princess," later a member of the Ukrainian government, who was accused of stealing a good measure of Russian gas during the murky times of the Ukrainian "velvet revolution."

A Russian woman could, if she wished, choose some other traditionally mannish occupation and become a pilot or a ship captain (don't women in uniform look sexy!), and should she attract the attention of the media, no doubt she would be treated as an oddity; but she wouldn't complain or file a lawsuit because she realizes that this world is still pretty masculine, even when "all men are equal" — you see, it's even hard to be politically correct using a standard expression!

But at least she has the other privileges of her sex, and most Russian women generally agree that they are the softer sex, for being softer means to be feminine, and nothing is wrong with that. Even feminism could be rounded off to some degree instead of being exaggerated out of proportion.

My Russian bosses sometimes interrupted our business conversations with a sudden compliment, and I was pleased, not insulted, that my appearance or attire was appreciated as well as my professional qualities — I don't have any self-doubts about the latter, but what woman could be tired of receiving com-

---

1 http://www.frbsf.org/publications/economics/letter/2007/el2007-17.html
2 Lewis Grizzard

pliments? A Russian woman won't take it as sexual harassment: it softens the moment; that sudden warmth in your heart melts away the stress of a hard day. Nothing is wrong with feeling that you are a woman, even in the workplace, especially if you are a woman who does her job well.

My American banker, a young Russian belle who smartly cultivated her resemblance to an Egyptian beauty, told me an illustrative story: at a party in the office one of their young colleagues commented that he would rather pour drinks for such good-looking girls at his place instead of celebrating in the sterile atmosphere of the bank. The Russian beauty smiled, and the American one smiled too — and reported it to their boss. The guy was fired; out of harm's way.

Though Penelope Trunk states in her article "The Five Biggest Workplace Myths":

> When you do report harassment, the most likely thing to happen is that you'll lose your job because of retaliation. Yes, that's illegal, but it's pretty much impossible to prove in court. But let's say you can sue and win: you'll get a settlement that's too small to allow you to retire, you'll be virtually unemployable in your field and career, and your harasser will probably do the same thing to your replacement. Before you accuse me of being indifferent to social justice, please know that I'm not saying this is OK. I'm saying that unless you're independently wealthy, you can't afford to single-handedly face down the injustice of sexual harassment laws.[1]

So much for intolerance of sexual transgression!

Yugoslav author Slavenka Drakulić wrote about a meeting with famous Western feminists before forming the first Yugoslavian feminist group: "We thought they were too radical when they told us that they were harassed by men on our streets. We don't even notice it, we said. Or when they talked about wearing high-heeled shoes as a sign of women's subordination. We didn't see it quite like that; we wore such shoes and even loved them. I remember how we gossiped about their greasy hair, no bra, no make-up."[2]

A young feminist from the Peace Corps was converted after just a month of Russian experience, as Vlad stated: "I was wheeling Alison's heavy luggage on our way to the airport, while Alison walked ahead, chatting and laughing with our American friend Jenny. Then Jenny apologized for their laughter, 'We were saying that in America, it is not customary for men to help women, but it's so easy to get used to such help!"

Slavic women are intolerant of harsh male chauvinism, but they are wary about feminism also.

"If you wear a Wonderbra, don't complain that we're looking at your breasts!" This plain American joke seems to make sense to me. Thankfully, women can't give up their ancient desire to be sexually attractive, but by the same token, they declare themselves almost "sexless equals" — even the usage of sex appeal in ad-

---

1 http://finance.yahoo.com/expert/article/careerist/35700
2 Slavenka Drakulić, *How We Survived Communism and Even Laughed*

vertisements is sometimes called wrong in America. How come? Well, maybe it is still a part of a woman's caprice, "Get out of this house forever! And don't you dare to be late for supper!"

After all, we are entitled to be contradictory — we are women.

No wonder when it comes to such a sensitive topic as "sexism," "not all women, however, see the issue the same way. Indeed, there are signs of civil war among women themselves on this question."[1]

But doesn't the "sexless" confusion hurt women? I can tell you a sad might-have-been-love story. Let's call it —

1 Charles J. Sykes, *A Nation of Victims*

A Woman at the Door

And it goes like this:

After dreaming about her for a year, he was on cloud nine when he finally got a chance to ask her to dinner. They went to a fine restaurant, and he held a door for her.

She froze on the spot.

"I am able to open a door for myself!" she hissed.

He said, "Okay," went inside and shut the door behind him.

They chatted amicably during the dinner, but afterwards he asked for separate checks. "If you are so emancipated, you can take care of your part."

Of course, she was angry, and that was *finita*. By the way, that American was of Slavic origin.

Indeed, those doors are hazardous. I tried in vain to train one of my American friends to open that damn heavy door of his old convertible for me, at least when he asked me out and it felt like a date. Once, when he habitually slid behind the wheel and I was still standing on the curb in front of the restaurant, it dawned on me: the car top was down, so I stepped inside without opening the door — fortunately, my physique allowed me to do that.

But all that "door business" is such a trivial matter in comparison with the situation when a female immigrant in America fights for a well-deserved professional job. Being a "double minority," she has to prove that she is at least twice as good as the rest of the jobseekers in order to get her foot in the door. In that situation gallantries are usually checked at that same door, for this is, indeed, "bidness."

My own experience was like a soap opera. I was invited to sit on a county committee, but the department received an anonymous letter which stated that

I could not possibly be on such a respectable board since I "didn't pay taxes," "didn't have any qualifications," and generally, was "not from here."

The first two were insinuations, but the last one was an unforgivable sin, I guess. The head of the department routed the letter to its proper destination in the wastebasket, but the county officials were puzzled about its authorship since the writer seemed to possess almost an insider's knowledge about the committee — things that hadn't been announced to the public yet.

The puzzle was solved when my gem of a husband verbalized statements from the anonymous letter. I was finally hired by the county, and that sent him flying off the handle: according to him, I was "good for nothing" — forget my graduate degree! — and no way should I gain any foothold in his small Southern hometown. I was shocked, but he seemed to think very sincerely that his letter and his insinuations, as well as the fact of meddling itself, were no big deal. Moreover, he explained that in his view I had never held a job — evidently, since journalism is not an 8:00 to 5:00 occupation, it simply couldn't be serious.

That incident was an eye-opener for me. I had believed that my dear Southerner might have had good intentions when he advised me, earlier, to turn down a state job proposal. I thought his opinion was based on a fair analysis of the job duties versus the compensation. His "consummate Southern gentleman" mask was very convincing. (Once a Russian friend admitted that he was jealous of some of my writings, but we were both in the same creative field, at least; and it was for good reason that those creative groups were called "terrariums of the like-minded" by one famous Russian theatrical director.)

Prelapsarian naivety was shedding off me like bark from the southern sycamores: it seemed that "a woman at the door" in America can't afford to be unwary; she has to be on guard. But that is so tiresome.

The Competition of Congregations, or Which Christian is more Christian?

"Do they believe in Christ in Russia?" my mother-in-law surprised me with the same question a Southern third-grader once asked. I explained that in Russia we even had quite an early start, and that we had celebrated the Millennium of Christianity in the 1980s.

"Oh my God!" said my in-law.

I knew for sure that she was familiar with Fabergé Easter eggs and pictures of famous Russian icons and cathedrals, but somehow the correlation between Christian symbols and Christianity wasn't made.

I admit that some Russian Orthodox traditions might be confusing for a foreigner. While most of the Christian world celebrates Christmas on December 25, the Russian Orthodox Church holds onto tradition, commemorating it on January 7. The discrepancy started in 1917 when most of the world was using the Gregorian calendar but the Russian Orthodox Church was still following the old Julian calendar, which is 13 days behind.

Once, during a holiday dinner, I tried explain to an American, upon his request, everything *ab ovo* — about the separation of the Churches, about the Julian and Gregorian calendars and consequently the differences of the Christmas dates; and guess what question Jim asked in the end?

"So, do they believe in Christ in Russia too?"

I downed a glass of champagne, sighed, and said, "Yes."

Although my dinner companion could not quite sort out those church distinctions, he was absolutely captivated by the unofficial Russian holiday oxymoronically named "Old New Year's Eve." It is celebrated on January 13; that would be New Year's Eve according to the old Julian calendar. Such a typically Russian idea: just give us a chance to celebrate something — anything at all — and we will go for it, the more the merrier. Though even the easily-carried-away Russians seem to know where to draw the line; no one ever tried to celebrate twice the anniversary of the Great October Socialist Revolution, which broke on October 26, according to the old style, or on November 7, according to the new — both dates were in our textbooks since the Revolution happened in that contradictory year 1917.

The Russian Church is austere in its services. As one Russian immigrant said, "Church in Russia reminds you about the recompense for your sins, about suffering, but in America, church is about joy and bliss."

To me, the Orthodox Church is reminiscent of that rageful mural *Dies Irae* in the Sistine Chapel — the transfixing, overwhelming and gigantic scene, where even Our Lady looks frightened of the wrath of her son. The less upsetting ceiling frescos would look more suitable for the Western denominations. I can imagine that if a poll were conducted in the Bible Belt, you could find modern supporters of the medieval idea of painting clothes on those "improperly naked" figures.

The Russian Orthodox Church is sensitive about the temptation of the body as well; women are obliged to cover their heads in church since the beauty of a woman's hair could tempt one toward sin, but that dress code has some gaps: on one magazine photo a pious starlet, a self-declared Russian sex symbol, posed holding a church candle and sporting an impressive overflowing cleavage dramatically emphasized by the mandatory head scarf.

An Orthodox church doesn't have pews — the congregation is supposed to remain standing during the service, and only the sick and pregnant are allowed to sit on benches that run along the back wall. And Orthodox services are very, very long. Now church weddings are in vogue in Russia, but some young couples have no idea what the ritual entails — home videos of those solemn ceremonies sometimes evidence how the excitement on the newlyweds' faces gradually gives way to obvious fatigue.

The Russian Orthodox Church, with its stern rules, traditionally was the dominant religious institute — which, of course, never missed a chance to interfere in national politics — a museum with amazing icons and architecture, a bearer of cultural traditions in literature and music but never much of a place for communal socializing. Russian newcomers sometimes compare American churches to social clubs — no wonder people shop around if they don't like their "church club" anymore. It reminds me of a joke — American, evidently — about a man who was cast away on a desert island. When the rescue party finally arrived, he proudly showed them his premises: the house he built, the barn for his domesticated animals, the church. "And what is on the yonder side, on the hill?" — "Oh, that's the church I used to go; I don't attend it anymore."

One charming Southern gentleman told me about his clash with a preacher who suggested he was going to take the gentleman's name out of the church books. That is a serious, even nasty threat toward people of venerable age, since proper dying — God forbid, of course, but we are not dateless — is so important in the South.

"I told him," said the gentleman, "that we didn't attend the church lately due to my wife's health condition, but if he wanted to take my name out of the books then I would take his name out of my checkbook and we'll be even. That worked!"

The gentleman added that some churches insist on checking the W-2 tax forms of their parishioners in order to make sure that the flock allots the Biblical tithe. I wonder if there should be anything in the Bible about inflation and the increasing cost of living. Really, "If the Lord wanted me to tithe that much, he wouldn't have made college so expensive."[1]

Traditionally, Russian churches abided by the principle that everybody gives what he can afford — I cannot imagine that an elderly Russian woman, a *babushka*, could be expected to bring a check stub from her meager pension to justify her tithing. Organized crime and criminals of all persuasions were the most generous church sponsors during the troubled transitional times of Soviet *perestroyka*. And the churches put the names of the sponsors — organized crime groups — on the memorial plaques. In America, I saw a curious sign on the Stanford University Church too: the name of the Lord, amusingly, was chiseled in much smaller letters that the names of the givers.

More than once in America — especially in the South — I've heard about preachers who bankrupt their churches with some wheeler-dealer financing, while catechizing and evangelizing from the pulpit. I remember a TV episode about a thieving preacher who built a nice fortune for himself and his multiple relatives from the church alms. While he was being placed under arrest, the preacher sermonized to the FBI agents, "God does not forbid being rich!" Interestingly, my electronic dictionary gives only a politically correct part of the Biblical proverb, "it's easier for a camel to go through the eye of a needle..." — in Russia the second part is usually quoted as well, "than for a rich man to enter the kingdom of heaven."

For some Southerners, churchgoing seems to be not so much about religion as it is a hypocritical attempt to elevate their social position by rubbing elbows with influential people they could not otherwise meet socially. Often it serves as a convenient dry-cleaning for the soul — evidently, I'm not the only one who is bothered by that: "The thing is, all [of that family] in this town have always gotten away with bloody murder. They run around and cheat and lie all week

---

1 Lewis Grizzard

long, then they stand up in church on Sunday in the front pew and sing louder n'
anybody — because everybody looks the other way."[1]

My husband's increasing fair-faced piousness was also alarming. The more
tricks he pulled, the more showy piety he demonstrated. Probably he was looking for an ultimate indulgence for his deeds, and the Baptist postulate "once saved
always saved" must have been helped a great deal. If one is "saved," then what is
the risk for his soul, in the big picture? Was he seeking support, or forgiveness for
lying and casting aspersions, for example?

Once I asked Martin what religion meant to him.

"It makes me feel better," my Baptist answered truthfully.

I thought that the main idea was to help somebody to become a better person.
But I agree that consumerist's approach must be convenient, especially considering that many congregations share the popular belief that salvation, once obtained, cannot be lost by bad behavior. Market competition has started a chain
reaction: Baptists are considered sectarians by the nearby church, which in its
turn has declared that only its congregation is destined for heaven.

I had an edifying experience at one of the local churches when I decided to
check their well-advertized divorce support group. The sessions were based on
videotaped lectures, which suggested some soothing solutions for aching souls,
and notebooks for homework and minutes were offered for sale, too. The propaganda of the church was very pushy, though whoever pays the piper calls the
tune, I guess.

But then the video unveiled rules, which defined when one shouldn't try to
save the marriage. Condemned partners included drunkards, drug addicts and
— unbelievable as it is — those who belonged to different denominations. That
made me almightily angry. It didn't sound very Christian that those of different
beliefs had been placed on the same level with drunkards and drug addicts. I
wondered, why, exactly — in fear of proselytizing, because they represented a
potential threat to convert the spouse's checkbook? I looked around: the group
obediently continued jotting down the "golden rules," nobody batted an eye.
They didn't question the absolutes — they were in church, after all.

But what about the Gospel, which calls for indifference to our neighbor's religion? Astounding how interpretations can differ from original texts, especially
if the originals are known only as interpretations. I didn't waste my breath trying
to educate anyone about panhuman values and secular laws, about spirituality
that is probably above any organized religion since it embraces the world as it is,
about legitimate respect for other religions and denominations.

> If Americans are ignorant of the facts behind religion, a goodly share of the
> blame belongs to mainstream churches and their ministers... churches remain
> places to believe, not places to think. Ministers rarely challenge congregations
> to ask questions, do research, think deeply or explore other faiths with anything

---

1 Mary- Kay Andrews, *Hissy Fit*

like an open mind. Rigorous thought is suspect. Intellectuals, especially intellectual women, are not particularly welcome. In my experience, ministers just want congregations to believe, obey and donate — generously.[1]

Even high-ranking church leaders seem to be "very poorly advised" when they throw oil on the smoldering embers, as Pope Benedict did during his Brazil tour, outraging Indian leaders with " 'arrogant and disrespectful' comments that the Roman Catholic Church had purified them and a revival of their religions would be a backward step... The Pope said the Church had not imposed itself on the indigenous peoples of the Americas. They had welcomed the arrival of European priests at the time of the conquest as they were 'silently longing' for Christianity... Several Indian groups said the Indians had suffered a 'process of genocide' since the first European colonizers had arrived. 'It's arrogant and disrespectful to consider our cultural heritage secondary to theirs,' said one of the Indian coordinators."[2]

The modern trend in American spirituality, when people, especially women, instead of going to church choose their personal spiritual contacts, on their own terms and at their own pace, is not catching on in the South. That people might choose not to declare their faith because they don't want anybody to think that they are trying to push their beliefs — that idea would look exotic there. But luckily, even among old-style Baptists there are more open-minded people. One African-American grandmother told her granddaughter, who had converted to Catholicism, "We all need to find our way to God. It doesn't matter how we get there."

American media and mainstream literature carry these messages over and over again, trying to sooth the aggressive battling for market share between different denominations:

> Once you have conquered all your sins, pride is the one which will conquer you. A man starts off deciding he is a good man because he makes good decisions. Next thing, he is convinced that whatever decisions he makes must be good because he is a good man. Most of the wars in the world are caused by people who think they have God on their side. Always stick with people who know they are flawed and ridiculous.[3]

Unfortunately, this advice is a drop in the bucket compared to massive attacks from ministers and politicians who capitalize on religion and religious issues. American history itself was never such a close marriage between church and state as Mr. G. W. Bush tries to enforce. Roger Williams fled from religious persecution in Boston and founded Rhode Island in 1635 — he believed in complete separation of church and state. Statesman Benjamin Franklin became a deist, believing in an abstract god. He wrote, "I think it seems required of me, and my duty as a man, to pay divine regards to something. [...] As to Jesus of

1 Letters, *Newsweek.* March 26, 2007
2 Raymond Colitt, "Brazil's Indians offended by Pope comments," Reuters, May 14, 2007
3 Helen Fielding, Olivia Joules *Overactive Imagination*

Nazareth [...] I have some doubts of his divinity, though it is a question I do not dogmatize upon. I see no harm, however, in its being believed, if that belief has the good consequence, as it probably has, of making his doctrines more respected and better observed."[1]

Ex-president Bill Clinton commented, in Aspen, "You know there is a reason that the framers gave us the separation of church and state."[2] He also said in one of his interviews, "I have these arguments with some of my most conservative Christian fundamentalist friends all the time [...] I don't agree [...] that we need to write Jesus into the government [...] St. Paul [...] said in the King James version, 'For now I see through a glass, darkly; but then face to face: now I know in part.'"[3]

An absolute truth is unachievable in human society, and a man's world can only be as big as his experience and knowledge about it, and so unrepentantly and truculently the biggest part of the world could be left out, cast out along with those of different beliefs.

But undeniably, a flock of non-thinking obedient individuals is much more easily governed. As one very churchy Southern lady told me, "I support the war in Iraq because the President decided to do so — since we elected him, we must follow." I did not remind her that Hitler was officially elected too, for I was sure she would take it too literally. Church, giving her a sense of order, of predictability, of calm and appeasement, lulled her into following a shepherd, always following, without thinking.

Just like a zealous Baptist from that divorce support group who asked me if I was "saved," if my husband was "saved," and in case he was a cheater, if his lover(s) were "saved" — I guess that could simply, firmly and finally determine where to point that Finger of Judgment. "Too many Americans feel they know everything they need [about the Bible]. These same Christians are quick to judge (first ones to cast a stone), and then wonder why Americans are so reviled in other parts of the world."[4]

A Guide to Naturalization states, "America becomes stronger when all of its citizens respect different opinions, cultures, ethnic groups, and religions, found in this country. Tolerance for differences is also a responsibility of citizenship."[5] But this is just for the newcomers — evidently, indigenous church citizens can afford to forgo all that stuff. Closing the church door behind me, I could quote an elderly Southern mountain woman, "The way some folk run they's churches, it take God right out'cha heart."[6]

---

1 John Bigelow, ed., *The Works of Benjamin Franklin*, quoted from World Policy Institute website
2 http://www.aspeninstitute.org
3 "Clinton's Crusade," *Ladies' Home Journal*, November 2005
4 "Letters," *Newsweek*. March 26, 2007
5 www.uscis.gov
6 David Baldacci, *Wish You Well*

The Baptist outlook on divorce seemed mind-boggling for me too. It doesn't matter if her soon-to-be-ex-husband is philandering left and right — the proper Southern Baptist female must chastely avoid socializing with men up to those fifteen months that precede a final divorce in North Carolina. Even if she is legally separated, even if she intends just to meet her childhood male friend for a cup of coffee in a public place. The only exception — of course — is the company of fellow-Baptists from her church. This period of continence long enough that one could bear a child is a legacy from the 18th century, as the extreme Baptist proudly told me. Though the Bible Belt is hardly Siberia, with its permafrost, there are certainly some well-preserved "mammoths" lurking under the surface.

That extreme Baptist would be surprised how close he was to Confucian ideas. He would definitely admire The Three Obediences: when a girl, obey your father; when a wife, obey your husband; and when a widow, obey your son. Or the Four Virtues, "which delineate woman's behavior, speech, carriage, and occupation: 'Be chaste and yielding, calm and upright in attitude; be quiet and agreeable in words; be restrained and exquisite in movements; be perfect in handiwork and embroidery.'"[1]

I was shocked when my Southerner explained to me that as a married woman, I must obey. Oh, sure — maybe, continuing with the Confucian codex, I should never show my teeth when I smile or raise my voice when talking to a man? In fact, I think some obedience could feel very sexy and romantic — unless one is forced into it — but that would imply inviting, involving, and seducing, not bluntly coercing.

Some ancient Indian beliefs even declared that "the woman is guilty of misconduct until proven innocent"[2] — the poor women had to walk on scorching coals in order to prove that they hadn't ruined their reputations. Such a ritual, for example, could have saved Martin the trouble of illegally gaining access to the business cell phone accounts of my department and to my separate bank account; digging through my purse and trash-diving into wastebaskets (including the bathroom's — yuck!) in vain attempts to find some dirt on me.

I had hoped that woman's liberation had made some headway, even in the South, but there must be "something rotten in Denmark" if the treatment of women and children is a touchstone of the true values of the community.

But on the other hand, what if that was my punishment from above for being too picky, and then saying "yes" to the wrong man?

---

1 Lisa See, op. cit.
2 Beena Kamlani, "Brandy Cake," from *Growing Up Ethnic in America*

ANALYZE THIS

I ponder whether I should hold Chinese restaurants responsible for my doomed marriage. While slyly pouring ancient Oriental wisdom, buffet-style, right into my stomach, they insistently whispered that I should marry a boar. A boar! The beast doesn't even seem attractive to me, but the description on paper placemats stated that the zodiac Boars are "sturdy, gallant, and thoughtful."

I am a Rabbit, fluffy and white, and allegedly, a perfect match for a Boar.

When I met my future American husband on a shady street in Spain, my built-in always-on-alert woman's intuition immediately reported, No! And it wasn't a small or tentative "no" — it was a pretty assertive one. Nothing seemed wrong with him, though: in his favorite everyday wear, a sweatshirt over a turtleneck, he looked like a young Episcopal priest, as my mother wittily observed when she saw his pictures later. He also had those fine chiseled features that usually turn out well in photos. Perhaps he was too skinny for my liking, or maybe the smile looked somehow alien on his face — as I found out later, he rarely smiles or laughs. Maybe his reddish hair raised my intuitive bristles, "Pigheaded, that's what it is. Red-haired men, God save us. You can't tell them anything."[1]

That first subconscious impression of a potential mate usually is the most accurate. In a split second, the inner computer can determine if this is your person or not, regardless of his appearance. That is the voice of lifetime experience and intuition, perhaps something more complicated than just pheromones sensors. Later, that first impression can be varnished or polished, even overturned if either party really tries hard. But that small voice couldn't be fooled: "Talk of woman's intuition, of the subliminal signals the sex is somehow able to pick up on, in the

---

1 Joanne Harris, *Chocolat*

way of the dog that knows its master is coming home when the car is still six blocks away."[1] (I guess for pet lovers the comparison between women and dogs is not impertinent.) Of course, intuition is not error free, but still it is better not to ignore it.

"Just give it a try!" coaxed my future mother-in-law.

But for me it wasn't "just a try" because I was the one who had to leave everything behind. No wonder I was reluctant. I decided to go home. And I stayed instead: I was literally "cried into a marriage." Aborting my packing, I got married exactly two days before my departure flight. The lady-magistrate asked us several times, in utter disbelief, about our rings — it didn't even occur to me until that moment that my darling, amid alarums and excursions, had dodged the obligatory rings, both engagement and wedding.

One has to be egoistic when it comes to one's own happiness; even my broken-hearted not yet husband said that I had to think about myself first. Perhaps that's what got me, precisely — it was so thoughtful of him. Watching his disappointment wasn't pleasant, either. Not that I hadn't turned down a proposal before, but I didn't witness the reaction so closely, hour after hour, being under the same roof. Poor thing didn't eat and didn't move; he was just disconsolate.

He tried that "wet trick" again later when he was seriously in the wrong, but I let him know that I can't be fooled twice with the same ruse — and the faucets were turned off in an instant. He possessed an impressive skill; were he in the acting career, he wouldn't need artificial tears.

My reluctance to marry had been based on more than just gut feelings, of course. I believe that inuring a seasoned bachelor to matrimony is a thankless task. A woman can't assume that all her predecessors were undeserving rejects or expect that she can serve as a universal solution, smoothing all the unavoidable frictions in the relationship by herself, so that everything will fall into place "automagically." Martin was a special case — not that he didn't want to get married, maybe he just didn't like those who wanted to marry him. I do sympathize with men who are imprisoned in their isolation, unable or afraid to express their feelings; but encrusted in their shell, they rarely care about feelings of others. If the bachelor is from a broken family, the doubts should be doubled, especially if his mother left the way my mother-in-law did — her son will always harbor a deep fear of abandonment and betrayal. These are not just my own reservations — many studies show that "adults whose own parents had split had nearly twice the risk of going through a divorce themselves."[2]

But sometimes you do what you know you shouldn't. Driving instructors always advise not to concentrate on the obstacle that a driver is just about to hit since it becomes a target. I knew I should swerve, but I didn't. My fault.

---

1 T.C. Boyle, *The Inner Circle*
2 "Family, More Than Genes, Helps Drive Divorce," by Carolyn Colwell, *Health Day News*

Definitely, Martin liked the idea of playing at being a couple, having a woman on his arm to show off to his friends and relatives, proving that he was capable of being a family man. He was trying his best, before slipping back into his habitual existence, when he saucily said, "Yes, I am boring!" He was aware of that. And surely he was not going to count his blessings every day because I came into his life — why would he? He wasn't happy either. As my mother-in-law said when she was just about to become my ex-, "You're too much of a woman for him."

WHEN MARTIANS AND VENUSIANS CLASH

When I was an outsider, it was easy for me to muse about the American "battle of the sexes." The very idea sounded silly. But don't you say it before you try it — soon after I had married my Southerner, I found myself in the trenches.

"Be nice to me! You'll get further that way!" signaled my Martian.

I transmitted back, as a real Venusian, "I've tried. Didn't seem to work."

And both of us were right in those contentions. Now I can look back and study "what killed the patient."

With Martin, I learned the hard way the literal sense of the American proverb, "give him an inch and he'll take a mile." While I didn't bother to argue about things that were, in my opinion, not important to fight over, I didn't realize that my Martian was keeping score: "I won this round — I should win every time." But I didn't want to be like a Laura Doyle's porcupine, "Disrespecting your husband's choices on a regular basis is like pricking him repeatedly with little pins. Imagine living with a porcupine."[1] I just didn't realize that my amiability would soon deprive me of choices altogether.

In the beginning, the differences in opinion seemed more funny than serious. Once we were chopping vegetables for supper, side by side, just a picture of marital bliss, when I asked Martin to make the cubes smaller. I didn't say, "Don't you know how to do it?" I didn't mimic, in reverse, his favorite ethnic teasing style, "Don't Americans know how to cook?" I simply explained why I was asking. But the result of my request was petrifying: Martin slammed the knife on the counter and stormed out of the kitchen, "Do it yourself then!"

His voice sounded strange, somehow womanish in anger. At that moment, I thought it wasn't a big deal — maybe the man was out of his element in the

---

1 Laura Doyle, *The Surrendered Wife*

kitchen. But the disproportion between the reason and the reaction was alarming. It was clearly not about vegetables. And when an issue arose that required discussion, there was no room for adjustment. It could be done only one way — his way. Period.

"You can go here or you can stay home," my "sovereign" declared with a thin-lipped smile, showing me a picture of a hotel when we "discussed" where to go for our first Christmas together.

I explained that I don't appreciate that approach. We didn't even have a heated argument, but Martin felt so offended by my "riot" that he boycotted me for three months after that episode. Even though "Martian specialists" advise Venusians to wait patiently till their sulking men finally decide to come out of their "caves," I would suggest that in some tough cases, a Venusian is entitled to forget her Martian's name if he makes her wait too long. In my case, it would have spared me a lot of wrecked nerves and a substantial chunk of wasted time at a very critical age for a woman.

Efforts "to save" a lonely Martian so very often are doomed and won't help the Martian and especially the Venusian — aliens' lives are tough. Besides, if a Venusian, especially of Russian origin, tries to make an unhappy person happy, she might become attached to him more then she would like to, even as she suspects at the same time that her heroic attempts might be self-damaging and nothing but a waste of her own life. Why should she bear responsibility for a pile of problems if the other person doesn't care to dig in from his end?

But I got off on the wrong foot, too — in the beginning, I was just a visiting guest with an obligatory polite "up-to-you" attitude. So when I adopted a marital role, I couldn't, in Martin's opinion, have a vote. As one American woman said, "They only clean up their acts until they've got us, then it's all downhill from there." When Martin was doing his best coaxing me into the marriage, he wrote a thoughtful letter accentuating that marriage is all about compromises and tolerance — I guess he just edited out the statement that compromises and tolerance are solely the woman's merits.

It has always been easier for me to deal with a strong person, one who feels self-sufficient and doesn't have to check every second if his turf has been invaded or if he is venerated enough. I had the privilege of working with such a man in Russia. Internationally acclaimed, he had a reputation of being a "lone wolf" but he invited me to be a peer — as I discovered, to my astonishment, he had put together a quite complete portfolio of my articles. A female technician, also strong-headed, joined our team, and we worked together so productively and happily that our television crowd was puzzled — how on earth could these three get along without fighting? Colleagues even admitted that they eavesdropped to find out if we were yelling at each other in an editing room and were disappointed that we weren't. In our work group, we cared about the best results, not its authorship. Evidently, such men could hardly be put off by a woman's critical facilities — more likely, they'll find those facilities useful and put them to good use.

In the sphere of personal relationships in the Soviet Union, a sharp woman was considered attractive; "winning" an intelligent woman tickled male's sensitivity. So it was strange for me to read in Maureen Dowd's article:

> Men, apparently, learn early to protect their eggshell egos from high-achieving women. The girls said they hid the fact that they go to Harvard from guys they meet, because it's the kiss of death. "The H-bomb," they call it.
>
> "As soon as you say Harvard Business School . . . that's the end of the conversation," Ani Vartanian said. "As soon as the guys say, 'Oh, I go to Harvard Business School,' all the girls start falling into them."[1]

In my private life, I was always grateful that my Russian male friends — not even "boyfriends," just friends — seemingly enjoyed brightening my life, impressing me, helping me. It made me thankful and happy for their company, and they took pleasure in it.

"You think they really enjoyed helping you?" Martin ironically asked me once, complaining that I "was spoiled by men." I tried to explain about exchanging care and warmth, but for him "being nice" was just an obligation.

I guess I didn't fulfill his expectations of a true Southern wife, either. "[I had to] remember to smile even when I didn't feel like it. I knew that while it was okay for [him] to dump his bad feelings on me, it was not okay for me to tell him mine — as the magazines instructed me that it was my duty to protect his fragile male ego, and any indication that I was less than happy would make him feel like less of a man."[2] I couldn't get it: why the male ego is supposed to be so fragile, what tempered it that way in America — I was used to Russian men's thinking, and they attributed hypersensitivity to the female domain. There also was a view that it made sense to make a woman happy, even if for the sake of a man's well being. A woman needs her triple-A's — adoration, admiration, and affection — just as she needs her vitamins.

But when a woman has too many good men around her, a dangerous illusion appears that a better man is still around the corner, perhaps around a further corner. Then she turns that corner — and voila! I had never been in an unhappy relationship until I got married, so I wasn't prepared.

With Martin, communication was doomed: our different ways of arguing made it impossible to solve issues. I preferred to stick to facts, but Martin could start with one thing, then switch to another, and finally soar to his favorite "you always!" — it didn't matter if something had happened once or even never occurred.

Once he complained to me, "Remember, you scratched the Mercedes and said, 'Well, it's just a car!' hopped in and drove away!" That puzzled me — I remem-

---

1 Maureen Dowd, "The Baby Bust," *New York Times*, April 10, 2002
2 Florence King

bered for sure that I said those words, but something was wrong with the picture. And then it struck me: I said that, all right — when he backed his van into the "baby car" and I was trying to solace him. But he depicted a completely different scene, keeping the cue but putting me behind the wheel. That was the move of a film director! It was interesting.

Martin's bursts of anger looked bizarre because his habitual distant disposition changed into rage in a heartbeat. Once he incautiously performed these hysterics in front of his friends, and jokingly asked us later, when we witnessed a child's tantrum in a park, "Did I sound like him?"

His quick natural sense of humor patched over and saved many moments, but everything is patchable only to some extent, and some things were hardly patchable: staking out my friends' houses (they were married people with grandkids, for Christ sake!), authorizing unglued rednecks to "straighten me out" in his absence, searching in vain for damning evidence, writing anonymous letters — all that looked too morbid. Martin presumed that since he was a Southerner and I was an alien, the law would be on his side.

"I've lived here all my life," he would remind me, "and you're nobody."

But instead these rogueries harmed the author: he got third degree for unauthorized access to the county's cell phone accounts; stalking brought his oddities out in the open; his helpers-trespassers ended up in a courtroom and got it good and proper. Of course, if the woman in my place had been some new arrival who didn't have any friends and support or couldn't stand up for herself, the outcome might have been quite different. The best advice I can give to alien women who find themselves in difficult conditions is to find help and refuse to be victimized.

Since I wasn't good at yelling or making a scene and didn't feel like studying those skills, I started smashing innocent artifacts when Martin crossed the line into the unacceptable.

"But you don't smash things!" said my mother incredulously.

But I had to — I didn't have a choice. Some say that launching flying saucers is a healthy way to vent one's feelings, but it certainly didn't work for me. Those articles were the products of someone's labor, after all, and destroying the nest doesn't feel natural for a woman. I started to take brisk walks after discovering that the expression "he makes my blood boil" is not just a trope.

Although in some ways we were compatible, Martin and I. I cannot imagine living under the same roof with some people whom I love and respect greatly, but I knew I could cohabit with him. Even during our worst times he was a polite enough "neighbor" and his hardened habit of being frozen and uncommunicative suited the situation just fine. He was tidy; I still respect that a lot — he even washed the exterior of the house after pollen season — and he didn't have a violent bone in his body. He cherished his dog and started feeding wild creatures after I insisted on getting bird feeders. He consistently opposed redneck-style deer hunting, when poor animals were annihilated in peoples' own backyards. But as Mary Buckley said, "Husbands are awkward things to deal with; even keeping them in hot water will not make them tender." So true.

Of course, American and Russian men, as well as men of other nationalities, share some of the same "slightly chauvinistic," features. For example, none of them really like to follow women's directions — literally. A friend of mine mentioned that his Seattle-based communications company, which records messages for phone systems, couldn't employ the trademark pleasant female voices for some of their Middle Eastern clients. No man will follow directions from a woman, they were told; the man would hang up before he even got to the instruction to press another button. Once, giving downhill ski lessons to a colleague, I took a break, leaving him on the slope with my friend. When I returned, the progress was obvious: "Your friend explained to me that I should do this and this," said the editor.

"But didn't I say the same?"

"You did, but it is much easier for me to take directions from a man," the editor explained. There was nothing I could do about that.

But some of the Martian-Venusian advice looks off-base to me. For example, "a woman gradually learns to relax and receive more." Why does a woman, allegedly, have to learn such a built-in skill as receiving something good from a man? Does she really have a "belief that she is unworthy to receive more"? Oh, my — that belief must have been acquired through some brutal training!

And not only a Martian has to be close and then "more distant before being close again."[1] As one Russian woman put it, "I don't know how we, women, cope: all the time that husband of yours is in front of your eyes..." She gestured showing how he moves back and forth in front of her, with one hand because in the other she was holding a *mojito* — we were talking on a Cuban beach, which meant that her husband was at the moment in the other hemisphere. I am sure that she went back home rejuvenated and missing him, but for some Martians tidal love waves surely recede — and then just stay low. In these cases, the graduation to the next level of relationship never occurs, and since it's humanly impossible just to hang onto that first stage when the initial excitement of love pursuit wears out, the surfers set off to catch yet another wave and another Venusian. And then another. And another.

Playing hard and working hard has been perfected, but love seems to have a hard time squeezing into this *modus operandi*. Dennis Wholey wrote, "Mental health is the ability to love, the ability to work, and the ability to play." Gauging mental health by the ability to love is a very interesting point. Nowadays people who cannot love usually don't reproduce, at least not by their choice, consequently letting nature weed them out. No wonder that people have more

---

1 John Gray, *Men are From Mars, Women are from Venice.*

chances to sustain their mental health in happy loving families since they feel psychologically protected. "Everybody craves romantic love, but Russia is quite a special country regarding relationship between sexes," says psychotherapist, professor, and sexologist Alexander Poleyev. "About three quarters of people are able to love, but the rest just lack some personal abilities: in particular, the ability to idealize the partner. Devotion, appreciation of the partner's qualities, empathy, and mutual assistance are very strong in marital love. One can simultaneously feel love and pity for somebody, and nothing is wrong with that."[1]

But pity and love don't fit the competitive professional world, and often draughts from that world filter into a family cell — some spouses seem to be more like business partners than lovers, even if for the sake of self-protection: "What if the marriage doesn't work out? We should minimize our risk. Don't let yourself get hurt. So the only way to avoid hurt and anger is not to get close."[2]

In America, this trick seems to be used too often. "Yes, your comfort zone might feel safe, but it is filled with compromise. If you're in a comfort zone, you are failing to meet your responsibilities in the relationship.... You get in a daily rut of going to work, coming home, eating a fast dinner, and then heading to your remote control, or your book. Whatever it is for you, you have a more intimate relationship with that than with your partner... You've stopped relying on your best instincts, values, talents, and wisdom."[3] In Russia, we call it *escapism* — we had to borrow the English word for the intention to avoid reality.

It's hard to adore this sneaky Martian trick: "A man gives you 'penalty points,' and takes all your score away when he feels bad about you." In the South, men can whisk off those points in a heartbeat. Martin and his tribesmen were also such accomplished gossipers that it made me wonder if they left any margin for the gals to surpass them. They could be sweet to one's face, spilling dirt behind a person's back the next minute; the transition from sugary to acrid was dizzying.

Of course, perfect humans are non-existent, luckily — such characters would be hopelessly flat, like good heroines from the old soaps. The minuses in one's personality just have to be balanced with good features.

But perhaps one of the most discouraging tribulations for women who are caught in a bind is living *alongside* a man when we are craving to live *with* that man and to be truly connected. A Russian woman told me about the communication gap that she was still trying to bridge with her American husband of many years. "He doesn't refuse to discuss problems or listen to me — he sits and listens patiently to what I have to say. But then comes that inevitable, 'I see your point, but I think...' — and here it goes, I could never convince him of anything."

1 Olga Ryabinina, "Lubov' – eto psikhicheskoe rasstroistvo." *AiF Zdorov'e*, August 2, 2007
2 Dennis Wholey
3 Phillip McGraw, *Relationship Rescue*

Will he ever be willing to change this behavior? At least their disagreements were non-abrasive, and he was getting the message that she was unhappy about something.

Another woman tried to explain to her husband that the adjustment to American life was not easy to her, saying, "Imagine that you had to work as a taxi driver in Vladivostok. You can drive, right? You would only have to deal with the language problem." To him, the idea of plunging into an unfamiliar environment didn't seem attractive, so she made her point. She recalled her first marriage to a Russian officer. "We did so many things together spontaneously. We could just walk to the cinema when we didn't have a car. It was so much fun." She missed that feeling of being united with her spouse, missed the relationship that wasn't filled with demands, expectations, and the constant need for approval as her American marriage was.

Though when we nostalgically recall our past, one Russian joke comes into mind: an old man, who had seen a lot in his life, was asked what was the best time period. He thought for a moment and announced that it was Stalin's regime.

"Why?"

"I was young then, you know..."

Youthfulness nowadays has become a very elastic concept; a consumer just has to have enough money for a surgical miracle. Lifestyles have changed dramatically also: according to new American standards, "forty is the new twenty, fifty is the new thirty," and so on, but nothing can still alter the fact that "women with mileage" are more realistic and mature. "There will be few men who will suit you. Most of us remain boys for as long as possible, beating back responsibilities that ought to come with adulthood, substituting whatever specious things we can conjure up as a way of staving off the quite reasonable demands of full-blown woman."[1] Little wonder that in modern Russia, much younger girls are considered a suitable match by older wealthy men — exchanging one's spouse for a newer model is the same matter of prestige for the Russian *nouveau riche* as updating his car. It is all about proper accessorizing.

Speaking of "the new young," I was absolutely charmed by these "old school" Southerners — he was 81 and was planning to marry his girlfriend next year. She was 75, and there was some talk that she "had a reputation." Isn't it remarkable — to have "a reputation" at 75? Some of my male widowed relatives got married in their golden age too, but mostly for the sake of mutual care and support, not to have someone to go on the cruise with. As Alexander Poleyev put it, "Getting older, we lose the ability to idealize and thus to love passionately. Elderly men and women often make couples because they are afraid to spend the remainders of their lives alone, so they make a rational marital union. They don't fall in

---

1 Robert James Waller, *High Plains Tango*

love with their withered age-mates spontaneously. They choose a partner that is befitting."[1]

In the musical "Fiddler on the Roof," Tevye asks his wife Golde if she loves him, and she recites that for all those years she washed his clothes, cooked his meals, cleaned his house:

> Do I love him?
> For twenty-five years I've lived with him,
> Fought him, starved with him.
> Twenty-five years my bed is his.
> If that's not love, what is?[2]

Isn't that mutual care the constitutive essence, sacred and precious, that helps to withstand the craziness of the outside world? If someone doesn't care selflessly about your happiness, your success, your comfort, your pleasure, there always will be these pangs of doubt: does my partner offer enough to balance out everything that I'm giving up?

1 Olga Ryabinina, "Lubov' – eto psikhicheskoe rasstroistvo." *AiF Zdorov'e*, August 2, 2007

2 http://www.demnos.com/lyrics/fiddlerontheroof.htm#10

Russian Men vs. Their Western Counterparts

More than once I have been asked about the nature of Russian men. Not surprisingly, American men's inquiries lay in practical spheres — when do their
Russian counterparts marry, what cars do they drive? Women gravitated more
toward questions in the relationship department — how are Russian men different from Americans, really?

Saving for later certain heated personal opinions and broad generalizations
from other Russians who discuss this touchy subject without reservation in the
chapter "Russians Talk," let us look at the impersonal facts first.

First of all, let me clarify that a man who was brought up during the Soviet
era, and established his priorities and values then, and a man who was born and
raised in today's Russia are quite different. Western researchers mention this in
the article "Marriage in Russia, a complex phenomenon poorly understood":

> The collapse of the socialist regimes in the USSR and Eastern Europe since 1989
> and the transition from a planned to a market society, which is still going on,
> led to a total change of life, which also will affect demographic behavior. In our
> data, there is some indication of changes taking place with respect to marriage
> and divorce, but the date of the micro census is too early to decide whether this
> implies a postponement or genuine structural change. Recent data could imply
> the latter possibility.[1]

Until just recently, Russians were holding fast on their traditional views on
family.

> The typical Eastern European marriage pattern of early and almost univer-
> sal marriage was remarkably stable. The major crisis, the Second World War,
> led to a postponement of marriage, but even though the female cohorts were
> confronted with an extremely unbalanced marriage market, the proportion of

---

1 Avdeev and Monnier 1999, Philipov 2001, Avdeev, A. and A. Monnier (1999): La nuptialité russe, une
complexité méconnue, *Population*, 54(4-5), 635-676.

never-married was remarkably low. In contrast to the West, where the marriage pattern underwent profound changes, in Russia early and almost universal marriage have remained typical. According to the latest 1994 micro census, only 6 percent of men and 5 percent of women were never married at age 50. The proportion of people getting married at very young ages even has been growing recently.[1]

Russia definitely was never a country of independent singles. Single women of childbearing age without children were quite exceptional; if a woman happened to have her first pregnancy at age 25, she was officially called in medical charts "old primipara." At age 23, an average statistical woman was supposed to be married to her average statistical husband, about 2–4 years older.

Interesting, that this age gap existed almost everywhere, including the US. The traditional rationale is that girls mature earlier universally; and traditionally, men have been providers for the family. Only in two countries in the world — in San Marino and France — wives are just so slightly older.

In the US, "the sex ratio (women per 100 men) is 104.5... Currently, 91.9% of men and 93.9% of women get married. [It] implies that the average number of wives per men is 1.07. This seems puzzling, given that polygyny has been illegal in the United States for more than a century. What is missing? A key observation is that men typically marry younger women."[2]

That is, their wives are from different age groups. And here international marriages make a substantial contributions. In Norway, where the standard age gap of 3.5 years was stable for 100 years.

> The increase in marriages where the man is a lot older than the woman is [due to] so called mail order marriages. Increasing globalization and international mobility have gradually affected the marriage market in Norway, and in more and more marriages one or both of the parties have an immigrant background. In 2002, 7 out of 10 marriages entered into were between two Norwegian citizens, 10 per cent were marriages between two immigrants, 7 per cent were between a Norwegian woman and a foreign man, and a total of 12 per cent were between a Norwegian man and a foreign woman.
>
> The latter group in particular has increased dramatically in recent years, with the majority of men marrying women from non-western countries, especially Thailand, Russia, and the Philippines. These women are often much younger than their Norwegian husbands. While the proportion of marriages where the man was at least 6 years older in marriages between two Norwegian citizens was only 20 per cent, the figure was almost 60 per cent for marriages between Norwegian men and foreign women. Additionally, in the increasing percentage of marriages between persons with an immigrant background, the man is often much older. The increasing proportion of marriages where the woman is older than the man is more prevalent in cases where women marry a foreign man.[3]

So the traditional stereotype becomes outdated: foreign men are also more frequently marrying Western partners. There is a popular belief that Western

---

1 Sergei Scherbov, Harrie van Vianen, "Marriage in Russia..." February 26, 2004; www.demographic-research.org
2 Michele Tertilt, "Dynamic Marriage Market Accounting." Stanford University, January 2004
3 Jan Erik Kristiansen, "Statistics Norway," January 31, 2005

women do it solely to try something exotic, but I think that those women who were successful must have a very different opinion.

Broad generalizations are hazardous, but it is safe to say there are certain trends. Indisputably, "classic" Russian men somehow possess much less fragile self-esteem than their Western counterparts. That is especially remarkable considering the Russian unisex tendency to talk freely about touchy subjects and serious life matters.

A traditional Russian man in love was often not afraid to be open and vulnerable, freely expressing his feelings and doing romantic, imprudent things. He was pleased if she gracefully accepted his offerings; for him it was just one more way to reach and "touch" her, and he did not expect that a woman should be indebted to him for life for his generosity. He was not calculating, and the growing trend among American men to deliberately seek a mate with the same or greater level of income would disturb a traditional Russian male who was brought up as a family provider and protector.

"What trend? Are you nuts?" flared one actively dating but not wealthy American when I mentioned this view. I offered him a quotation, including Christine B. Whelan's credentials: she is a New York-based author, journalist, and commentator with a master's and a doctorate's degrees from Oxford University:

> Since the 1930s, researchers have been asking men and women what they want in a spouse. And my, how times have changed. While today's young man ranks love and attraction as most important, a few generations ago it didn't even make the top three. A dependable, sweet lady who had skills in the kitchen was the prized catch in the 1930s; these days, guys are looking for brains, beauty — and a sizeable paycheck seems to sweeten the deal.
>
> [In the 30s], a woman's financial prospects were second-to-last on the ranking of 18 characteristics, just slightly more important than her political background. [Now] if she has a fantastic job and makes a lot of money, most men report, then it's a great bonus.

But women seem to be drifting in the opposite direction: "[In the 30s], a man's professional status, income, and family background might very well outweigh love. But by the 1990s, less than 10% of women said they'd marry someone without love. Why the drastic change of opinion? One explanation is that as women gained access to power, education, and money themselves, they could shift their focus in choice of a partner away from economic considerations toward love and attraction. It's still a little too soon to say for sure, but it's a trend worth watching."[1] In 2001, 72 percent of women filling out the questionnaire at American marriage agencies specified that they prefer men with high income, and only 31 percent of men mentioned the income of their potential mate. In 2006, the proportion had changed: a high income of the potential partner was requested by 57 percent of women and 51 percent of men.

---

1 *Busted Halo* magazine, http://www.bustedhalo.com/features/PureSexPureLove40WhatWomenand-MenareLookingforBustedHalo.com.htm

A popular Russian actor, director, and producer Oleg Tabakov told an interviewer, "A male can be called 'man' only if he is able to support his wife and children. If he cannot, then it should be written in his documents: 'Sex: neuter.'"[1] Despite his harsh words, he did not mean that his much younger spouse, a talented popular actress, must become just a housewife. But the principle is that "her money is her money, his money is family money."

The American man who suggested that his ex-wife should have bought him a car "since she had money" would not be understood by a "classic" Russian man. The plot of the Oscar-winning Russian movie "Moscow Does Not Believe in Tears" is based on a romantic story that takes a dramatic twist when the main hero discovers that his love is not just a single, middle-age woman with a child but a successful business woman, general manager of a big factory. The hero has to reconsider his potential as a breadwinner, which is traumatic for him: unlike his antipode, a romantic villain, the man is not a sugar-mommy seeker.

Relying on a wife to shoulder the financial burdens of the household has been considered un-manly by generations of Soviet men, but again, the economic conditions — free medical care, free education, affordable day-care for small children, low-cost housing, subsidized and widespread public transportation, and paid vacations provided by the work place — could sustain such a position. Though even during Soviet times not many women chose to stay at home — the social status of a career woman looked more attractive, life more eventful, and money was still useful. Now, many wealthy Russians can easily afford the swank life for their families and relatives. They fly to pricey European winter resorts with their nannies in tow, and their mothers-in-law parade newly presented full-length mink coats. Keeping the best affordable lifestyle for his family has always been important to a male's pride.

If a traditional Russian man left his family, especially if he was at fault, he might walk out with just the proverbial "suitcase with a couple of shirts." A man was expected to build his life again, and quarrelling over household items was considered unmanly. Now, parting is not that simple, especially when multimillionaire estates are involved.

Narcissism used to be an exception among Russian men; loving wholeheartedly was their trademark. A man once thanked me for teaching him to love the woman, not his reflection in a woman. But modern Russian metrosexuals are hardly different from their Western counterparts.

***

Recently, I witnessed two Russian families on a shopping spree — that is, the men were picking outfits for their women.

"I don't need another coat — I just got one!" protested one of the ladies while her athletic, blond, broad-shouldered cavalier was towing her to the coat rack.

---

1 Olga Shablinskaya, "Veriu v neporotoe pokolenie", *Argumenti I Facti*, #33, 2005

I realized that in America, I had forgotten altogether how it feels when a man actually insists on buying something for you and you have to restrain him from unnecessary purchases. That was so Russian!

The other man recommended to his wife, "You need black boots — these will look good on you and will go with more of your outfits." He sent his wife to the dressing room, bringing her armloads of clothes to try on — he didn't have to ask what size she needed. On the sly, I watched his selection — he did very well, finding for her some interesting French outfits that emphasized her slim long-legged figure.

"Impossible to beat European style," the man explained his selections. Then he returned with the younger couple in tow, who already had gone through check-out, to show them some unusual coat. He had just bought one for his wife, spending no more than five minutes picking the style and color, asking her to try it on and making the decision.

These men were a stark contrast to the regular sulking male customers who slumber on chairs, waiting for their significant others at department stores. The store associates who helped the Russians wore those amused smiles that people may have in church, witnessing a touching wedding ceremony. Indeed, it was nice to watch these people who hadn't the slightest intentions of making a show — they were just following their family routine.

THE LAND OF LONELINESS

The interviewee, Bollywood actress Aishwarya Rai, was strikingly beautiful. The American interviewer didn't hide his surprise at the fact that the 33-year-old star, who was single at that time, lived with her parents. She politely smiled and explained that actors are nomads, so she didn't have a chance to see her family much anyway.

For the popular American show, Aishwarya didn't bother explaining about close-knit traditional families. She belonged to the other world — Bollywood, Makharashtra, not Hollywood, California, where one strikingly handsome actor shares his roof with a potbellied pig — that cute eccentricity would be more understandable for American viewers.

"The American pleasure in privacy and independence is strange to many refugees. To them, our autonomy simply feels lonely," wrote Pipher.

It seems lonely or it is lonely? When the autonomy of an individual becomes an end in itself — where is that borderline?

For outsiders from traditional cultures, the modern life of metrosexual singles who party in order not to feel lonely might seem to being lacking a meaningful core. When the party is over, what is in the sediment? Are singles really so happy to be single? The craving for companionship can bring singles together for a while, but the centrifugal force of yearning for autonomy tears them apart again. One needs human warmth, but at the same time is tiresomely on guard lest something impinge that precious sovereignty, checking constantly to see if it has been compromised. The dichotomy might be quite painful until it becomes second nature, when a hard-core single will seek another individual just for short-term satisfaction.

Boosting hormones make a person feel alive, but real feelings seem dangerous — they make one vulnerable, a person may get hurt. In the well-groomed land of the blooming Narcissuses, short-term practical love affairs substitute for deeper relationships — sex instead of love, partners instead of family.

And then people wonder about why they are unhappy. Satisfying sexual intercourse can chemically unchain a burst of positive emotions, but it does not come close to real happiness since that is based on quite different values. "Americans are mixed up about their sexuality. [...] I would teach the true place of sexual intercourse in a relationship. Happiness really is based on fundamental values like mutual understanding, empathy, sympathy, adjustment, compromise of little elements without its being called compromise, and having a mutual goal. Something is wrong with the academic process if people think emotional sex is an equivalent of happiness."[1]

And rarely lonely people come from happy extended families, where generations learned to live together without fighting for supremacy but respecting each other's needs, rights, and feelings. Of course, if generations are crammed together because they cannot afford separate living then all idyllic sentiments go out the window and life become rough, but I knew a Russian editor-in-chief who shared an apartment with his mother-in-law. That was quite unusual — in-laws are a laughing matter in Russian culture as well — but the family found a balance in their life, and when the editor accepted a job offer in another city, it was clear that they were going to relocate all together. The older woman helped to raise her granddaughter, and the family members, sharing the housework and burden of everyday chores, had built visibly happy and harmonic relationships.

Just like another family, from a different culture, but with the same ability to blend their lives together for some meaningful purposes: "They live together and while the couple works, the older women cook, care for the house, and supervise the daughter after school. The mother told me, 'Our mothers have gentled our daughter. If they hadn't been with us, I think she would have trouble in junior high. But they were waiting for her after school with snacks, attention, and affection. They held her life in place.'"[2]

"You marry the family" can hold so much truth. When a Western woman marries a Russian, the experience may come as a pleasant surprise. "The Russian spouse's family and friends also usually provide much stronger emotional support than is true of American families in the United States. [...] 'Once Andrey was born I don't know what I would have done without [mother-in-law]. She was absolutely great in helping with the baby so that I could keep on working. I don't think I'd be able to have this kind of a relationship with my own mother — I certainly couldn't live with her and Ivan!'"[3]

---

1 Dennis Wholey
2 Mary Pipher
3 Lynn Visson

Russian parents usually cherish the fleeting moments of their kids' babyhood. If a woman can afford it, she might very well choose to take a break and stay home bringing up the children instead of pursuing career goals and leaving the kids to professional care: "Immigrants wonder why we, in such a rich country, leave our babies with strangers."[1] The elderly expect to be revered and taken care of also: "The American notion of raising a child to become independent — and move out on his own — is diametrically opposed to the Russian notion of parents supporting their children as long as possible and the children becoming their mainstay in old age."[2] Nursing homes do exist in Russia, as well, but mostly for the elderly who have no immediate family. Generally, Russian society doesn't approve of transferring elderly parents to nursing homes.

Western families with grown-up children sometimes remind me of a submarine in distress: the partitions are sealed, each compartment fights for life separately. As a teenager says in a book, "They never said, Here's the deal, we look after you till you are not cute anymore, then you're on your own."[3] The author doesn't imply that parents have to sacrifice for the sake of their children, either. "Just about the only duty parents have towards their children, it seemed to me, is to enjoy their life. After all, here they are in the prime of this life they've given us, and if they don't like it, what hope is there for us? [...] Me, I'd sooner make the good world for myself and let the children do what they have to do when their turn comes."

Setting the example is a gift from parents to their children. I knew a family of Muscovites who demonstrated such an obvious and warm connection when gathering together for their family meals — the TV was in the other room — that I wasn't surprised when their son built another close-knit relation, with his in-laws living under the same roof and helping to rear his much-loved children. Financial arrangements in families like this might look unusual for foreigners: the parents sold their spacious family nest and simply presented a separate flat — a super-expensive asset in Moscow — to their son's family. No loans, no expectations to be paid back — that was just a gift, a natural thing to do.

The other source of warmth comes from good teachers who can "give children lap time, pats, and nonverbal reassurance that they are going to be okay... A hug has a universal meaning,"[4] wrote a psychologist. But the reality deals with different standards: Sybil, a substitute teacher of German origin was unpleasantly surprised when she was told that she could not hug a child or have any other physical contact with her students.

---

1 Mary Pipher
2 Lynn Vissoan
3 William Nicholson. *Society of Others.*
4 Mary Pipher

"I shouldn't hug and solace a crying child?" the mother of three couldn't believe it, "They are just third-graders, they are small and fragile, they need as much warmth and compassion as they can get!"

But solacing hugs were considered inappropriate conduct in that Southern school — better to be on the safe side. At school in Illinois, two hugs equaled two days of detention for 13-year-old Megan who violated a school policy, which banned public displays of affection, when she hugged two friends at Mascoutah Middle School. "'I was just giving them a hug goodbye for the weekend,' she said. Megan's mother said the embraces weren't even real hugs — just an arm around the shoulder and slight squeeze."[1] Isn't that quite ridiculous?

American parents invest a lot of time rearing their children, but in a different manner than Russian. Parents are chauffeurs, schlepping kids from one activity to another. They are managers, dealing with conflict of schedules in their kids' busy calendars. They are agents, arranging play dates for their offspring. Everything seems to be so highly regulated in American kids' lives that it reminds of some version of a corporate environment marketed for children. And when all events were attended, all deadlines were met and the children became older, families grow to be not close anymore.

But could the independent way that American children are raised in be a compensation for the constant over-the-shoulder guarding in childhood? By law, American children have be supervised well into the age when in other cultures they are already a quite substantial help and have their own daily chores, including, ironically, baby-sitting for their younger siblings. How amazing the independence of Japanese children looks, in comparison: their precious young are supposed to get to schools using public transportation in huge busy cities. And imagine, kids manage!

"Children from traditional cultures are raised to have great respect for adults... Old and young enjoy each other's company... Refugees are amazed how American teenagers treat their parents and grandparents... Many of the ELL teens plan to live at home until they are married."[2]

That is the way of life in some traditional cultures: a person goes from one family, of his parents, into another — of his own. It doesn't mean, of course, that those marriages stay intact, but it definitely helps to manage skills of living together. Though for us, it sure looks like a person should carve some "single's time-out" in between.

A practical former "Russian bride" Svetlana said, "I would never opt for a forty-some-year-old man who indicates that he is 'single, never married': that type is just hopeless. I would look for a man with children, even if those children are

---

1 Associated Press, "Ill. student gets detention for hugging," Tuesday, November 6, 2007
2 Mary Pipher

a pain in the neck. At least he knows what family life is about." She married a divorced American lawyer, consciously choosing her lifestyle.

Hard to argue with this statement: "The ethnic community can become a feather bed, a little bit too soft and difficult to climb out of. To really succeed in America, refugees must learn to deal with Americans. The best way is to somehow hold onto the good from the old culture while taking advantage of the new, which is more difficult in practice than in theory." Immigrants, and especially refugees, help each other on a level that is unheard of among "authentic" Americans: people do not mind sharing "food, clothes, bicycles, cars, and money with their countrymen." Once, trying to cut through Chinatown in San Francisco, I lost my bearings and discovered, to my amazement, that I was not really in an American city anymore — the people around me didn't understand English. Luckily, I was able to order a cup of green tea using my meager Chinese vocabulary — if not for that, I would have to resort to a dumb show. I was inside a large community, with all the necessary accoutrements — stores, shops, doctors' offices, street vendors etc. — all completely and absolutely ethnic. These people had not just emigrated to the US — they brought their own bubble of national environment and evidently didn't care too much for the world outside. Operating on that level, they don't have to really deal with Americans, at least with Americans of non-Chinese origin. That situation reminded me of a Russian Jewish immigrants' joke. "Abram, we have lived seven years in Brighton Beach already, and these New Yorkers still don't speak Russian!" Many American businessmen in Moscow live in a similar "bubble," not mingling with Russians.

On the roadside in hi-tech Seattle, suburban signs advertised something for those who can read Tagalog — the rest, evidently, should not care and were not invited. Asian communities are homogeneous, loyal to insiders and wary of people of different descent. And these people know the strength of communal life: living in North Carolina, I watched Hmongs overflowing the nearby city park every weekend. The place became as busy as Beijing Square during rush hour: only black-haired heads, no Caucasian co-workers or acquaintances could be found in that crowd. They played volleyball and soccer, ate and laughed, while the kids formed small flocks with a serious, slightly older girl in charge. That happened every weekend, weather permitting. They didn't stay at home all day watching sports on TV as so many Americans do — they played sports by themselves, with their kids on the sidelines. Those impressive, numerous, family-oriented Asian gatherings at the park were diametrically opposite to the signature American loneliness.

"Loneliness in America is an epidemic disorder. TV is the principal contributor. [Now TV has a rival — 64 percent of Americans said that "they spend more time with their computer than with their significant other."[1]] What happens if family "gets together" alone? They do not communicate — they watch TV," wrote Dennis Wholey. A Russian scientist who used to work in the United States remembered those "TV parties." "We got beer, chips — that was not the bad part, though I would prefer normal food any time — and then we sat, chewing and staring at the screen, so we could pat each other on the back after the movie saying, 'That was good! We should do it again soon!' But what about companionship, sociability? Is it just watching TV side by side?"

I could see why that is called a party — at least the people were watching the same show in the same room. It gets worse when married couples relax in front of different TV sets, better yet on different floors of the house. A partner doesn't have any chance competing against a favorite soap character.

"Traditional cultures value interdependence and cooperation, whereas Americans place a high value on individual autonomy. As D.H. Lawrence wrote, 'America is the homeland of the pocket, not the blood.'"[2]

So no wonder the average American blood in the near future is not expected to be Caucasian. "In fact, the Hispanic-origin population would contribute 39 percent of the Nation's population growth from 2000 to 2010, 45 percent from 2010 to 2030, and 60 percent from 2030 to 2050." That growth won't be just due to the net immigration: "After 2011, the number of births each year would exceed the highest annual number of births ever achieved in the United States."[3]

Thanks to Hispanics, the USA will have an increase of population, even if the structure of the population will change significantly. Russian sociologist Vadim Aliev pointed out that the demographers associate the decrease of birthrate in the most of developed countries with urbanization, growing prosperity, and woman's emancipation.

> The proportion of urban population, especially in developed countries, grew significantly, and the city dweller has more egoistic views than the country folk; in the city, one has more temptation to live for himself. As for wealth, the popular belief that the growing prosperity stimulates the birthrate is false. On the contrary, in poor countries, the birth rates are usually higher. It might seem illogical that in a poor eastern country a woman doesn't go to work to help the family but bears children. But isn't it even more illogical that a prosperous woman prefers to work and to build a career instead of caring for her children? Here the other logic is applicable: it is not so much about emancipation as an accomplishment of the civilization, but about emancipation as an egoistic moral of individualism, when a Western liberated woman forgot about her mission and concentrated only on herself.[4]

That was a Russian sociologist, and this is the *New York Times* review "The Baby Bust" by Maureen Dowd:

---

1 Lamont Wood, "When Your Most Significant Other is a Computer," LiveScience.com; http://news.
  yahoo.com/s/livescience/20071008/sc_livescience/whenyourmostsignificantotherisacomputer
2 Mary Pipher
3 Jennifer Cheeseman Day, "National Population Projections," National Census Bureau, 2001
4 Vadim Aliev, "Rossia vimiraet," *AiF Dolgoizitel*', March, 24, 2006

The cover story [of *Time* magazine] chronicles the new baby bust — women who focus too much on their careers suddenly realizing they've squandered their fertility... *Time* offers the scariest statistics for women since *Newsweek* declared in 1986 that a 40-year-old woman was more likely to be killed by a terrorist than to tie the knot...] Sylvia Ann Hewlett, an economist, conducted a survey and found that 55 percent of 35-year-old career women are childless. Between a third and half of 40-year-old professional women are childless. The number of childless women age 40 to 44 has doubled in the past 20 years. And among corporate executives who earn $100,000 or more, she says, 49 percent of the women did not have children... Ms. Hewlett, the author of 'Creating a Life: Professional Women and the Quest for Children,' observes..., "Nowadays, the rule of thumb seems to be that the more successful the woman, the less likely it is she will find a husband or bear a child."

In this midst, many smart metrosexuals of both sexes are doomed to lonely brooding — it was determined a long time ago that "an increase of knowledge is an increase of sorrow."[1]

I omit the second part, "for in much wisdom is much grief," since I am not sure in which ballpark wisdom is — perhaps in the court of old-fashioned kindness, forgiveness, and love.

---

1 Ecclesiastes 1:18

Meanings and Means: "Just a Click Away"

An Internet search for the keywords "Foreign wife" brought up more than five thousands results — Googling for "palmtop computers" harvested hundreds times less than that.

Most of the references were for the dating web-sites/agencies that have mushroomed tremendously. Russian ladies host many of them, or so the web-sites allege, and these ladies supposedly live their happy lives in the USA with their happy American husbands. One site featured dozens of pictures of the "hostess" — a languid young peroxide blonde, model type, who scrupulously posed in different outfits but obviously on the same day, even unemotionally embracing a young "son" before the camera so the prospective husband wouldn't have to force his imagination envisioning a Russian beauty installed in his living room or bedroom.

"They've cheapened my expectations by that frank sex demonstration," one might-have-been customer told me, "though I admit I checked those web-sites when I was considering a way to override the 'local traps,' the limits of the local resources — bars, clubs, school, and work. I thought that there must be some way to get a logical match, perhaps with web-site assistance, if it takes into consideration one's interests, values and hobbies."

Of course, it doesn't mean that all of those international cyber-matches-unions are doomed to unhappiness — after all, not all marriages lead to divorce. In America, just about 50 percent, in general.

But uprooted people live on highly charged ground, and sometimes even reading Russian immigrants' forums on the Web makes me uncomfortable, so much bitterness and anger throb there. I do not imply that some kind of manual "How to Handle Your Foreign Wife" could possibly be created, but at least one can learn from the mistakes and achievements of others.

So why do they go for it — why do people try to find happiness with a foreigner?

The foreign-wife seekers are a motley crew, but even multimillionaires like Donald Trump are looking more or less for the same qualities as humble hourly workers. There are many categories of seekers, and usually they are a combination — after all, life rarely gives us pure characters, pure angels or pure villains.

One educated American tried to prove to me that if a man were to marry, then it should not be to an American woman. I was bewildered by his logic: he had been married twice, both times to non-Americans, and both his marriages failed. So I doubted that the nationality was the stumbling block. I guessed that probably he could have been happy with some of his American students. But then I learned that the man had fathered a child with a Russian colleague he had been dating on and off for ten years. And he turned out to be an absolutely fanatical father. I am not sure how happy his partner was, but he couldn't get enough of his precious child.

Pico Iyer's explanation is at the same time realistic and poetic, just like the subject itself, "Whenever a Westerner meets an Easterner… it awakens in us both the lover and would-be-conqueror… Each finds himself drawn to the other, yet mystified; each projects his romantic hopes on the stranger, as well as his designs; and each pursues both his illusions and his vested interests with a curious mix of innocence and calculation that shifts with every step."[1]

These unions of Easterners and Westerners might be pure romantic love stories — those might still happen not only in soap operas. Some people like to feel that tickling sensation of something exotic, and she might be as exotic for him as vice versa; so that may hold a relationship for a while. As one tour instructor put it, "The girls from the other group are always more attractive."

But even here the attraction ranges from sincere admiration and more or less pure curiosity of all shades to the simple opinion that "the cute accent makes you feel like you are dealing with an innocent girl." Jim, who was so tickled at the "cute virginal touch," was almost an octogenarian. But young and beautiful Sarika Dani, of Indian descent, also wrote, "Growing up, I always assumed that I lacked the gene that made Indians of the opposite sex appealing to me. They seemed immature, unexciting, and too close to home to be attractive. It was hard to understand how I could be connected to my culture but disconnected from the guys who populated it. I now know that when it comes to dating, the desire for the novel and exotic [feels right] for me."[2] At least it was so for some time.

---

1 Pico Iyer, *Video Night in Katmandu*, quoted in Lynn Visson, *Wedded Strangers*
2 Sarika Dani, "Two of a Kind," *Tango* magazine, June 2, 2007

A pretty Russian she-cajoler might be a formidable weapon and a perfect answer for a male midlife crisis: "As for American men...wanting to marry Russian women, they tended to be middle-aged. Their fiancées were usually pretty and well-groomed tour guides, translators or secretaries who showered them with attention and flattered their egos. Foreign spouses also act as magnets for social misfits, very shy or unattractive people, and products of unhappy families. A relatively homely US citizen soon finds that an American passport makes him or her much more popular in Russia than in his own country," Lynn Visson observes in *Wedded Strangers*. Peter, a smart Californian, admitted that all of a sudden a man feels such a pleasant sensation — he again can date and even marry a girl he might have been able to attract several decades ago, so a young foreign beauty serves as a nice-looking "time machine."

The other witty gentleman, Rick, who had a family "to the south of the border," explained, "In Seattle, I am an old guy with a potbelly — in Mexico I am a gringo with green eyes!"

A former naval officer Patrick, who saw enough of Oriental–Western marriages while stationed in the Philippines, admitted, "These men expect to capitalize on a vulnerable, 'needy' female to gain leverage in the sexual attraction game. They expect to move it up a notch in terms of the attractiveness and youthfulness of their prey — even the best of males have an innate predatory trait. No doubt there is an American arrogance as well. The guys think they are saving the Russian girls from some horrible existence in their home country, offering them a relative life of luxury in the good ole USA. But this is more of a tool rather than a genuine concern. The overriding issue for the men is sex, pure and simple. Maybe that's stark and despicable, but nonetheless real and understandable. [But surprisingly, sex is not necessarily the main agenda.] Americans would tend to assume that the Russian-wife hunters are basically losers, either physically or socially too ugly to succeed in attracting an American woman. Or they are looking for a woman who will be more compliant than American women — less bitchy, more controllable, more dependent, and certainly more sexually willing."

"They may try to marry a woman from Eastern Europe in pure desperation or in the hope that the women may be willing to compromise for the sake of living in the US," echoed his compatriot.

But one has to consider that "the desire to 'marry America' — and to go there — is not the only reason why Russian women are attracted to American men."[1] That was also written by an American — and by a woman, be it said incidentally. Yet another testimony indicates that those reasons are not strictly linear. She translated from a popular Russian newspaper, "Sob stories told by stunning Russian girls of drunken husbands who mistreated their children, fears of the return of Soviet totalitarianism, and assurances of a great interest in America, the

---

1 Lynn Visson

outdoors, family barbeques and family values are highly successful with balding, middle-aged farmers and timid insurance agents who have never in their wildest fantasies been the subjects of so much adoring female attention."[1]

The desire to have a "fresh start" with a good-looking foreign woman can have a sociological rationale. "People who choose a spouse from a different culture often do so because they are unable to find a place in their own society, reject its values, or seek a niche elsewhere and would prefer a mate unaware of their alienation," wrote David Klimek.[2] In the first stage of those out-of-the-ordinary marriages, many participants are brimming with hope, emotions, and illusions, especially women, who often claim, or maybe are, or at least try to be, in love with their American fiancés. The fiancés may feel elated, too: they are idealized and their imperfections are irrelevant. Some of them will sincerely try to become better partners — before falling back into old routines.

Dugan Romano stated, "Generally, people who enter into an intercultural marriage have already distanced themselves somewhat from a strict adherence to the predominant values of their own societies."[3] The parties must be adventurers, risk-takers, often buying into something sight unseen, relying on often unreliable, handsomely airbrushed self-descriptions.

> "Anyone who orders a mail-order bride over the Internet deserves more or less who they get," Lawrence Toppman points out, "The bride may or may not be looking forward to a lifetime as a loving and devoted spouse, but she is certainly looking forward to an air ticket, a visa, and citizenship in a Western democracy. Would-be husbands who do not understand this probably believe that beautiful women gladly offer themselves sight unseen to men merely because they have mastered such skills as logging on, typing, and possessing a credit card. Yet hope springs eternal."[4]

If a Russian woman has a child, she may say that she is going to sacrifice her dreams and desires for the sake of her offspring. Again, that might be not the whole truth, but I would say that the self-denying Russian parent is something rarely seen in the West. Some Russian parents are devoted to their children to the extreme, to the last penny and to the last breath, literally, making every possible effort to make their children's lives better.

"Our generation is just a fertilizer for our children," a talented Russian writer, father of two, told me to my astonishment. He made me think of spawning salmon that fertilizes the environment for its offspring by its own flesh. And there were generations and generations of Russian parents like him. Though he alleged that he would not live in a foreign country under any circumstances, his blunt expression applies to the immigrants as well: the first generation of newcomers

---

1 Janet Collins and Dmitrii Kotov, "Zanevestit'sya po-amerikanski," *Moskovskii komsomolets*, 8/30/96, p.8

2 David Klimek, *Beneath Mate Selection and Marriage* and Dugan Romano, *Intercultural Marriage: Promises and Pitfalls*

3 Dugan Romano

4 Lawrence Toppman, "'Birthday Girl' a piece of cake," *Charlotte Observer*, February 1, 2002.

is not that often successful on foreign soil, but their offspring have a much better chance.

Some women, judging the American life from audio-visual resources, hope that they really can fulfill an American dream of their own — if even the "Pretty Woman" could. After all, "American dreams are strongest in the hearts of those who have seen America only in their dreams."[1] For some it turns out to be a great disappointment, but other can really achieve more on American soil. Here, again, it depends, if their men are just the "means of transportation" to a better life or the real-life partners.

Natasha was a unique case: a tactical, calculating Russian woman, she married Tim, who had just reached lawful age — he was her junior by seven years (now, isn't that great!). They had started a real estate business, thanks to her excellent business acumen. He was converted from a computer whiz to an investment specialist, and she, an engineer by education, became a broker. They are not just a family — they are a team, though she still speaks to him in her "little girl's voice."

Some women may be fascinated with the American style, and with American men, for that matter. After all, it could be a part of the old tradition — the Russian aristocracy periodically brought into vogue one foreign style or another. There were periods of Anglophilia and Francophilia in Russian history, so Hollywood and Disneyland could set a new king on a throne — one with a loud and demanding lifestyle. "I wanted to visit Russia before McDonalds and Disneyworlds invaded it, because imperialism doesn't come on the tips of bayonets — it comes on Mickey Mouse's ears," told me Frank, a trailblazer-importer of young Russian brides.

On the other side, an American man must feel like a child in a candy store, browsing the Internet and looking at all those pictures of beautiful Russian women, who seem to be so available and "just a click away."

Most of the women, on the other hand, no doubt feel that time is getting short and they had better make an extraordinary effort to find a man and start a family. And preferably in a place where the sun in brighter and the grass is greener: "You think that same glorious happiness of fortune, fame, and triumph will be yours at any minute, that you are about to take your place among great men and lovely women in a life more fortunate and happy than any you have ever known — that it is all here, somehow, waiting for you and only an inch away if you will touch it, only a word away if you will speak it, only a wall, a door, a stride from you if you only knew the place where you may enter," as a great Southerner wrote.[2]

A woman's life can be instantly and utterly transformed by the magic of the "right" ring. Self-made women sometimes "find it appalling" and say that those

1 Pico Iyer
2 Thomas Wolf, *No Door*

brides are looking for "an excuse to never have to do anything with their lives except trade on their youth."[1]

A tame but tough Russian woman, Nina spent twelve years of her life pursuing that goal, purposefully handpicking her American match. She knew exactly what she was after: she needed a kind and generous man, who would be willing to share his income and father a child. Finally, she found one, but after a test-drive Michael sent her back. She was able to convince him from Russia that he was perhaps too hasty — and he finally married her. They have a child, and now she doesn't even want to recall those twelve years of pursuit. That woman must have sifted through tons of "human ore" because the majority of foreign bride-seekers are not the type of men that their own compatriots considered ideal marriage material.

So those in the most resourceful category, the Western Life Huntresses, have to go through an ordeal, though their prey doesn't have a chance — he might think that she is follows his rules, but as another Russian proverb states, "a man is the head of the family, but a wife is the neck" (here comes an absolutely new definition for necking, I guess). Peter, a small business owner, thought he was training his "young blonde" wife Alyona as free labor for his company. She clenched her teeth and dug in, all the while obtaining the qualifications necessary for a good life without him. She succeeded, and her income now surpasses his.

I would not blame lady-huntresses exclusively for their poor luck, though. As the great Russian poet Alexander Pushkin said, "It is easy to fool me — I am happy to deceive myself."

Here we go.

---

1 Dorothea Benton Frank, *Shem Creek*

In order to go to the United States, a Russian citizen has to obtain a visa — everybody knows that. Accordingly, an American has to get a Russian visa for a trip to Russia — that surprised some Americans.

I was told to pick up my first US visa at a boiler-plant.

"Sure," my witty friend Boris said, driving me there. "Where else one goes for the American visas? To a steam-shop."

That's the way it worked in my case because a kind lady, a complete stranger, worked there. A member of our sports team simply asked her at the airport to carry my documents to our hometown: fast, secure, and free delivery. I cannot imagine asking a similar favor in America, but for Soviets it was not unusual. I recall those times with nostalgia: in a pre-9/11 world, people could trust a stranger on a train to take their child to the destination where the relatives would pick up the kid, and if something happened and the family couldn't make it on time to the train station, the person in charge took care of the child until his relatives caught up. No wonder my passport made a safe trip.

One can easily spot a US consulate in Russia even without looking for the Star-Spangled Banner since, more than likely, it will be the only wheelchair-accessible building. Sadly, Russian bureaucrats are not fastidious about the ordinances for the handicapped. Those islands of American territory may look all buttoned-up in Moscow and unkempt, to some degree, in provincial Russia. And American officials don't let their hair down only when it comes to grounds keeping. Sometimes they could be as unjust as they pleased to foreign citizens. I had such an episode when I went to apply for one of my following US visas: a vice-consul, a young woman, bluntly accused me, "You have been working illegally during your previous visit to America!"

That was an accusation of a crime I did not commit.

"Is that a question or a statement?" I asked, seething.

Her icy light -blue eyes looked at me as if through a gun sight. It was the first and so far the last time when I saw a textbook image of a "potential enemy." I didn't care that I might be black-listed for future visas and explained what I thought of such treatment.

The little people of the world, American visas applicants, share their ludicrous and sad stories on the Web. A Georgian woman was stopped by consulate security because of her excessive luggage — she showed the amazed officers that all her luggage consisted of papers to prove her relationship with her American husband.

Long, patient queues still line up in front of the US Embassy in Moscow, though the times of great friendship between Russian Conductor Boris Yeltsin and American Saxophonist Bill Clinton are history. (Yeltsin was nicknamed after directing a military band during his visit to Germany. I wonder if George W. Bush knew that — he "conducted" some bands, too.) Russian policemen, *militsioneri*, guard entrances to the American diplomatic offices now, so right in front of the Moscow embassy one can see a demonstration of the rudeness and arrogance of Russian law enforcement. Inside the embassy, American security takes over. I remember a very green and very ginger marine, gawking at Russians with childish, wide-open, orange-lashed eyes. He had a spectacle before him, indeed — a never-ending parade of beautiful Russian girls on their way to make his countrymen happy.

Muscovite Irina worked as a tour agent and on the side as a Russian auxiliary of a New York lawyer; her duty was to instruct the lawyer's clients before they go for their visas.

"I got an eyeful here — enough for a paperback novel. Mostly I work with brides, the majority of them are young girls who have never been to America, and they don't have a clue what is awaiting them there. So all that evidence that their American fiancés have to file in order to obtain the US visas for their brides are not bureaucratic cavils, but attempts to protect the girls as much as possible. Usually the fiancés are at least twelve–fifteen years senior and the young ladies are supposed to prove that they are madly in love with their bridegrooms. What skilful actresses they must be, convincing the consulate officers!

"I remember one bride who brought a picture where her fiancé was standing next to her mother. The fiancé was of Mexican descent, very obese, and so much older that I caught myself thinking that he wasn't a match even for her mother — he was simply too old. But what could I say?

"The other asked me to analyze her fiancé's bank statements and other documents because she thought that his stories about his prosperity were doubtful. I refused to do that — I don't want to get involved. Many of those girls don't speak

English — their children, girlfriends, and interpreters help them. Sometimes it turns out to be very moving; even consulate officers empathize: for example, kids chose a husband for one woman who placed her ad on the Internet. She was inclining towards another candidate, but her children stayed firm, 'We want this one!' She obeyed, and said that she doesn't regret the choice."

At the embassy, these brides must feel that getting a visa is the hardest part of the deal, and once they are abroad, everything will be easy. Mila, a young bleached blonde from Kazakhstan, was very nervous. "This is my fiancé: I brought our pictures from Thailand. [The photos looked like advertisements — a beautiful young couple in lavish tropical landscapes.] We met for the first time four years ago, and since then I went to Thailand twice to meet him. All his family is against our marriage, and his commanders object severely. He is in the military, stationed on some base with missiles. Everybody tells him, 'Marry whoever, but not a Russian!'"

After anxious waiting, Mila nervously asked the consulate officer, "So, all the papers that he sent me are not good at all?"

That didn't seem fair — as *The Wall Street Journal* reported, "In 1991, five of the American inspectors assigned in Votkinsk to monitor Russian compliance with the 1987 intermediate-range nuclear missile treaty married Russian women from the escort unit assigned to them." Beauty is a formidable force.

Another bleached blonde, Nina, in her mid-forties, was sporting a mini skirt that did not suit her, but she didn't mind, in the typical American attitude — Russian women usually are much more cautious about even minor flaws in their appearance.

"I'm not a bride," Nina explained, "I'm a grandmother, trying to visit my daughter who went to California as a tourist and got married there. I got a refusal three times already, but who knows, maybe this time I'll be lucky? My grandson is growing up there without me, my daughter needs my help — but they don't give me a visa."

A very young beautiful mother, a petite girl clad in tight blue jeans and a scoop-neck sweater with feather trim, brought her tiny-tot daughter. To my delight, the little thing approached me, took a seat, and initiated a lengthy serious conversation in her baby talk lingo.

"My American fiancé has a son of the same age," the young beauty said, "He just got divorced six months ago. We spent three months together when he came to work in the Ukraine."

In a while, she was happily floating like a breeze to the subway station, her helper trying her best to keep up, carrying the little girl in her arms.

"I'm afraid that the ticket offices might be closing soon — I'm flying to Connecticut tomorrow!"

Of course, there is a great difference between a long-distance relationship and actually living with somebody. It's easy to imagine how most of those international couples, divided by oceans and continents, spend hours on the phone, nurturing their connection, trying to find out more about each other's habits, likes and dislikes. How women come home from work, feed their kids, and go to the computer, composing letters, flirting, fighting with a foreign language. Most of them are eager to take a test-drive, no doubt. If it looks like somebody is ready to move heaven and earth to get his woman, it must be for real, right?

At that point, the obstructionism of US Immigration looks like the main impediment to the pursuit of happiness: once that dragon is slain, everything is going to be fine.

Knowing the romantic nature of Russian women, one can safely say that many firmly believe that destiny has something better in store for them than the life they have at the moment. Of course, somewhere there must be an ideal knight in shining armor for each of them, and, most likely, he lives overseas — where else? These beliefs somehow survive the toughest experiences. As Anita Brookner put it, this is "why novels were written — to give ordinary men and women a better idea of themselves, and, more importantly, to show how fate might take a hand even when the given circumstances appeared to militate against a significant outcome." So they try.

The Declaration of Independence guarantees the rights to life, liberty and the pursuit of happiness in America. Perfect wording: just a realistic right of pursuit.

So run, lady, run — and the best of luck to you.

And the Huntresses prepare for their hunt too. They dress in the style of sexual aggressiveness. They calculate their shock tactics, target their simple prey, put on "war paint." Their goals are not subtle; they are not looking for happiness in some fata-morgana of a personal relationship. They know what they are after; they have structured plans, and they are equipped to achieve their personal success. Putting sentiments aside, they adapt to life abroad with ease. But some of them may get in serious trouble on their journey to success — alas, things do happen.

TECHNICALLY SPEAKING

As outlined by the US Department of State Bureau of Consular Affairs, an American man has two choices for bringing his foreign love into the country.[1] He can marry her outside of the US and file a petition I-130 for his foreign spouse to immigrate to the United States — as an immediate relative, she is instantly eligible for an immigrant visa upon approval. The petition can be filed either with the Citizen and Immigration Service in the United States, or, in some cases, at US

---

1 Robert J. Scholes (with assistance of Anchalee Phataralaoha), The "Mail-Order Bride" Industry and Its Impact on US Immigration, http://www.uscis.gov

Embassies or Consulates abroad. Consulates and embassies have differing policies, so the availability of that service has to be confirmed.

In many cases, this procedure takes longer than the alternative method, the so-called "fiancée" visa, or K-1. But the immigrant visa doesn't require additional processing in the US. (Additional information can be found through the US Embassy and Consulate links page, as well as from the brochure of the Bureau of Consular Affairs "Tips for US Visas: Family-Based Immigrants" and from the Office of Citizens' Consular Services brochure "Marriage of US Citizens Abroad.") The marriage ceremony that takes place abroad, no matter how exotic and impressive it may be, has to be legal and valid.

The alternative includes an engagement — though engagement is virtually a nonexistent institution in modern Russia — and a "test-drive" first, so that an American fiancé can become a sponsor for a so-called K-1 visa. The process, which usually takes anywhere from 6 to 12 months, begins when a US citizen files an I-129F petition with the USCIS for a K-1 fiancée visa. Then a consulate or embassy in the fiancée's country receives a petition filed in the United States and approved by the Attorney General (now, doesn't that sound serious!). Unmarried children of the foreign fiancée, who are under twenty-one years of age, are also eligible to enter the country.

But this petition can only be approved upon "satisfactory evidence": namely, the parties have to prove that they previously met in person, within two years of the date of filing the petition. So the vintage "picture bride" technique, matching parties who have never met before, wouldn't work now — the foreign woman must present actual pictures of herself together with her fiancé to an American consulate officer. Only the Attorney General may step in and at his discretion waive the requirement that the parties must have met in person, in cases of "long-established customs of the citizen/alien fiancé(e)'s foreign culture or social practice."[1] (More information about K-1 visas may be found in the Bureau of Consular Affairs' brochure "Tips For U. S. Visas: Fiancé(e)s.")

The parties have to prove also that they have a bona fide intention to marry — in other words, that he is going to stay faithfully unmarried until her arrival to the US and that she is coming as a prospective wife, not as a skilled professional for his company or a maid, and that they are legally able and willing to conclude a valid marriage in the United States within ninety days after the alien's arrival.

Ninety days; not much time for soul-searching.

By the way, legal permanent residents are not eligible for the "test-drive" method and cannot apply for K-1 visas, but they can marry abroad and then file an I-130 petition for the immigration of their new alien spouse.

> Procedurally, the process works like this. The US citizen or permanent resident must submit a visa petition (form I-130) to the appropriate local INS office to prove that the marriage is bona fide, that is, entered into for love rather than

---

1 Wayne State University Law School, *The Wayne Law Review* 2004

simply for the foreign-born spouse to obtain a green card. Attached to the visa petition are the following items: (1) Biographical forms (forms G-325A) for both the husband and the wife with photos attached; (2) Proof of the citizenship status of the petitioner. This can take the form of a US passport, a Certificate of Naturalization or Citizenship or a certified copy of the citizen's birth certificate; (3) A certified copy of the marriage certificate; (4) Certified copies of the documents that terminated any previous marriages of the husband or wife, including final divorce decrees, and certificates of annulment or death; and, in the case of a permanent resident alien, proof of such status.

Simultaneously, the foreign-born spouse must submit an application for adjustment of status (form I-485) which is an application for a green card. Items which must accompany the green card application are a completed fingerprint chart and green card photographs, and other INS forms may be required. The spouse can also file an OF-230 with the consulate and be issued an immigrant visa. In both the immigrant visa and adjustment of status cases, the petitioning US citizen or Legal Permanent Resident must also complete an affidavit of support, INS form I-864, on behalf of the alien spouse. In the case of a mail-order bride, a permanent resident alien would most likely marry the person abroad and then file the I-130. It would be possible for the woman to enter as a visitor or in another nonimmigrant category so the marriage could occur in the United States. The US citizen spouse would then file the I-130 and the bride would file for adjustment of status using INS form I-485.[1]

---

1 Robert J. Scholes, Anchalee Phataralaoha

What the Statistics Reveal

It might seem that Russian fiancées are arriving in formidable Operation Invasion formations — large contingents of irresistible young beauties are on their way, dispatched by a click of the mouse. But how many of them succeed in their matrimonial intentions, and who are their American grooms?

The Citizen and Immigration Services — formerly Immigration and Naturalization Services — published a case study with the data from a questionnaire polling the men who were looking for a wife via marriage agencies. The INS asked 607 men to fill in the questionnaire, and 206 of them responded. Among these men, 94 percent were white Americans with some college education, 50 percent had at least a two-year degree or higher, and 6 percent held M.D.'s or Ph.D.'s. Only five of the men had not completed high school. (Such surprisingly high educational standards perhaps could be attributed to the fact that the Internet was not really a factor at the time of the INS study.)

Overall, the men had conservative political and ideological views. Among the participants, 64 percent reported income above $20,000; 42 percent held high managerial positions. They represented 44 states, and 22 percent were Californians; 84 percent lived in big cities. Also, 57 percent had been married at least once, most had been divorced after an average of seven years of marriage, 35 percent had at least one child, and 75 percent wished to father more children.

The average age was 37. Older men were choosing younger ladies without college education.[1] That seems logical if, as Glodava and Onizuka discovered, they were looking for a foreign woman who was "happy to be the homemaker and ask[ed] for nothing more than husband, home, and family."

---

1 David Jedlicka, 1988, cited in Robert J. Scholes, Anchalee Phataralaoha

The report shows that "of the 30 mail-order bride couples... encountered between 1986 and 1993, only two were close in age (4–6 years difference)". In the other 28 couples, there was a 20–50 year difference in age. Older men, says Glodava, often want women "they can mold" and therefore do not want those who are too educated. "They would just become like any other American woman," they said. She concludes, "It is apparent that power and control are critical for the men."

Interestingly, that same tendency exists in Eastern countries as well: for example, the report cites "Taiwan Moves to Boost Women's Marriage Prospects" (The Associated Press, Aug. 30, 1996, by Annie Huang):

> Many Taiwanese men prefer brides from other Asian countries because they feel Taiwanese women — who tend to be better educated and more affluent — expect too much from their husbands. Due to this attitude, Taiwan has imposed a limit on the number of brides from certain countries that can enter Taiwan each year — 360 from Indonesia, 420 from Burma, and 1,080 from China. On the women's side, many of them are seeking Western men since, they say, Taiwanese men want to marry only hard-working obedient drudges while Taiwanese women have discarded this traditional role and are seeking equality and mutual respect in marriage.

The current USCIS regulations established limit for American men as well: only one mail-order bride per man per year. Some of the "hunters" were too eager to write for as many beauties as they could afford.

The Philippines are the most attractive for American mail-order bride seekers: quoting the case study, "of the foreign men who married Filipinos, 44 percent were US citizens. According to a report from the Commission on Filipinos Overseas (Paredes-Maceda, 1995) mail-order brides constitute 10 percent of the marriages between Filipinos and foreign nationals. Between 1989 and 1994, 95,000 Filipino men and women were engaged to be married to foreigners, the great majority of whom met their partners through work or personal introductions."

Based on these data, the report estimated that 4 percent of the 100,000 to 150,000 women seeking US husbands through international services find them — that is, "mail-order bride" and e-mail correspondence services result in 4,000 to 6,000 marriages between US men and foreign brides each year.

This figure was up 200 percent from 1990, and researchers attributed it "to the recent increase in both e-mail correspondence services and the agencies specializing in Russian and Ukrainian women" as well.

In any case, "the women who immigrate through international correspondence agencies represent less than 6 percent of the new citizens. The majority of the women who gain permanent resident alien status through marriage do so through more traditional means, such as by meeting their spouse at work or in school or through marriage to US servicemen stationed overseas." Luckily, nature can still take its course in natural, traditional ways as well.

But what is the success rate for marriages arranged through agencies? Success statistics do not exist, but the National Center for Health Statistics shows the number of marriages in the US for year 2001 as 2,327,000. The marriage rate was 8.4 per 1,000 total population, and the divorce rate was 4.0 per 1,000 population.

This is a tendency of the modern world: the rate of marriages/divorces is similar in Russia as well. A UNICEF report found that an average of "seven couples get married in Russia each year per 1,000 people. But Russians are also the most likely to get divorced, with a record of six couples per 1,000 people getting divorced in 2002." In the countries of the former Soviet Union bloc, "next in the divorce stakes are Estonians (almost 70 percent), while the lowest divorce rate among the countries surveyed is in Tajikistan (7 percent)."[1]

So "statistically speaking," the overall risk of failing in an international marriage seems to be about the same as in a domestic one for Russian mail-order brides — and that's when both parties to the international union are aiming for a happy marriage to begin with, of course.

Dealing with average numbers, I always recall a grim Russian joke that an average temperature of the hospital patients is 98.6 degrees Fahrenheit because some have a high fever, and some are already stiff. So, since reliable data about the success of international marriages do not exist, I would rather prefer to share my own opinion, based on personal observations: less than 50 percent of first international marriages survive the proverbially stormy three- and five-year anniversaries.

---

1 *The St. Petersburg Times*, Tuesday, December 14, 2004

Often international marriages occur with the help of marriage agencies, and this fact shames many women into denial.

"Why does she have to make up stories about how we met?" Tom wondered about his Ukrainian wife. "I don't mind telling people that I found her through a marriage agency."

His giddy young wife Anna could not even remember what she was saying to whom, so one day the story was that they had met "via the Internet." According to another version, she was just visiting her friend, a marriage agency employee, and her future husband happened to be there and fell for her on the spot. In yet another version, Anna met him in Europe while traveling with her friends — she evidently forgot that she had often divulged that her first trip abroad was to the United States, hand-in-hand with her American fiancé. Little wonder that when the fiancé turned into an ex-husband, the ex-bride started telling sob stories that their marriage was ruined by his drinking problems — naturally, non-existent.

But even otherwise trustworthy ladies try to dissemble, saying that they were just keeping their girlfriends company, attending a marriage agency party without having any matrimonial intentions of their own, or that their future husbands were "just traveling," and a translator/tour guide/helper introduced them to each other. Though it is hard to explain, for example, why all of a sudden an eccentric past middle-aged divorced lawyer Rick — and coincidentally, not a great-looking man either — would find himself taking a trip to some ordinary Ukrainian town where some young and coincidentally single Slavic woman Yana so conveniently resides.

Those women probably deny their dealings with marriage agencies so fiercely because it makes them feel like they were merchandise pitched for sale. "We have first-class goods — buy here! Try one, and you'll be buying more! We have experience in this market, we supply only first-class goods — buy only from us!" promised a disgraceful, badly printed brochure. Most of the featured ladies were from Southeast Asia, some from the former Soviet Union. The Asians looked more natural, except for the platinum blondes, and most of their Caucasian sisters were heavily made up. Several used a deadly weapon: one picture featured a beauty in lapping waves, in a wet white tee shirt, all her charms on display. At least this "respectable" publication omitted the nude pictures.

A former immigration attorney for the much bigger agency, Foreign Affair, mentioned, "When this started 10 years ago, you had wholesome pictures of beautiful women... Now you go on their Web site and you see low-cut blouses and high skirts."[1] The reporters unveiled a strange coincidence: the former address of the company, which is the current address of a house owned by a company director and mother of one of the co-founders of the agency, is listed by a producer of adult Web sites as its headquarters. Another profitable franchise?

> Fees paid by male clients to the matchmaker services vary widely; costs can climb into five figures when the men go on organized trips to such destinations as Ukraine or Russia. Encounters International, a Bethesda, Maryland-based service, charges men $1,850 for access to addresses and phone numbers of several hundred women in the former Soviet Union whose photos are posted on the Internet.[2]

The mail-order bride phenomenon is not new — "picture brides," as they were called then, have existed since the time when Anglo-Saxon bachelors sailed off, expanding the borders of the British empire. Evidently, the men had enough stress and probably too much exoticism in their lives, so they preferred to marry recognizable, modest British lasses who could mitigate the men's pangs of nostalgia. Very wise thing to do, indeed, considering that their families had become islands of their native culture installed in foreign surroundings.

But they didn't have the Internet then. Now the usual model is an older Anglo-Saxon bachelor looking for an exotic bride. The amplitude of this business started to earn it official attention. In 1996, Congress requested a report in 1996, entitled "International Matchmaking Organizations." However, it was not available to the public until February of 1999 — that in itself is a sign of its seriousness, or perhaps its rather heavy lobbyism.

American lawmakers were not alone in their concerns: in 1989, the Swedish government appointed an Ombudsman Against Ethnic Discrimination to conduct an investigation of the mail-order bride business. The Ombudsman found that the business was neither unethical nor unlawful, concluding that "Some people simply prefer meeting their partners through an agency. Just because the

---

1 "Marriage brokers scrutinized," Associated Press, Oct 24, 2005
2 David Crary, "Mail-Order Bride Bill In Works," Associated Press, New York, July, 5 2003

agencies make money is not enough cause for condemnation ... It would be too difficult to decide on where to draw the line in a free society."[1]

That is really a tricky situation: if citizens prefer foreigners, who, and on what grounds, can stop them? If the matchmaking industry makes money domestically, who can prevent them?

"These businesses can be highly profitable. Bob Burrows, president of Cherry Blossoms, reports that his agency serves over 1,000 men per month who pay up to $200 each."[2] The accuracy of statistics related to the international matchmaking industry is difficult to verify since the agencies are mushrooming, but roughly up to 150,000 women from different countries use marriage agencies each year in a search for a foreign husband. Lately, Filipinos have yielded precedence to Ukrainians.

"Mail-order brides" web-sites prefer to be called "international pen-pal services." They offer ladies' names, photos, and addresses via catalogs or the Internet. Most of the agencies do not charge women for enlisting, and men have to pay a few dollars for each chosen address. After the initial contact, the potential couple is on its own. Interestingly enough, some agencies are now selling men's addresses to women as well. Emancipation, or gender equality, if you wish, has finally penetrated even this sphere. Technically speaking, those gentlemen could be called "mail-order grooms," but I doubt the term will ever enter the vernacular.

Other marriage agencies arrange special tours, "To Russia for love," so to speak. These parties are gaining popularity, and though they sound just like singles clubs' parties, familiar to American bachelors, seasoned participants advise freshmen not to pin their hopes on those gatherings. They warn that just a few lucky ones will be able to establish some meaningful contacts. The sources from the other side of the border agree: they recommend just relaxing and flirting, dancing, enjoying the champagne, and brushing up on a foreign language (that applies to the women, of course. Who would expect an American customer to speak a foreign language, especially one like Russian?).

Here are three recollections of Russian gals who married foreigners through those services. One woman supposedly became engaged right on the spot, after a party. Her style in this excerpt from a web-site is left intact: the simplicity of the approach is puzzling.

> Before attending the event, tell yourself that you are going to have fun first. In that case, you will not be very disappointed if you don't meet anyone whom you like... Many girls prefer to be dressed up in bright colors to attract men's attention. I was in a black suit and now am happily married.
>
> Do not smile at everyone. Maybe it is not very polite, but if you do not want to speak to a person, you will just waste his and your own time. You don't have time to make a mistake. Define for yourself what is good in him and what is not. Try to imagine your future family with him. Do you think you could marry him?

1 Wayne State University Law School
2 Robert J. Scholes, Anchalee Phataralaoha

Is he kind? Is he sincere? Note that even if he spends a lot of money on you now, it does not mean that he will be the same after your wedding.

Consider that he may suggest going to his hotel room. What will you do? My future husband said that we "needed to fill out some paperwork for a fiancée visa" in his hotel room. I did not believe it and refused. He insisted. He promised "no sex." There was only one way to check what he was really after, so I decided to go. We went to his hotel room. He gave me beautiful roses and we filled out the papers. No sex! He was a real gentlemen and I appreciated this.

Then I decided to check if he was greedy. He asked me for a date. I was working that day. I said that if I did not go to work I would lose my pay. He asked how much, and paid me. He gave more than I told him, but I only took the sum that I mentioned. I didn't want him to think that I was using him.

He stayed two days longer. I appreciated that too. When he said that he was going to see my parents, I decided that he was a right man for me.

That was a swift decision for a young woman, but more experienced women are prone to swift or careless choices just as well. "My American husband is 52 years old," a woman wrote in her letter to a popular Russian newspaper. "Three years ago he divorced his second wife and sunk into depression. He quit his job and found me via the Internet. At that time I lived in Moscow, had a good career, and everything in my life was just fine: I had a beautiful, smart daughter, a nice flat, but I wanted to get married so badly — and somehow I couldn't find a husband. Now I live in this heavenly place in America, but I'm not happy. The cost of living is extremely high, and we live on a shoestring. My husband is very nervous and blames me for all his problems. He yells all the time. I've tried to help — I learned English and found a job, but that made things even worse. My husband can't stand that I am succeeding in my life here and he is threatening to kick me out of the country. I am shocked and very offended."[1]

Another woman warned rookies in a practical and realistic manner on a website "Russian women abroad":

Though I married an American and don't regret it, I would like to emphasize that I don't want to advocate a "brides drain" from Russia, the Ukraine, Belarus etc. (hereafter 'Russia'). Because, first, there are great men in these countries, and second, not all of those women who tried were successful in finding happiness in the USA. So you have to think twice whether leaving Russia really is the best way to solve your problems, and even if so, are you sure that a marriage is the best solution?

I won't recommend you to get on with marriage agencies — everything they do you can do by yourself, using just the Internet and basic English skills. Plus, the Americans who use the services of marriage agencies are all fat, old, poor, and have broods of kids. Of course, some good agencies exist, but better steer clear anyway. After all, you don't want to feel like you are merchandise. Trust me, an American who dreams about a Russian wife is not the best type of man. In reality, even if he doesn't admit it to himself, he wants a submissive housewife, and American women en masse are independent, proud, and willful, so the guy starts looking towards the east in the search of obedient women.

---

1 Pavel Konov, "Seks-obmanshiki-2," *Komsomolskaya Pravda*, 03.11.2005

Let's conclude from the facts just cited: when describing yourself as a woman who enjoys being a homemaker, don't overdo it. You might be not willful, but still proud and independent. You are not dreaming of going to America to iron shirts and cook dinners — you could do that at home just as well.

Write your texts by yourself, without the help of a girlfriend-English teacher. Even if the language is simple and primitive, it is your own. So later, answering the letters, you'll be doing it by yourself. It's unethical to translate private letters with somebody's help, right? And don't leave out all other countries except the USA — after all, you are looking for a spouse, not for an airplane ticket from Russia to America.

Don't let him think that he is saving you from something horrible — in his eyes it may oblige you to be grateful till your last breath. Better consider that you are lucky to have a nice view from your Russian apartment or a fabulous forest lake near your *dacha* [a summer cabin]. Don't omit to mention things like that, because in reality you are going to part with your family, friends, job, and break your entire life in two unequal parts. Once in America, many times you will wish you could go back![1]

This advice works for those women who don't fit the Procrustean bed of stereotypes promoted by marriage agencies: even though Kristina met her American husband at one of those notorious marriage agencies parties, she gave her story an interesting twist. She set the meeting with the man neither in a public place nor at her home — she made him wait in the reception room while she was giving instructions to her assistants; she wanted him to see what she would sacrifice by leaving for America. She had a nice career, but had grown tired of fighting for everything by herself. And her American doctor-fiancé got the message after seeing Kristina in her full shining glory — certainly, she didn't just fall off the turnip truck.

One agency cited the reasons why American bachelors should look for a foreign bride: "American women can have attitudes that are difficult to deal with. They are often demanding and hard to please. Russian women, on the other hand, are so unspoiled. In many less-developed countries, like countries of the former Soviet Union, women have a much lower social status than men. Russian men are often abusive and disrespectful toward women. This is what Russian women are used to. Compared to that, the life you can give her will make her so happy and grateful. Russian women tend to be devoted adoring wives."

Those advertisement writers would be better off not trying to prove this to any of the "Russian women with much lower social status," for they might get a big surprise.

Most web-sites pitches follow a pattern. After clearing the scene of those "so-frustrating" American females, the flow of sugary language starts. It goes something like this.

---

1 http://www.russianwomenabroad.com/page380.html

Hook #1: Appreciation

"In western societies, women have an equal status to men, as it should be." Here is a curtsy towards the norms of Western society — "as it should be" — baited with a hint that not all societies, luckily, stick to that rule. "Russian women see American men as kind, sensitive, respectful, understanding, compassionate, and dependable, and for the most part American men are this way. Many American women take these qualities in American men for granted. However, because of what Russian women are used to, they will never take these qualities for granted. These qualities make American men very appealing to Russian women."

Superiority over an entire nation of Russian males that are portrayed as undependable, insensitive, and heartless should make an American customer feel much better already. Another matchmaking service puts it this way: "The Russian woman has not been exposed to the world of rampant feminism that asserts its rights in America... She is the weaker gender and knows it."

The term "weak gender" has an entirely different meaning in the Russian culture, but the agency does not go into that discussion — the goal is to dangle bright prospects before males' eyes.

Hook #2: Appearance

The National Institutes of Health indicate that 61.9 percent of women over 20 years old are overweight and 33.4 percent are obese. Thus a male customer of one popular American dating web-site observed, "If a woman writes that she has an "average" body type — she is size 12–14, at least."

"Russian women in contrast are rarely overweight." Here the web-site tells the truth. "They seem more concerned with their appearance. Russians do not have many of the high-fat convenience foods we have. They tend to eat more whole foods, whole grain breads, and in general have lower-fat diets. Most Russians cannot afford cars and must walk most places they go. Very attractive women are common in countries of the former Soviet Union."

One can picture a vast plain, just like in "Doctor Zhivago," where crowds of beautiful women are milling about, in a Serengeti-like style, waiting for a foreign groom.

Hook #3: Dating Statistics Will Not Let You Down — Guaranteed

"Internet dating in the United States for a man is tough. Most singles' web-sites in the US have 2–3 men for every woman-member. However, Western men wishing to meet Russian/Eastern European women average about 5–10 women for every man. The demographics are much more favorable."

Hook #4: She Will Relocate Anywhere

> "The Internet is a fabulous resource for 'meeting' and getting to know women from anywhere in the United States. But when it comes to marriage, if they live far away, this can be a problem. Many American women own houses, have careers they do not wish to leave, or have kids that are set in their lives there. Convincing a woman in those situations to relocate to where you live can be difficult. With a Russian woman this will never be a problem. She will want to come to America or Western Europe and be with you."

Does that mean she will come to share a shack in the desert, as long as it is an American desert and an American shack? Or that she'll come to live with a lunatic, as long as it's a Western lunatic? Sadly, in some cases the answer is yes.

Hook #5. The Legendary Success of Marriages

"Perhaps the best evidence that Russian women make good wives and life companions is the low divorce rate between American men and Russian women. Russian women also don't mind marrying a Western man who is much older than they are."

There are no reliable statistics to prove the success of those marriages, but the age discrepancy sometimes is astonishing. Some of the American grooms are so ripe it would be unseemly of them to court their prospective Russian mothers-in-law.

Hook # 6: We Have What You Need

> "Russian women, wishing to marry Western men, tend to be a cut above the average Russian woman. They tend to be better educated and know at least some English. There are so many Russian women wishing to marry Western men that if you desire a thin, attractive, well educated woman, who knows English and has no children, or any other set of exacting requirements, you can probably find one."

I remember a group of nice American gentlemen gathered around a teak table onboard a yacht in a West Palm Beach marina. The oldest, Jake, was listening intensely to his friend — listening literally open-mouthed, leaning across the table, cupping his ear with the palm of his hand to hear better. The topic he was so keenly interested in was "trips for Russian brides."

His friend was telling how his neighbor went to Russia and a marriage agency arranged an audition for him. The competitors for the honor to become his fiancée were led one by one into a room where the gentleman was sitting at a table, interviewing, with the help of a translator, the aspirants for his hand, heart, and (maybe) bank account. Then he made his selection. The candidate he had chosen, for some reason, couldn't master English even when she came to America, but that hardly bothered the happy husband — evidently, he wasn't that much after heart-to-heart conversations.

The elderly gentleman, who was listening to the story with such great gusto, ran like a stag to his car and came back with a stack of hundreds profiles of

Russian brides that he had printed from the Internet. He and his companions ogled the tasteful pictures of lovely young Russian ladies — engineers, teachers, doctors...

Years later, the industrious seeker reported that he had found an ex-military woman from Siberia, half his age, who was eager to share the ties of marriage with him. Jake went to Russia to meet her, and they had a great time — at least from his point of view — traveling from Moscow to St. Petersburg by train. I asked how they communicated, since she did not speak English, but he smugly assured that "the language of love" is universal. I brought him down to earth with a question about how he planned to bring his love to the US if he didn't even have a home — he lived with his relatives. That didn't worry him either. "Anyway, she's never been abroad, so she has to get a passport first, and then — we'll see!"

Evidently, his goal was just to have a good time and to make a good impression, pampering his male ego with an easy victory. Later he became quite well-known in the local Russian diaspora for his continuous attempts to court single Russian women, posing as a wealthy American entrepreneur.

Another gentleman, Paul, shared with me a delicate problem. His co-worker, knowing that Paul was in contact with people of Russian origin, had asked for help in communicating with a Russian woman. "I know him well enough," said Paul, "He is sloppy, quite rude, and shallow, so I feel sorry for that woman — she seems to be way too sophisticated for him. Why does she even care?" Paul felt relieved when the Russian woman was refused a fiancée visa due to some technical problems. Her pen-pal tried to argue with the American consulate in Moscow, but in vain. Two years later, the woman somehow obtained her visa, but once she crossed the threshold of the spacious house of her long-distance American love, their disagreements started piling up. They argued almost constantly and she left before her three-month visa expired, but later started to regret it — perhaps because from a distance everything looked less dramatic, and besides, she had invested so much time and effort in the mission; maybe, after all, he was her prince, just in frog's skin? Her American boyfriend, being more pragmatic, declined her offer of a sequel.

Why do grown-up women prefer to shut their eyes tight when facing evidently hopeless deals? Partially, the romantic nature of Russian women is to blame. They really are more compassionate, more giving of themselves, and less defensive than Western women are. They foolishly and desperately wish to believe in the romantic stories they have created in their own heads, and when their frog-prince is overseas, he looks much better from far away. Sometimes, when Russian wives have complained bitterly to me about the very evident demerits of their American spouses, I asked them why on earth they had rushed headlong into a marriage abroad, without even first visiting the country where they were supposed to spend the rest of their lives — and if everything is so bad, then why to eliminate the option of going back home before investing too much time and effort?

Only once I heard the age-old sorrowful reply, sprinkled with bitter tears, "I feel so lonely here, but in my apartment in Odessa, I will be alone, too. Here I am at least loved, or sometimes it seems so."

But even though she "seemed to be loved," it was not in the manner she was craving for, which she needed in order to feel happy: "Love may be universal but its construction in each culture is defined, both literally and figuratively, in different languages."[1] And it is harder to adopt those languages than to learn linguistic instruments.

The reality hits women cruelly, piling nostalgia on top of adjustment issues, and they pay dearly for their intentional or unintentional delusions or pragmatic goals to gain a piece of the "American pie." A Russian newspaper published the "Six Principles of a Trickster Groom," found on the Internet forum where American "cowboys" share their experiences: "I'm not ashamed of my male desires; I walk through life without excuses and apologies; I don't need a woman — a woman needs me; I don't argue with a woman and I don't try to please her — I just listen to her, and gently, but firmly, follow my own plan and do with her what I want; a woman so beautiful that she can become my wife doesn't exist; I don't know which lady will be my last one — before I bed her."[2]

The newspaper offered women who had suffered ugly experiences to post their cautionary tales at http://www.antidate.org. They collected quite a gallery there. Each of the "cowboys" from 48 countries had at least two victims in his portfolio, and each profile had photos and descriptions of the tricks and methods he used.

I cannot believe that the instinct of self-preservation does not cause women to push the panic button in such cases. In this excerpt from a Russian newspaper, a party thrown by an international marriage agency is described. Their narrator was introduced as "Helen Loran, ex-Russian Bride Lena, now the wife of a successful Canadian businessman."

> Friday, hotel lobby, 3 p.m.
>
> The hotel staff grinningly watches the group of fifty "brides," all in their early 20-s, wandering about the lobby in their high stiletto heels, nervously wrinkling invitations to the "special party." Finally the girls are let in the conference room, and there, at the tables, they finally view a dozen beat-up "cowboys." Comfortably seated, the "cowboys" are looking devouringly at the pretty girls, who begin strolling around, obediently smiling non-stop. A "fiancé" points to a potential mate, and the interpreter springs up with questions: "How old are you? Nineteen? Fine! That respectable gentleman would like to meet you!" That "respectable gentleman" turns out to be an electrician from Arkansas who had three failed marriages and who does not want to have any kids. But for those girls the guy seems to be a ticket to a happy life.

1 Esther Perel, *Mating in Captivity*
2 Pavel Konov, "Seks-obmanshiki-2," *Komsomolskaya Pravda*, 03.11.2005.

The "fiancé" asks the girl to take a picture "for the future evidence for your visa": the seedy Lovelace hardly reaches the shoulder of the Russian beauty he hugs. More likely, he is going just to show the photo to his buddies in some Arkansas bar, as a trophy, "That's how cool my trip to Russia was!"

The girls at the gentleman's table come in a flow: a bosomy blonde, a striking Cindy Crawford-like brunette, a charming red-head.

The translator logs girls' names and phone numbers into gentlemen's notebooks, and Americans make dates, competing with each other: Bolshoi Theatre, restaurant, "Moscow by Night" tour ...

The same day, 3 hours later.

Tired but satisfied, the foreigners, arm-in-arm with their chosen beauties, leave for restaurants. The girls who were not so lucky head towards the subway station. Tomorrow they will come again, in hopes of finding their happiness.

Sunday, 10 a.m., breakfast room.

Two elderly gentlemen share pictures on their digital cameras.

"Look, such a beauty!" brags one. "I took her to a restaurant yesterday!"

"I know, she's lovely — she is in my room right now."[1]

Even factoring in the newspaper's exaggerations, I cannot picture a normal woman tolerating such incredible humiliation as the aforementioned "party." A more typical Russian woman would be shocked by such degrading exercises or TV shows like "How to Marry a Millionaire." An American tube-viewer probably would not give it a thought, but the Russian girl, unexposed to that segment of pop culture, was shocked. This is how she described her impression:

> Somebody with a wicked sense of humor decided to launch a national search for a wife for a millionaire without disclosing any information or even a picture of that 40-year old presumptive millionaire, and a whole troop of lovely young ladies fought for that noble gentleman and heavenly love. The guy was sitting backstage during the competition, pushing the button and eliminating the less desirable ones,... Then the chap came out, straight to one blonde, and kissed her on the lips (!). Immediately she was robed in a bridal outfit and wed right on the spot. I couldn't believe my eyes, I was scared and disgusted.... To mock the holy of holies, marriage and love, on a national broadcast? Of course, it was all fake.

Indeed, the popular "dating" shows that America has visited upon us all are hardly any different from the humiliating "interviews" that foreign brides-to-be suffer.

---

1 Pavel Konov

CREATING A VICTIM

The mail-order bride industry's main marketing hook is a recipe for disaster. "When someone is marketing relationships that by design involve a dominant party and a subservient party, the likelihood of violence is greater," said Layli Miller-Muro, executive director of the Tahirih Justice Center.[1]

The agencies pitch men with images of docile, submissive foreign women, and to foreign women they offer portraits of wealthy and benevolent American men with strong family values. False expectations arise, and dramatic collisions occur.

Sometimes even the agencies themselves get involved in those collisions: one "docile" Ukrainian client sued her agency for counseling that she would be inevitably deported should she leave her abusive husband. Evidently, she had been Americanized enough to see through that lie; but not all women are aware that they have rights in this country even if they are not yet citizens or even permanent residents. Most of them are very much afraid that anything they do may harm their immigration case, and these fears have some reasonable basis.

Immigration rules were changed in 1986 to reduce the number of foreigners seeking marriage solely as a pathway to US citizenship. Robert J. Scholes and Anchalee Phataralaoha indicated in their chapter "Fraud":

> There is no question that many of the alien women who advertise for US husbands are far more interested in gaining permanent residence alien status than in gaining a good marriage.... we cannot know what is in the woman's mind, but a reading of the self-descriptions they offer and their willingness to marry men of advanced age and dubious character attests to this intention. The true character of the men is well expressed in Glodava and Onizuka (1994:26), who note,

1 Mail-Order Bride Bill In Works, Associated Press, New York, July 5, 2003

"those who have used the mail-order bride route to find a mate have control in mind rather than a loving and enduring relationship."

The most common times for mail-order brides to leave the marriage, according to Martin, are "immediately, 3 months after marriage (receipt of the green card), and 2 years after marriage (receipt of nonconditional permanent residence)."

The aforementioned schedule is a relic. The time frame now has been stretched so dramatically that it doesn't make sense anymore for a woman to wait for the slow-moving wheels of the immigration services: bureaucracy has effectively beaten the fraud. Considering the piles of legal forms which have to be filled out, the uncertain years which have to be spent waiting, and the significant amounts of money which have to be paid, only quite a seasoned couple can apply for the petition for a permanent resident status adjustment.

So the pathway to permanent resident status has been defended, more or less, from abuse, but are the individual applicants defended from abuse? These aspirants for permanent resident status are often dealing with a very special cohort of Americans: some men used to file multiple requests for fiancée visas with the Bureau of Citizenship and Immigration, so they could "simply choose to marry the first woman who is approved!"[1] No doubt, they were very much in love...

Sumiko Hennessy, executive director of the Asian Pacific Development Center, mentioned, "What you have are older men, people with three divorces, alcohol problems . . . some of whom have a history of domestic abuse or problems with the law."[2]

Representative Louise M. Slaughter testified before the House Judiciary Committee on Immigration, Refugees, and International Law that many battered "conditional residents" had no viable legal options, and she introduced a bill, passed in 1990, which provided that "battery and extreme cruelty, if alleged and proven, could qualify a conditional resident for a waiver during the waiting period."[3]

As Senator Maria Caldwell put it, "It is critical for legal immigrants to know that they don't have to suffer abuse or work without pay to remain in this country. The Violence Against Women Act provided some safeguards for these female immigrants, ensuring that in cases of abuse a woman's immigration petition may proceed without the sponsorship of her abuser."[4]

So, an abuser *may not* be in control of the immigration status of the person he abuses, but here is one substantial difference: while US social workers recognize psychological abuse, the rules and regulations of Citizen and Immigration Ser-

---

1 Statement of Sen. Maria Cantwell Upon Introduction of International Marriage Broker Regulation Act, source: the office of Maria Cantwell

2 "The Health Care Response to Domestic Violence" (anon. 1994), from Robert J. Scholes, PhD (assistance of Anchalee Phataralaoha, MA), "The "Mail-Order Bride" Industry and Its Impact on US Immigration," http://www.uscis.gov

3 Robert J. Scholes, Anchalee Phataralaoha

4 Statement of Sen. Maria Cantwell

vices do not. Sensitivity to psychological issues seems to be a privilege of a citizen, though studies show that far more American women are emotionally abused than battered: "Within the last year, 7 percent of American women (3.9 million) who are married or are living with someone as a couple were physically abused, and 37 percent (20.7 million) were verbally or emotionally abused by their spouse or partner."[1]

Since this data is from the research sponsored by the USCIS — then INS — itself, it is hard to believe that such an issue could be unintentionally overlooked. The respective clause in the USCIS form includes the wording "extreme cruelty" — not "extreme mental cruelty."

When I asked several immigration lawyers what they could read into that formula, they explained that without suffering physical abuse or outright psycho-type cruelty a foreign wife doesn't really have a chance to stand up for herself in her immigration case.

"A foreign spouse is an ultimate souvenir... it cannot be easily returned, exchanged, stuffed into closet, or consigned to the wastebasket," wrote Lynn Visson. But some men try to do just that. Alien wives are believed to be at a higher risk for abuse.

> Though no data exist on the abuse of alien wives, there is every reason to believe that the incidence is higher in this population than for the nation as a whole. Authorities agree that abuse in these marriages can be expected based on the men's desire for a submissive wife and the women's desire for a better life. At some point, after the alien bride has had time to adjust to the new environment, to make new friends, and to become comfortable with the language, her new independence and his domination are bound to conflict. The problem... is largely due to the men's unrealistic expectations. While many state a desire for a submissive wife, they find that such dependence becomes a burden. To provide some relief, the husband seeks ways (friends, activities) to get the wife "out of the house" on occasion. The resulting independence then angers the husband who manifests the anger on the wife, who may have only been guilty of trying to please her husband.[2]

It's hard to expect that a woman will indefinitely try to please somebody who is cruel, no matter how docile she is. Sooner or later, she'll try to leave; and leaving could turn into a deadly dangerous act.

A Filipina, Susanna met her husband through an international marriage agency. She left him within a few months and filed for a divorce, having been physically abused on a regular basis. They had been separated for more than a year when Timothy Blackwell learned that she was pregnant with another man's child. On the final day of the divorce proceedings, Timothy Blackwell shot and killed Susanna, her unborn child and two of her friends who were waiting just outside of the Seattle courtroom.

---

1 Robert J. Scholes, Anchalee Phataralaoha
2 Ibid.

The new International Marriage Broker Regulation Act means to shield for-eign women from potential abuse, though it is hard to imagine that a male client of a marriage agency would voluntarily submit information on "any previous his-tory of domestic violence and their past marital history to all prospective fiancées they contact." But maybe that covers the agency from liability. Ken Agee, one of the founders of an agency Foreign Affair, sarcastically commented that conduct-ing a background check on their clients would be like forcing a man to provide a background check to women that he meets at a bar — evidently, Agee doesn't see any difference between his enterprise and a bar scene. Interesting that all three founders of the agency allegedly found their Russian wives through their own firm.

More serious is the demand that a client provide the same information to the Bureau of Citizenship and Immigration Services when he files a petition for a fiancée visa. The Act also "requires that US citizens sponsoring a foreign fiancée undergo a criminal background check. Information on domestic violence convic-tions and civil restraining orders would be relayed to the visa applicant by the consular official, along with information on their legal rights should they find themselves in an abusive relationship." That would be a good sobering moment for some naïve prospective fiancées.

In the case of Anastasia Solovieva, a young bride who was murdered in Seattle, that would have yielded the vital information that her American groom Indle King had been married just one year ago to another mail-order bride who had to seek a protection order against him. While plotting to kill Anastasia, Indle King was already searching for the next bride. "The case ... generated much public attention about the safety of mail-order brides and inspired lawmakers to pro-pose state and federal legislation [but] [l]egislation by Democratic US Sen. Maria Cantwell to regulate the industry died in committee last year," wrote *Seattle Times* correspondent Brian Alexander.

"The women are the product, and they are treated like chattel," said Layli Mill-er-Muro, who helped craft the legislation. "many international marriage brokers... are an easy conduit for predatory abusers to find the next victims."[1]

Until the International Marriage Broker Regulation Act emerged, an Ameri-can who was seeking to marry someone through a marriage agency held all of the cards.

> The American client has the benefit of a complete background check on his future wife, a requirement of the immigration process. In addition, the IMBs provide clients extensive information about the women they offer, everything from their favorite movies and hobbies to whether they are sexually promiscu-ous. Conversely, the foreign fiancée only gets whatever information her future spouse wants to share. These women have no way of confirming what they are

---

1 "Marriage brokers scrutinized," Associated Press, Oct 24, 2005

told about previous marriages or relationships or the American client's criminal history"[1]

International marriage brokers strongly oppose the act, which was finally signed into law on January 2006, complaining that it would "hurt their business," and "drive marriage broker companies offshore."

It is a growing business, indeed, and some have added new features: "IMBs also are being used as a cover for those seeking servants. That's what happened to Helen Clemente, a Filipino brought to the US by retired Seattle-area police officer Eldon Doty and his wife, Sally. Eldon and Sally Doty had divorced to allow Eldon to marry Helen Clemente. However, Eldon and Sally Doty continued to live as man and wife, forcing Helen Clemente to work as their servant. After three years, Helen ran away. The Dotys have worked with INS in exchange for de facto immunity, while Helen Clemente continues to fight deportation."[2]

Evidently, Helen Clemente was not recognized as a subject of cruel treatment by USCIS standards — maybe "bizarre," but not cruel.

There are reports of a different kind of fraud, when women are recruited into prostitution through the international matchmaking services. "This new slave trade has not, however, to the author's knowledge, occurred in the United States, although it is a well documented trade involving Russian women imported into Israel (Specter, 1998)."[3]

According to the other source, a good number of young women are brought into the US just to be trapped into real slavery. In 2002 over 60,000 young women from post-Soviet countries, mainly Russians and Ukrainians, were reported missing in the USA. Though a majority leaves Russia legally, "only a few exceptionally lucky girls can get back home — others cannot afford the trip, or have been robbed of their papers, or are in fear of their lives. The number of Russian and other Eastern European girls who did not come back last year is roughly estimated at 175,000. said Maria Mokhova, manager of the Moscow-based independent care center for victims of rape and sexual harassment."[4]

The United States even used to have special centers in Russian metropolises, offering training for women who were leaving for the US and enlightening those potential victims on possible outcomes of their American dreams.

---

1 Statement of Sen. Maria Cantwell
2 Statement of Sen. Maria Cantwell
3 Robert J. Scholes, Anchalee Phataralaoha
4 Russian Information Agency Novosti, January 23, 2002

TACTICS OF VIOLENCE

Some women simply refuse to be victimized. Jennifer, now happily married, recalled, "My second husband had a quick temper and a black belt in karate, so just his bare hands could be lethal weapons. When our marriage was falling apart and our blood was up, I told him that if he ever laid a hand on me, he had better never fall asleep at home." She was neither violent nor hysterical type, but her tactic worked — who knows what those serious ladies might do in self-defense.

Nobody is implying that all women of foreign origin are complacent about violence while all American ladies are strong in self-defense — domestic violence doesn't acknowledge race or nationality. In the documentary "American Tears of Russian Wives," Nadezhda said about her American husband, "He jumped at me one time, simmering with anger, but I told him that if he ever dared to touch me I would kill him at night. Terrible thing to say, I know, but it cured him on the spot — he never jumped or swung at me again."[1] Evidently, she was a woman of the same breed as Jennifer.

Still, many female newcomers can grievously confirm that their slice of the sacramental American pie comes from the pie chart "Power and Control Tactics Used Against Immigrant Women" published by the Domestic Abuse Intervention Project.[2] In the center of that "wheel of fortune" is the button "Power and Control" and the outer hoop describes the methods of physical abuse. The description is meticulous; physical abuse may include, but evidently is not limited to, pushing, shoving, hitting, slapping, choking, pulling hair, punching, kicking, grabbing, twisting arms, tripping, biting, beating, throwing the victim down, and, of course, using a weapon against her. Isolation and emotional abuse crown

1 Mikhail Fainshtein, "Amerikanskie slezi russkikh zen"
2 The Domestic Abuse Intervention Project in Duluth, Minnesota

the "wheel." Putting a victim under a house arrest, isolating his "property" from her friends, relatives, and anybody else who speaks her language is easy.

Lying about her immigration status is an extremely popular and effective method: most of the women don't have access to legal help and don't have a clear understanding of their status anyway.

Another trick is a threat to write to her family about her "promiscuous behavior." Sounds weird, but I knew one high-flying citizen who said he was going to write to the girl's family in Puerto Rico. Luckily, he never got around to it and contented himself with calling her *puta negra*. Insults, obscene and racist names are common, as well as flinging out the "mail-order bride" label. Even the form for a US visa includes a question about practicing prostitution.

Some women are stripped of their documents and their credentials may even be destroyed: Nina got her Russian passport back from her abusive husband only in the courtroom. In "lighter" versions, men throw away all the women's possessions they brought from home.

Schooling or jobs are banned even if the woman could bring some consequential financial advantages, because gaining outside contacts poses an immediate threat. The women might pick up some dangerous ideas, and, god forbid, gain financial independence.

But the favorite threats are those associated with men's privileges as permanent residents or citizens and the role that they play in women's immigration cases. In even slightly troubled unions those waters, more likely, will be tested. Almost every immigration form has to be accompanied with a check, and sums vary from fifty dollars to more than five hundred. Now throw in a sizable fee for the immigration lawyer — a dependent woman would sure feel trapped and bounded.

If she is battered or is subjected to extreme cruelty by a US citizen or lawful permanent resident, she can file a self-petition, though "self-petitioning can only be done while a couple is still married. If a divorce takes place, this form of immigration relief is no longer available to the victim. The victim will then only have cancellation of removal as a means of relief."[1]

But the all-time favorite, striking below-the-belt, is the threat to separate the woman from her children. Enslaved illegal immigrants may be threatened with a promise to report their children to immigration authorities, and "mail-older brides" blackmailed with a promise of deportation and separation from their American-born children. For a credulous woman, this is the worst menace possible. Inna, a woman of Oriental origin, panicked when she was threatened that her baby would be taken away from her. She felt that her suspicions were well-founded when, during her custody battle, a judge repeatedly asked her if she was

---

1 Reva Gupta, Policy and Advocacy Coordinator, Illinois Coalition for Immigrant and Refugee Rights, http://www.ilcadv.org/legal/special_imgr.htm

a Muslim. If an elderly Southern judge could allow himself such unconstitutional questions about personal beliefs in his courtroom, what should she expect from the judicial system?

TECHNICALLY SPEAKING

To find a local battered women's shelter, a woman may call 1-800-799-7233; Family Violence Prevention Fund may help with immigration-related questions at info@endabuse.org or (415) 252-8900; useful information could be found on the web-site for immigrant women wttp://endabuse.org. Here is the list from a self-help brochure: Legal Aid for Abused Women and Children (703) 820-8393; AYUDA (202) 387-4848; National Coalition Against Trafficking in Women (814) 685-1447; NOW (707) 255-2516; and the Asian Pacific Development Center (303) 220-3398. The brochure "You Can Be Free" also gives practical recommendations about managing finances, lawyers, and counselors.

Practical American divorce web-sites advise women to take half of the money from joint savings and checking accounts and warn her that she may find that the locks have been changed, the money is gone, and her name taken off credit cards once she leaves the house. (In some states, the lock-changing would be qualified as a "malicious turning out-of-doors" but that doesn't mean it can't happen.) Among other practical recommendations are to get hold of all one's credentials, passports and visas, documents from any public assistance programs, rental agreements, checkbooks, credit cards, paycheck stubs, marriage license, copies of tax returns — both for the woman and her partner — and to copy her partner's credentials or at least write down the information from those. The site endabuse.org also reminds women to keep documents in a safe place or even at a friend's house.

A call to the police can be useful in future legal battles only if a police report about the incident is completed, with the incident report number and the police officer's name, so the woman can get a copy of it. Usually the police do not turn in a woman who reports domestic violence to the immigration services, which is a different department. So the idea that one must tolerate battering in fear of "immediate deportation," as some "slave masters" threaten, is quite groundless.

According to Russian data, if a woman can hold her ground when she faces her partner's violence for the first time, overcoming the strong shock she usually feels, the violence is not likely to be repeated.[1] I have never been in a violent relationship but I have been violently attacked by strangers, and luckily have never been harmed anyhow. Even in a serial criminal case I was the only one who escaped unharmed, and perhaps that was exactly because I did not behave as a "proper" victim, making the attackers vacillate — their hesitation gave me a chance to escape.

---

1 Anna Hasina, "Muz i zena = nasilie?" *AiF "Zdorovie"* #6, 2002.

Russian women may be afraid of scandal when facing domestic violence, as a psychologist from the Moscow crisis center ANNa pointed out. They don't like to wash their dirty laundry in public. But in those situations people outside her family can be a real help, and a woman in a critical situation needs all the help and support she can get. If she is reluctant to talk to other people, she can consult specialists in crisis centers or women's centers.

When foreign women surrender all financial control, the "provider" tool may be used very heavily. Many men-providers work hard and are quite successful, but they like to emphasize that the women are interested in the relationship just as "consumers" — the man is the breadwinner, and the woman just takes advantage of him, providing "nothing of value," only taking care of their house and family, so she has no "voting rights" or role in financial decisions. Some men say they take that approach out of a fear that their family fortunes would be blown in endless shopping sprees because "all women do it."

Elvira, a little Oriental woman, was married to a formidable man. She found my phone number through mutual acquaintances and called me. In a while, my phone rang again — it was Elvira's husband, who inquired why this number had showed up on his home phone caller ID. I explained that I had a conversation with his wife and inquired, in my turn, why he was checking the number — was there any problem? — and courteously asked if I could talk to his wife again. He just as politely informed me that everything was okay and that she had just stepped outside for a moment, and we said our goodbyes. That looked like a big trouble, right from the beginning. Later, Elvira took a ride in a squad car to a shelter for battered women.

Elvira's abuser needed her, needed the soothing company of a woman, and since he was accustomed to control everything, he hated to think that his need of a woman's company gave her some power over him. He was afraid that his meek wife would leave him once she gained her legal status and some independence. But she forgave him instead, and came back after he almost killed her. She wanted to have a relationship, at any price, and believed that a man should keep his woman under control.

Misogynists behave sweetly sometimes, putting women off guard with sincere-looking repentance, and that works up to a degree. Typical self-deceiving excuses: we are all humans; he is so sorry; I have to give him another chance. And another. And many more.

My own American suitor, when we were traveling in Italy, let himself yell at me for a mistake that he had made. He apologized, explaining that he was so out of his element, feeling confused and stressed. At that moment, being more observant than emotionally attached, I mentioned that the worst part in this incident was that he was capable of such behavior. But he tried his very best to put me off guard, and evidently, he succeeded.

His next hysteria occurred on American soil, after we were married. Out of the blue, he yelled at me over the phone and hung up, depriving me of the opportunity to read him chapter and verse. "Eating my words has never given me indigestion," said Winston Churchill, but it in my case my digestive system literally shut down due to unexpected shock during lunch, so on the following day I was a candidate for outpatient surgery with a preliminary diagnosis of ulcer — luckily, not confirmed. Hard to believe that mean words, coming out of the blue at the wrong moment, can hurt so literally.

Later, when our marriage was clearly crumbling, Martin would intentionally try to pick a fight at dinner. Recognizing the ugly trick, I just smiled radiantly. I guess it was hard to feel any satisfaction facing an impassive, calm "victim." So every cruel tactic has a counter-tactic.

But the main point is to recognize when one simply has to turn around and leave — preferably, with as little damage as possible, both for oneself and one's abuser — before it is too late.

Love: Russian Style

When I first heard her deep sultry voice over the phone, I pictured Svetlana as a middle-aged brunette of generous proportions, but a slim young barefoot bleached blonde with a ponytail answered the door. So much for my powers of imagination.

We talked in that traditional locus for cordial Russian communing — in the kitchen, flooded with sunlight and lit up with a bouquet of daffodils. The place had been just a standard Russian flat before it was given radical facelift — the walls were moved and heated floors were installed, and the latter sure felt good considering the harsh Russian climate.

"This is all Nicolay's design and choice, from the cutlery and any small kitchen things to the reconstruction plan," explained Svetlana. Definitely, her busy Russian businessman had a taste for home improvement.

"I see, the ladies are gossiping!" Nicolay commented, showing up for a while and leaving again. You would never mistake this red-haired man for Brad Pitt, but how much does appearance matter, really? Anyway, we were not going to "gossip" about him but about her American stories.

This is what Svetlana told me.

* * *

Usually my "American romances" started as business acquaintances [Svetlana used to work as a translator]. And I would say that you have to really impress the American man in order to get from him, let's say, a warm glance. Though there are some open-minded, emotional, and warm men, they are a rarity in America, I think, at least judging from my experience.

The father of my child is an American who was single for a long time and got accustomed to being alone. Though he damaged my life, I believe that everything that happens to us works eventually for our own good. We met when he was visiting Russia, and he was able to convince me that he was tired of being alone, that he wanted to start a family. I bought it, though I pondered over it a great deal — I had just graduated from the institute and had received some interesting job proposals.

Of course, I would have made different decisions now, but I was twenty-one then, and he was past forty. I decided to start a family. He returned to Alaska and called me every day. Every day we spent an hour on the phone, and our plans became more and more grandiose — he asked me where would I like to deliver our baby, in Hawaii or in London? And at that time I was ashamed to go out of the flat, being pregnant outside of wedlock. When I was "big as a tick," my potential brother-in-law, an orthodox deacon, came to visit a new church in our region. I obligingly ironed his cassock every morning — later he was expelled, though, because of drugs and alcohol addiction.

Then the father of my child disappeared. He happened to have drinking problems as well. I couldn't reach him because he didn't have a house then — for the last twenty years he traveled through Alaska — a sort of Leonard Peltier, but of Aleutian descent. Undoubtedly, he had made his contribution to the well being of the minorities, their activists have achieved a lot. Their hospital in Anchorage is a state of the art facility, and the healthcare is free. Everybody who has at least twenty-five percent Aleutian blood is entitled to annual financial aid. But I couldn't get any financial help from him — we were not married, and though our countries have a juridical agreement, the paperwork is way too complicated. So I decided that it was not such a big deal: I've got a child, and the rest is not important. I registered as a single mother to get some financial support from the Russian state, if not from the father of my child. My boy got a birth certificate when he was more than one year old.

The father came to see us two years later, very proud of himself. He told me that according to his theory, the mother is more important to a child of this age. He approved my maternal skills. I threw him out.

Of course, it wasn't easy for me because our romance had been quite public, and everybody knew that the father of my child was a foreigner who had abandoned us. But eventually you come to the conclusion that what people think or say about you is not important. It's not smart, to live in fear of gossips. The only thing that matters is your real personality, and sooner or later people will recognize you by who you are.

Two years later, the father of my child resurfaced again. He was over fifty, and he was starting to long for a family again. He asked me to bring his son to Alaska so we could go somewhere for a vacation as a family. He reasoned that the child should see the country, in case he decided to go to school in America.

My goal was to help my son to create a positive attitude towards his father, so when the boy is mature enough he can make his own judgment about our story. I think it is important for a child to know the truth about his father, and I didn't even consider using one of those clumsy explanations about tragically perished pilots.

It was quite a story how I obtained a visa to go visit his father — I was asked why I was applying for a business visa if I intended to take a child along. I explained that I wanted to show him the country, and when I indicated that his father was an American, I thought it would be a reason for visa denial. But the consul was a much-emancipated lady, and she advised me to find the father of my child and told me about my rights and what I should do.

Sure enough, we didn't do any family-style traveling but spent all the time in Anchorage. I detested that place. I couldn't expect any help from the man who was so used to his emancipated American ladies: here's the key to the house — do whatever you want. I absolutely didn't need that kind of emancipation; I like to be cared for, and I like to feel that I'm a woman. I was close to hysterics: I was an alien in a foreign country and sometimes even riding a bus was a problem.

Luckily, I discovered a Russian store nearby that served as a club for Russian wives, and that helped me to survive in Anchorage. The owner was a Russian woman who had never had an intention "to marry an American passport," but her marriage hadn't survived either, and her problems were similar to mine. I was astonished when she told me that before her divorce was final, she was allowed to keep her child only two days a week. I can imagine how that Russian mother felt, especially considering that her child was a girl. [In Russia, the custody of a young child customarily is given to the mother.]

Of course, some ladies from the former Soviet Union lead active lives in Alaska. Some teach Russian at schools, but I met others who were brought there just to do the housekeeping. A girl I knew from the institute lived in a small mining town. They didn't even have asphalt there — the community didn't want visitors. Moose roamed around the house, leaving droppings on the property.

But at least we saw Alaska, some. There is an opinion that the Alaskan nature and that of our Russian Far East are very similar, but I don't think so; Alaska seems too picturesque for me.

Anyway, the father of my son noted my cleaning and cooking, so he decided that family life suited him: "I won't let you to go back."

I have to admit that he established a good relationship with our child, and they started to understand each other. Of course, the father was very proud of his son, who was an ideal child by American standards.

I took my son to his cousin's birthday party, and that was a very funny experience. When we arrived with our gifts, we found out that only the cousin's father was present. Finally their mother arrived, with some guests. The children showed up, the mother put a cake on the table in the dusty living room, inflated a couple of balloons and asked the guests, "Who wants a beer? There are some hot-dogs in the fridge, too."

Though my son enjoyed his stay in the United States for the cartoons and hamburgers, after a month he declared, "We have to go back to Russia! Of course, I am sorry for Father, he's so lonely here... But we can take him with us, can't we?" This little dumpling, stepping out of the airplane when we arrived back in Russia, cried, "The Motherland! Russia! My city!" I had never even discussed these concepts with him. The Russian frontier guards — women, were impressed. "Such a good boy!"

We got home to our place in Russia in the midst of one of our famous blackouts. We didn't have electricity for hours and it was cold, but you couldn't find a happier person than me. And my son was happy too. I don't know, maybe we are just genetically patriotic? The Russian ladies who gathered together in that Russian store in Anchorage said that my story was typical. They told me to bear it. But why should I bear it — just to have the freedom to travel around the world with an American passport? I don't need that — I have my family and friends here. I don't blame anybody for their decisions, but I don't need their "happiness."

* * *

Here my woman's intuition detected something. "Could your determination to come back have had something to do with a romance here?"

"Oh well, frankly, yes," Svetlana laughed.

"Then how on the earth did he let you go to the US?" (Any sensible male would surely fight for such a girl.)

"I am a very strong and independent person. I decided that I must give my son the opportunity to see his father, and that was the most important thing. When I was asked if I would be coming back, I said I didn't know. Though I had doubts about that my 'American story' could have a happy ending, I wanted to give it a try. So I did. That was the end of my major 'American romance.' Now the father of my child calls me at work and asks my colleagues or whoever answers the phone if they know that he fathered my child."

"And how do you react?"

"I don't mind, now. Whose business is it, anyway? But it was hard for the first three years, I have to admit."

"You've mentioned that it was your major romance. So there were others?"

"Because of my occupation as an interpreter, for some time I had even more American acquaintances than Russian. Every time it started as a business relationship, but I guess Russian women are so different that American men are really touched. I communicated with one American friend for six years. He even spoke Russian; he was an interesting, sophisticated person, I did my best to help him with his business in Russia. We were kindred spirits — he was of Irish descent, and we Russians have some similarity with Irish souls."

"Sure — some kind of tragic outlook, for example."

"Exactly! To find a problem and stew about it! We assumed that feelings could be developed eventually because we had so much in common. You know how it happens sometimes — people may be so madly in love, but later they discover that they are absolutely incompatible. We had quite the opposite situation: I just couldn't get beyond my strictly friendly feelings towards him. We even made a trip to California, but it wasn't a romantic getaway; we remained just friends.

"He had a similar experience with his former girlfriend. They lived together, but led absolutely independent lives. I think in America, they don't have an understanding about really close family relationships. My friend sent me an invitation to apply for a visa, but I don't think I will go for it. I don't want to encourage him in vain. I guess it's not my destiny to live in America. You know that good expression in English — 'peace of mind.' That's the most important thing for me, and it doesn't depend on my surroundings. I can talk heart to heart in my friend's shabby kitchen and feel so happy! I understand that even if I get a hold of all of my practical sense — and I don't have too much of that either — and force myself into a sensible, not an emotional, decision, considering what is better for my future or the future of my child, inevitably I would fall into terrible nostalgia abroad.

"Of course, I respect American order and I like how they keep it in their country. However, I dislike that they tell on each other, and that is normal in their society. Even a child can inform against his parents for 'cruel treatment' if they punish him for misbehaving.

"Being an absolutely straight woman, I looked at our Russian ladies with awe after my trips to America. They might buy their outfits from a flea market, not a boutique, but they are stylish and make themselves look so special."

"How would you determine the difference between Russian and American men?"

"I can't count myself as an expert, of course, but the greediness of some American men is astonishing. They can easily treat themselves to some useless but expensive trinkets, yet they will be in anguish over buying something essential for you. He takes care of himself, but if it's about you — it's your problem.

"Our Russian men are more passionate. Americans are too afraid of showing their vulnerability. Though again, I'm not an expert. For Russians, love is an all-encompassing concept — American men seem to be sex freaks, in the way that they like to talk about sex, but not actually practice it. They are just so proud that there are no forbidden themes.

"But somehow they are very gallant, irrespective of upbringing. If they open a door for you and they see that you like it — they are ready to turn inside out for you. I don't know why American ladies don't appreciate the gallant behavior. I would think they would cry with joy accepting all kinds of help from their men if they had experienced the life of Russian women who had endured the War."

[Here Svetlana refers to the Second World War — in Russia we call it the Great Patriotic War — when virtually all the men were at the front. The Russian territory was under fascist occupation for four years — to my astonishment, this fact is barely known abroad, thanks in part to politically skewed textbooks. French novelist Maurice Druon said, "I think that the Second World War was won by English stubbornness, American enginery, and Russian blood... June, 22, 1941, had been a 'holiday' for France because the hope sprang within us when we found out that Hitler had committed an insane act attacking the Soviet Union: we understood that now we would certainly be freed of fascist occupation."[1] But thanks to Hollywood, the majority of Americans probably are dead sure that Private Ryan saved the world.]

"On the other hand, some Russian men think that your real attitude and feelings toward them should be tested with pain: how much he can wound you, how much you can endure — that is how they try to check if the feelings are 'real.' But I think that it is much better to try women with kindness."

"Are you happy now here?"

"Yes. I like that my man needs my care, and I enjoy his attention. I like my life and I cherish every day. Because who knows — what if this is the last day of your life or the lives of your loved ones? So I would advise not to accumulate kindness but to spend it, so there will be more happiness in the world."

* * *

Sometimes it looks like some people and some events came into our lives for a reason. Looking back, you may wonder if fate was leaving hints for you.

When I talked to Svetlana, I found out that we were supposed to be at the US embassy on the same day to obtain our next American visas. But she opted for a vacation in Thailand with her Russian admirer instead. Later I heard that she took a maternity leave, bore a baby girl, and evidently lived happily with Nicolay.

I'm not implying that Svetlana was a prophet sent to me from above, but I certainly felt strange about it. What did that "prophet with a ponytail" say — everything happens to us for a reason?

Was I meant to write this, then?

---

1 Elena Joli, "Maurice Druon: "I worship your veterans." *Argumentu i Facti*, #34, August, 24, 2005

A Young Wife's Diary

He runs a small plant on the outskirts of Seattle and is very patient with his Mexican workers. He looks like a big softie, a good guy. Good to everybody but his petite foreign wife. She knows what he is capable of, and his four American ex-wives know that too. All these ladies made their respective choices, and the ex-s' and the foreign wife's decisions are so very different.

Here are the excerpts from her diary.

* * *

June 12, Kazakhstan, Astana

Our engagement party was held at the Ceremonial Hall. About 50 guests attended. My fiancé drunk more than two bottles of vodka in three hours — he could hardly stand, people had to hold him up. Afterwards, he was delivered to the hotel.

At 2 a.m. he took out his drugs — Remeron, Clonazepam, Viagra — shook tablets from all three bottles in his palm and tried to wash them all down with Pepsi. I dug as much as I could out of his mouth and called an ambulance. They said, "Watch him, if he feels any worse — let us know." Clonazepam is for post-traumatic syndrome, Remizon is an antidepressant, both marked as "incompatible with alcohol."

Several times at night he fell down on his way to the bathroom. I helped him to get up. He bruised his nose, forehead, broke a toenail. He threw up in the bed and wet it.

August 24, Seattle

I'm pregnant.

Our neighbor stopped me when I walked the dog and engaged me in a conversation. We talked for three minutes. My husband saw us from the balcony. When I came home, he started yelling, accusing me that I had come here to find someone else. I noted that the neighbor is an elderly man, and it would be impolite to ignore him, not to stop for a small talk.

My husband stormed out of the apartment but came back in five minutes. I was eating dinner in front of the TV. He kicked the coffee table — it shattered into splinters, plates and silverware flew every which way.

He calmed down in three hours.

November, California

He and his friend, whom we went to visit, drank two bottles of vodka. I said I was hungry. His friend took us to a restaurant. He drove and I sat on my husband's lap, since it was a roadster. It was a twenty-minute ride and we made it, fortunately.

November, Ritz-Carlton

My husband went to the bathroom at midnight. There he sat on the floor for twenty minutes. He wasn't able to even call me. He came back all soaking in a cold sweat, complaining that he felt dizzy. I offered to call a doctor, but he took that as an offense, saying that I didn't want to take care of him.

December 25

I'm upset that we are going to visit his relatives empty-handed, without any gifts at all. He said that he'd write checks for them. I tried anyway to find something in the house that could pass for a gift. He got mad, threw all the shoes from the hallway into our bedroom yelling that I had smeared expensive tile with shoe polish.

February 25

I'm almost eight months pregnant. He taught me to drive for three hours. I said that it's hard for me physically — I cannot react adequately, my stomach is bulging. He yelled profanities and made me continue. When we came home, he threw the phone receiver on the floor, yelling that I will never ever be able to drive.

I said that it's hard for me now. Just to sit behind the wheel is hard, and it is better for the baby if I take a break.

March 20

I have problems feeding my newborn daughter. She is a big baby, so she demands her milk every hour and a half. My husband insists on feeding her at intervals of three or four hours. "Let her cry, and when she cries, don't soothe her!"

He yelled something, and the baby started crying. I asked, "Please, don't frighten her." He got mad and was pouting for four hours. He said that he was playing with the baby, not yelling at her.

June 29

The baby was crying. He took her to the nursery, put her in the chair and let her cry for fifty minutes. He didn't let me hold her, saying that when she calmed down, he'd rock her in his arms. He added, "Do you know what jealousy is? You are busy with her all the time — it's not fair!"

Finally I couldn't stand it anymore. I fed her and she stopped crying. Later I consulted a doctor and was told that it's dangerous to let the baby cry more than fifteen minutes since it could cause an umbilical hernia.

July 2

I was breast-feeding the baby in a rocker. He entered the bedroom and asked me angrily why I didn't let her cry; why I don't obey him. I said, "Please, leave me alone." He grabbed my throat and knee. I was scared. The baby started crying. He let me go, but threatened that he'll send me back to Kazakhstan and the baby will remain with him.

When I put her to bed and came out of the bedroom, he yelled that none of his wives ever told him to leave them alone, and that he pays for everything. He asked what good have I done for him? I said that I bore him a baby. He said, "Your f***— baby cost me eight thousand dollars!"

Then he slipped his wedding ring off his finger and told me that I wasn't his wife anymore, that he was going to call the immigration service and I would be deported without my baby.

I went to the spare bedroom and lay down. He came in, grabbed my hand and dragged me to the front door. I balked, telling him that I wouldn't go anywhere. He dragged me into our bedroom and threw me on the bed. Our dog started barking, jumping on him. He came to his senses and left me alone.

I was able to soothe him in an hour. He promised not to manhandle me anymore.

July 3

His son with his wife came to visit us. I gauged the right moment and told them what had happened yesterday. Mary said, "You are not his slave — should something like that happen again, call 911. He treated his son badly too, that's why we didn't communicate with him for a long time." I asked if he beat his son. She said, "Probably."

My husband didn't hear from his son for five months before that. Then they met at the dealership because they had to sell a car. Then no contacts, again. My husband called his son and left a message on the answering machine asking for forgiveness and saying that he wants them to come to visit us. I left at least three messages, too, inviting them to come for his father's 50th birthday anniversary, but he didn't come and didn't even call.

July 14

I cannot lull the baby to sleep. I handed her to her father and she started crying even harder. He got mad, said that I spoiled her, that she prefers me to him.

I went to the nursery. He kept opening the door by hitting it with his fist and broke a decorative bell on the door. The baby cried louder and louder with each of his intrusions. I decided to take her outside to calm her down, but when I reached the door, he caught up with me, grabbed my hand, snatched my glasses off and threw them on the floor. I returned to the nursery again. He opened the door with a blow, threw my glasses down, shouting, "Never leave the house without my permission!"

September 1

We are going to the beach. When I sat down to eat, he started to complain, "Better pack cell phones! It's not a meal time!" He shouted to his mother that she shouldn't waste time cooking for me. I explained that if I don't eat, I will deprive the baby of the breast milk.

September 25

My husband is in a good mood. Said that he was controlling me all the time and that it's wrong, that love means trust. He said that he didn't send my documents to the immigration office because he is afraid that I'll leave him once I obtain my legal status. He said that every time I go out for a walk, he thinks that I'm leaving him forever.

I reminded him that in Kazakhstan I could hardly support myself and wasn't able to afford to have a baby, so why does he have these thoughts?

He said that he has a bad temper and he cannot help controlling me and since all his wives left him, he thinks I might leave him, too. He said that he behaves that way because he loves me, because he is too old for me, because he realizes that I would have more fun if I were with a younger man. He said that he hates himself and wonders how I can stand him.

September 28

My friend Nina has called. He hates her because she offered to find free medical help when I was pregnant and offered to help with my immigration forms. He asked me who'd called. I said that it was Irina, from Seattle. He checked the number and got so mad — for two days afterwards he was yelling obscenities, calling me a liar. I had the jitters. He checked every number in my address book, tore out Nina's and Irina's addresses and burned them, threatening to send me back to Kazakhstan and take my baby away from me.

October 1

My friend Maria called. He interrogated her, demanding explanations: who is she and why is she calling me? She said that she wanted to give me the phone number of a Russian woman whose name is Sonya.

When I came back after visiting a neighbor's family, he met me at the door, yelling, "So now you want to leave me for a woman with four children!"

I was taken aback. I said that I didn't even know such a woman. When he said her name, I realized that this is a woman who has three children and who is expecting again.

"You're lying to me, as always!" he shouted, "Get out of here!"

I went to prepare his pills — I always did that, it was my duty. He didn't even remember if he took his medications or not.

He came inside, too, locked the door and started approaching me with a strange expression on his face — evil and crazy.

He cornered me in the kitchen — I had the baby in my arms — assumed a boxer's position and hit me in my face four times. My glasses fell on the floor and broke. The baby started crying. The baby was hitting me, yelling, "You are cheating on me! You're a liar!" Then he squeezed my throat. I was so frightened I soiled myself. The baby started screaming and he backed up. He grabbed the phone and threw it on the floor — it shattered. I darted to the back door and ran across the lawn to the neighbors' house. He tried to catch me, but didn't go out.

I ran into the neighbors' house and locked the door behind me. The neighbor asked me what happened. I begged him to call the police. I was so scared, I was stuttering. The police arrived in five minutes when I still was in the bathroom cleaning myself.

At the police station, a lady-policeman took my statement. She saw my reaction and ordered that my husband be taken away from the glass partition where he was standing, watching me.

October 27

My husband took my baby. He got the court order for temporary custody. The baby was still breast-feeding. My relatives from Kazakhstan sent me $2,655 to pay for a lawyer so I could fight for custody.

How he controlled me:

He picked out what I could read and threw away all my Russian magazines. He chose what I could watch on TV and what I could not. I was to watch only the movies he had chosen. If an envelope in the mail was addressed to me, I shouldn't open it by myself but give it to him unopened.

When he was at home, I had to get his permission to take the baby for a walk or to go to visit a neighbor. When I came back after a visit, he asked me, "What did you talk about? I bet you were telling them about my bad temper!" And then he'd get mad.

He chose the girlfriends I was allowed to talk to and checked the phone calls, asking who had called and what they wanted — and called them back.

He checked all the phone numbers in my address book. He controlled what I wore before I went outside. He demanded that I always call him when I was going out of the house in his absence.

My documents were at the immigration lawyer's office for a year. He said that he didn't have the money to pay the lawyer. When one of my friends offered to help me to fill out the papers, he called her and told her that she was causing marital problems so she shouldn't contact me anymore. Then he collected my documents from the lawyer's office, so I couldn't get back my passport, birth certificate, and other documents. He took my address book, too.

Looking for a translator for the court hearing, I called one but she said she could not work for me on ethical reasons: "I used to work for your husband — he asked me to translate e-mails you sent to your relatives."

* * *

During the custody trial, the judge asked this woman several times if she was a Muslim — luckily, she had started to attend a local church with her new boyfriend.

She was awarded principal custody and decent alimony and child support. Her neighbor helped her get into a nice apartment complex under the subsidy program. Her boyfriend was supportive, but she was constantly probing him, testing the borders of his tolerance and softness, and finally he left her "because of her psychological instability," as he explained. She found out that she couldn't cope by herself and returned to live with her husband: she seemed to have a need for a "strong hand," for a difficult, even dysfunctional man who would tell her what to do.

The baby grew into a nervous, clinging child who couldn't let her mother out of her sight.

FROM THE HORSE'S MOUTH, OR SO THE HORSE SAYS

One American husband of a young Russian wife tried to make the point that all the deserving American women are married, so he and other poor American fellows are forced to seek a match overseas.

I asked the ex-husband of yet another Russian to share with me his theory. At that moment Patrick was divorced, but still in the process of analyzing the pitfalls of his international marriage and quite ready to jump into another adventure of that sort.

They were a strange looking couple, Patrick and his ex-wife — a very short bald man and a sharp, petite blonde a couple of decades his junior. My own American husband, who couldn't stand a disparity — at least in physical appearances — gossiped with an immigration officer about similar couples, "They just don't match!"

Here is Patrick speaking, so don't blame the messenger if something seems illogical now and then — I'm not correcting words out of the horse's mouth. I have only grouped his observations according to subject, including his first-hand opinion about the notorious tours "to Russia for love."

Still, I can't resist chiming in with my own comments here and there.

"Good Russian Women" Versus "Difficult American Ladies"

I guess the answer to that question — why would I rather prefer not to deal with a partner from my own culture? — is not easy. That's why I was trying to dodge it.

In theory, the American woman has more in common with the American man, but right now I actually think I have changed so much that I have more in common with the Russian woman — single, divorced, or separated. I suppose that somewhere in the haystack is my tiny little needle, an American woman who is waiting for me, but at present, I really think I am better prepared to cope with the ups and downs of the Russian woman companion.

I tried finding a good match with American ladies for ten years after my divorce. These relationships were certainly not difficult to start, but most ended after three months. A few longer relationships rarely exceeded one year due to lack of a real match, or an interest or devotion to make a long-term commitment. I know, they usually say the same about males, but my life just seems to be the mirror reflection of the experiences of most women.

Of course, it is easier to talk to an American woman since we speak the same language, but the relationship with the American woman is a constant struggle, especially in the area of finances and dominance. The good news is that America leads in women's rights. The bad news is that most of our women want a fifty-fifty split in absolutely everything. This much democracy is difficult to achieve. For example, what do you think of little girls playing soccer, or women who box or wrestle? It seems strange to me, but not to most American women.

So, I still have the dream of finding a wonderful woman who has the lovely qualities of intelligence, grace, femininity, and charm, which I think is more typical of Russian women than American. Most American females really don't like sex; they think it's disgusting and dirty. And I know that most Russian women really have a very different idea in this area, and I like it much, much better.

Of course, there are plenty of single women in the USA, and past the age of 45, American ladies seem to keep their attractive appearance better than the Russians. At least those Russians who are still in Russia — this is most likely due to climate, diet, and the stress of dealing with Russian men.

There is even a mailing list service where hungry American males exchange all kinds of ideas, lies, and rumors about Russian women. Most of it is pretty boring, guys trying to see who splashed more testosterone around in the Ukraine and the like. Over and over, guys ask "what is the K-1 visa?", "are these beautiful women for real?" Most of the men are starry-eyed dreamers, just like I was once. When somebody has a real problem with a Russian woman and tries to discuss it, they mostly ridicule him until he gets angry and leaves the group.

I think Russian women can learn enough about their partner, and can make a true decision of commitment in a shorter period of time, let's say six to twelve months, or maybe even in three months. My interest is in getting on with life, I'd rather prefer not to spend three years being psychoanalyzed by my American girlfriend's shrink, and all her friends, or wait until all of the planets line up, and all of the caveats can be fully explored in depth, and so on and so forth. American women are really keen on having long term dating relationships, two to three years, before making a commitment.

Now about my "Russian Wife Plan": I know my choice was screwy, but I definitely think that was a fluke, my blindness to "red flag" signals. But I have seen several successful American-Russian marriages, and when they are successful, they are very, very happy. It would be very nice to have one like that.

However, I know that a Russian wife faces a "cultural shock" that puts the process at big risk. That is principally about language and food, but also about making the adjustments for living with the American male.

"Price Factor"

This last factor makes me think that it is probably desirable to seek out a "veteran," or someone who is already in America, not only because of the frustrating immigration delays, but also because she would simply be more comfortable with the American culture, plus she would know more about how to accurately read and interpret the American male than the Russian woman who is still in Russia.

American women are definitely "higher maintenance" than Russian, at least until that moment when Russian women start making friends with American women and start getting ideas. The problem with Russian women's "maintenance" is just getting accustomed to their needs, all those signs of appreciation like flowers, gifts, etc. This is a lot easier to provide than the requirements of that dominant Americans. I think I'd still rather take my chances next time with another Russian.

Change of Heart

When I jumped on a singles web-site right after my divorce, I noticed a substantial number of divorced Russian women living in California. I'll bet that site alone is listing a hundred Russian women living in America. Interesting.

The gals from Russia I correspond with now are getting very impatient and want me to come to visit. I guess they all want to marry me, and most likely for a piece of that supposedly wonderful American pie. This correspondence occupies too much of my time, besides I have to make a million first and then retire to Izmail or Sochi, and just watch the lovelies go by every day... No more marriages for me, at least not in this decade — only friends and girlfriends. I don't mean to sound cynical, I'm just starting to get more realistic. Once you've invested a certain amount of time, emotion and energy, you just are afraid to turn back.

[So here my expert makes a 180° turn from his previous musing that Russian gals can make a quick decision, but he apparently enjoys making somebody wait impatiently for him.]

Next time I will definitely take more time to get to know my prospective fiancée. Spending two vacations together and having ninety days to decide upon marriage, according to the immigration timetable, is simply not normal — I think it takes more, like three to six months, or even one year to get to know someone and to show each other the full range of the ups and downs of one's temperament. This has to be done in spite of the stupid constraints of the Immigration and Naturalization Service, with crazy rules and laws that actually increase the likelihood of divorce.

Some of the best advice I got from my divorce recovery group was to just "journal" — to write down all those "red flags" that were detected before, during the courtship and after the divorce. In my mental state during our separation, I would have already jumped on the plane and gone to Russia to meet one of these virtual pen-pals, increasing my credit card balances. But now I am just waiting until I feel really comfortable again and more in peace with myself.

I've been out of a serious relationship for about six months now, and I think that just taking more time is also a good idea. No more offers of marriage, and no lifetime promises. Just kind of gentle friendship. Not getting emotionally involved is also wise, I'm going just to take care of my own health, house, and business.

I will not again, like a hungry child, rush to the first woman who is willing to be affectionate. I will be sure we are comfortable with all our differences, especially the important differences which may or may not include age, religion, spirituality, activity level, home care, preferred forms of entertainment, and compatibility with each other's family and friends.

They Are Cheating!

After three years of marriage to my American wife, I discovered she was having one affair after another. I just kept hoping it would change, separating and reconciling for about ten years. Finally, we divorced. I was single another ten years before I remarried, and I was hoping this marriage would be the miracle I had been hoping for. Now I can see that I ignored many "red flags," and actually allowed myself to be used because I was so hopeful for success in my second marriage.

When I discovered that my second wife was having affairs, I was shocked. I was not going to repeat the ten years of begging and pleading, like in my first marriage. I invited her to have counseling, or see a pastor, or try to understand

and communicate our problems. She immediately demanded a separation. I filed for the divorce about three weeks after she moved out. Now, after five months, I am finally feeling peaceful, and actually grateful that she has left. The truth is that we had friction, just constantly, about everything. My life is so much simpler now. But I still miss the companionship of having a nice friend close by, someone to speak to, and someone to share my heart with.

Marriage Tours: to Russia for Love

I visited Russia with a tour group trying to find out if Russian manufacturing business planners would like our production-scheduling software.

I went to the bewildering "marriage parties," and made no connection at all. We had about twelve men and about sixty women sitting at a dozen tables. The arrangements were made so that at each table was one man, one translator and five women. You were introduced to each woman. You had about fifteen minutes of conversation at the table. Then they made us move to the next table. In other words, they wanted us to have about three minutes with each of the women.

The women definitely did not like the experience of competing like hungry alligators that had been forced to jump for dangling meat. It was a humiliating experience for everyone. A few men just ignored the marriage agency staff and started talking to just one woman for the entire evening, and these were the guys who made the connections.

The rest of us, trying to be cooperative with the program, met many girls and posed for the advertising photos with them, and that was about all I got out of it. I enjoyed speaking with the translators and made friends with some of them.

In other words, these tour parties fail entirely. Only three or four girls out of sixty got meaningful dates. The rest got a good dinner and some champagne, so maybe it was a consolation prize for them.

I also participated in an "intimate party," which meant that the ratio was closer to one-to-one, and I met two or three women who later became friends. But at least the agency passed out photos of women that they had not downloaded onto the Internet site yet. From those I picked a few and had some dates, and it was a lot more enjoyable than the group party. But I never "clicked" or "matched" with any woman on this trip.

The most fun I had in St. Petersburg was when I crashed a party in the hotel, and I sat at a table next to a pretty lady who spoke a little bit of English. They started serving dinner, so I just stayed. Can you believe it? It turned out to be a Jewish Passover dinner. I was amazed how rich the people and dinner looked. Nothing like those poor Russian Jewish people that you can meet in Brooklyn and Brighton Beach.

Anyway, it was a great dinner, and I made friends with this lady, Svetlana

Kuznetsova. She took me around the city and we saw a lot of the sights together. She was forty, quite beautiful, and was kind of a "rescuer" for unfortunate souls: she had even married her best friends' son, just officially (he was twenty years younger) in order to allow this boy to reenter the country from Finland to visit his mother. The boy had lost his Russian citizenship because he went to live with his father in Finland for five years. It shows that the most interesting experiences, more than likely, will be the ones that you find on your own, rather than canned events on a tour.

Smart and Cute

I had been writing to Maria, and hoped to meet her, but she could not get off work to go to St. Petersburg for those parties.

So I returned to Russia later, mostly just to meet her, and we did have a "match," but I still wasn't entirely convinced. I visited with a few of the ladies I met on the first trip but still did not "click" with anyone else. After another month of letters, I decided to invite Maria to meet me in Italy. We had a very good time, and our hosts let us use their apartment in Rome. We became engaged.

Maria worked as an economist in Yekaterinburg with a big construction company for nine years, doing tax planning. She was making $800 a month, which was very good money for a Russian.

In America, I had her to do accounting for my business and I also trained her in software testing. In Silicon Valley, there has always been a big demand for this career. For some reason, Russian people are excellent in this work: it does not require accurate English writing, only a determination to take a computer program and criticize every aspect of it. In criticism and logic, Russians seem to have no equal.

Anyway, I paid for Maria's school and her certification as a Quality Assurance Engineer, as well as courses in database and Visual Basic. With these skills, she was ready to start interviewing for a job. At that time, the Bay Area still had a booming job market, with 3,000 unfilled jobs for QA Engineers just in San Mateo County. She received three offers, and I taught her how to play them off against each other, so she got an even higher salary, and after one year she got a ten percent raise — right at the time we separated.

Math and Money

How do I know that I spent about 150K on her and her son? The cost of living here is extremely high. You need a minimum of $2,000 per month for every family member just in order to survive. If you multiply the cost of keeping her and her son, at least $3,000 per month, times the 40 months we were together, you get the 120K that I lost on this failed marriage [Patrick forgets that she had a high-paying job at least for the last year of their marriage, and she did the accounting for his company for free], but you should also add the cost of the lavish 30K I spent on our courtship with three trips to Russia [so these "dating parties" should be on her tab too?], and two trips to Italy for all of us.

Her wedding ring was a modest $300 diamond. I gave Maria a modest diamond necklace and other jewelry on our wedding anniversaries, again not exorbitant, but at least thoughtful. Her Quality Assurance education was about $6K because it was taught at a rate of $50 per hour, in Russian, by Russian specialists in QA in the Bay Area. But her courses at the community college were only $300.

This means if I had never spent any of this money and just saved it, I would today be 150K richer. And that would be just about half of the mortgage on my house.

But that's stretching the truth, because even if I stayed single and kept dating here in the USA over those four years, I'm sure I would have probably spent at least $1K per month on a dating and social life — the cost in the Bay Area is high.

[And I doubt that in the Bay Area he will ever be able to get a partner who looks so strikingly different from him.]

The Evidence

I was starting to get a little bit suspicious about my wife's activities because she had adopted the habit of going out with her Russian girlfriend to a local pub where they had some disco dancing, and they always stayed out so late, and she was never reachable on her cell phone.

I also saw her rapidly changing something on her computer screen when I walked into the bedroom abruptly.

Once I picked up her cell phone, started skipping through her phone book, and was amazed to see several men's telephone numbers — I had no idea who these people were. I noted the phone numbers, and started checking the cell phone bill. As I found out, she was spending more time on the phone with these men than with her son or me. I noticed that she had consistently started exceeding the monthly cell phone minutes, but I didn't think much about it in the beginning.

I decided to hire an investigator who confirmed that indeed, she was certainly seeing other men. Next, I searched the house and her car, where I discovered some diamond gifts and love letters which dated back several months. When I confronted her with the evidence, she immediately demanded a separation.

When I asked her to go to counseling, she just snorted and shook her head in amazement.

If It Looks Too Good to Be True...

Maria's main attraction was that she looked like a knockout babe that guys like me can only dream about, like one of those girls you can meet in your youth.

She also had an accounting career, so we had common business interests. But most importantly, her Internet listing stated that "a gentleman's age and the color of his eyes or hair are not important to me." I thought this might be a miracle just for me...

Initially, I had proposed that she would try to help me sell my software to local businesses in Russia. [Is that where American men look for business associates — in the international marriage agency databases?] But after we met, it wasn't long before she made it clear she was interested in a lot more than being my local software reseller. Since I am a gullible, horny guy, it didn't take her long to bed me down. And now, of course, I recognize that I should have listened to that still, small voice inside my head that kept saying, Watch out Patrick, this is just too good to be true.

In addition, I also overlooked many other "red flags" as well. I did ask my Russian lady-friends from my prior visits with the marriage agency to chat with Maria and give me their opinions. They all came back with glowing endorsements of high praise for Maria. But now, in retrospect, I realize that it was strange that they all said almost identical things. I can now believe that Maria was so smart and deceptive that she instantly saw the "interviews" coming, and was extraordinarily skillful at passing herself off as the "little gray mouse from Yekaterinburg who only wants to have a husband who truly loves her." And then there were many, many other "red flags" both before and after we got married.

So now I know for sure that one has to pay attention to common sense, and just because you are dealing with people from another country really doesn't mean that everything is different. It is different only on the surface. You just need to recognize that if a woman that normally would grimace just to give you the time of day agrees to date you, then something is wrong, and you better pay attention to that "still, small voice" inside your own head.

Indeed, if one starts thinking that this is just too good to be true, then it probably is.

I have come across a few of Maria's current dating ads on the Internet, and now, since she is all set in America, her dating requirements indicate that a man's age, height, weight, and the color of his hair are all very important to her.

Something Good

I should say that Maria always told our friends nice things about me, like "Patrick always provides for me and my son Yura, takes the best care of us, makes sure we are correct with our immigration papers," etc. Of course, I was always flattered when I heard this. Now it makes me wonder how much of this was sincere and how much was intended to administer an anesthetic to the critical lobes of the brain, so as to deflect attention from any "trace evidence" of her extra-marital activities. How much was genuine gratitude and how much was the art of deception? I will probably never know for sure. But I am convinced that the mixture did exist and might have been about fifty-fifty.

Yura was the bright spot of our marriage. From the time I first invited him to play soccer with me, in Italy, his wide open eyes showed me a genuine gratitude to share the kind of fatherly play that his natural father had never given him. I taught him how to throw a baseball and football. And I got him into the CYSO (California Youth Soccer Organization). This is the tough gang, not like the patsies in the AYSO (American Youth Soccer Organization), where little boys play against little girls and never keep score to avoid the feeling of competition. Yura is very competitive; I am very proud of his athletic ability. His academic skills and ability to focus or concentrate in school are simply absent — he is pretty bright, but I doubt if he will ever apply for college, or advanced classes in anything.

Maria admitted once that one of her key goal for coming to the USA was to keep Yura out of the mandatory Russian military draft, since many boys got maimed or even killed in the army. If I saved Yura, then at least this was a good deed that came from our marriage."

* * *

I'm very grateful that Patrick had the bravery to write in detail. He pretty much outlined all of the contradictions by himself. Having not the easiest character, he was still trying to find a "miracle," but who can cast a stone at a person for that desire? John Lennon said, "You may say I'm a dreamer, but I'm not the only one." Though dreamers come in different shades — this one showed a full spectrum of male coquetry in his self-evaluation of the chase-and-conquer game, but he's paid for that already. And I don't mean the $150,000.

HE SAYS — SHE SAYS

These two couples, chosen for the parallel portraits, are in different stages: "Just hitched" and "A Voice of Experience" — no wonder that the woman-veteran wrote such a lengthy essay. Both of these young ladies seem to be inclined to the father-daughter type of relationship, and they both sought assurances and protection from their American spouses. But don't assume that they are an impersonation of that mystical "typical Russian woman."

Mike and Marina

Mike: I was interested in Russian women because a friend of mine had a Russian wife. I was sort of amazed at the number of women that I found on the website where I bought Marina's address. There were so many ladies that I didn't have the time to look at all the areas. I just researched the women in St. Petersburg and Moscow and decided to respond to those who wrote back by e-mail, and Marina was one of them. I guess I was extremely lucky because I met her right at the beginning of my search and we seemed to hit off right from the start. That is probably not the way it works out all the time.

Marina had a translator on her computer and could translate my e-mails into Russian and then would write back by starting in Russian and translating into English. She spoke English very well and when I called we were able to communicate — I would not have continued with her if she had not been able to speak with me without an interpreter.

But I think that the adjustment time is going to be a lot longer than either of us expected: Marina has been here for three months now and we have been married almost a month. She has some problems with being homesick and it does affect her mood, especially after we have had some misunderstanding.

There are cultural differences, definitely. She doesn't listen to our music very much yet. We don't watch too much TV, and that is a big change for me. That is because her English is not at a level that will allow her to keep up and understand enough to enjoy it. She is now going to English classes to work on that. But until she reads and writes better, she won't be able to learn how to drive and it will be hard for her to find a job if that is what she wants to do.

Marina: My husband found my profile at an approved web-site. But those men from the Internet were so different: some wanted just to chat, some were looking for a cheap exotic woman for sex, but the majority was so nice and really wanted to get married.

I intensively exchanged e-mails with Mike for two months. Finally he flew to St. Petersburg and in six days we were engaged. My English was fluent, so we didn't have a language barrier, but in my new family I have other major problems. His mother lives with us, and her constant presence in the kitchen and in the living room, plus her full-blast TV all day long irritates me. As well as his conservatism, he constantly reminds me that we have to save money. But I realize if I don't focus on that, my life in America will be nice and wonderful. My husband loves me and tries to understand. We are both very emotional, both like nature, animals, a healthy lifestyle, kisses and hugs, and sex. He likes my spontaneity a lot. When I smile, he beams with pleasure because he knows that I smile with all my soul. If I am upset, it pains him.

I don't know what nostalgia is about. When I start to miss home and friends, I remind myself that friends are just a part of the soul and distance doesn't matter at all, and that it is better Here [sic] and that I can help my mother and daughter from Here better.

My American is a big, calculating child. My experience with Russian men proved that they are adults who intend to get the best of a bargain when dealing with a woman. So I decided to look for a foreign man — I wanted to have a husband who would relieve me from all those impossible burdens of problems that Russian women have to endure in their everyday life.

* * *

So Mike omits the problem that seriously bothers Marina (living with an in-law), but gives away the problem which Marina denies (feeling homesick). The more practical Mike said, "It won't be easy." And what if she does not like American TV?

Tom and Lena

Tom: At that time there were many websites — more than ten [compared to thousands of them now!] — which provided names and personal information about ladies from around the world. Most of them were from former Soviet bloc countries and Russia, and I was primarily interested in Russian and Ukrainian ladies. I was online about six months looking for possibilities when I started to communicate with Lena by e-mail. Her English was sufficient from the beginning.

Several things irritated me during the adjustment time. Initially she wore enough clothes to bed to survive in a tent in the Arctic. She tried to feed me the previous night's dinner remains again in the morning for breakfast. At first she would not answer the telephone. Our relationship was severely tested when I tried to teach her how to drive... I don't recommend that — better to hire a professional driving instructor. But she seldom expressed homesickness, and cultural differences didn't cause any serious troubles.

Just the struggle of getting her a fiancée visa created a sense of accomplishment and victory over the various government agencies which seemed intent on preventing our relationship. So that obstacle became a Closeness Improver. It gives you an impression that you are doing something daring and unusual — friends are asking questions about your sanity, and you feel like you are doing something for World Peace.

We have common interests — travel and exotic vacations, fine dining and wine, videos, music, parties with friends, sensual adventures, massages, and the Internet.

Some things, luckily, changed in the course of our life together: she now sleeps nude (except in cold bedrooms) and answers the telephone. I stopped trying to be the driving instructor. She feels that American men, in general, are less distant than Russian men in relationships, but this may only be her perception based on personal experience.

I feel that Russian women have a clearer understanding of what pleases the typical man. They also seem to have fewer anti-male agendas and are more tolerant of their man's shortcomings. Russian women seem to be more supportive and less adversarial than American women. They don't expect to compete with men as many American women do, especially the current generation.

I did not have to change my existing circle of friends, but did enlarge it with similar Russian–American couples who had similar stories to tell. For a few months we even had a regular "dinner club" going when we lived in Seattle. We were four couples who seemed to enjoy getting together to share common experiences and trade favors. It was fun while it lasted. Unfortunately, one of the couples seemed to take offense with us. We never knew the cause. We continued to meet with the other two, but somehow the group energy changed.

It is my belief that the main differences between American and Russian women are in the expectations: American women, especially those who are well educated and of the last two generations, have developed a set of expectations that are competitive with their male counterparts. A woman who competes is admired. A woman who is supportive is ignored.

It is as if women feel that men are somehow predisposed to take advantage of them and do them ill. No doubt there are many examples of boorish men who have done just that. However, once the crusade against men is honed by the media and taught in the classroom, it becomes more than just awareness. It becomes a weapon that is wielded by women in general against men in general.

American society has been fundamentally affected by the woman's movement and not all of the effect has been positive for American relationships. When the married couple enters the relationship with attitudes of confrontation what can be expected of the outcome? There are enough challenges in marriage without adding a set of feminist's challenges to the mix.

Clever women have always known how to persuade men and balance the control in a relationship without using the confrontational tactics that seemed to be in vogue today. No amount of legal action or legislative involvement will ever make a happy, lasting marriage. Prevailing in court is no guarantee of success in love.

By now I believe the reader can draw his own conclusion about my personal choice for a Russian wife. Aside from the very human tendency to want what is on the other side of the fence, my interest in a foreign woman was to avoid the confrontations that I was finding in my own culture.

From just a very few experiences with Russians I detected a significant and refreshing difference in the way Russian women viewed their role with a man. And of course, I found them to be, as a whole, quite attractive and well educated. They had something to offer besides a pretty face and a list of requirements.

Lena: I would like to start from the very beginning — why I had decided to start this "American Husband Project" in the first place.

My first husband was an intolerable distant programmer-"workaholic" who worked 12 hours every day, including weekends. When I divorced him, I decided to refresh myself a little bit and to go to see the world, and at the same time, if that were possible, to restore my self-esteem which was pretty wibbly-wobbly during the last years of my marriage.

So I went... guess where? To Paris! And this travel exceeded all my expectations, especially about restoring my female amour-propre. Later I went to France again, this time to Nice. It was the end of September, a beatific sunny time — I could write a story in Fransuaza Sagan style about that.

These trips were the best present I have ever given myself. I found out that the world could be abundant, pleasant and hospitable and men could be smiling, attentive, and be ready to do whatever in order to please you.

Then I came back to my cold Siberia, thinking why people in countries like France live happily and comfortably, but I have to freeze in the icy-cold rain, and suffer the rudeness of our services, and so on.

At that critical time of my epiphany, I had tried to find the "Mister Right." I even published an ad in a newspaper, but that came off in a couple of short-term disappointing romances. One "dark and handsome" happened to be an alcoholic. That was hard to guess — he was a successful businessman and he looked all right. The other happened to be a womanizer, absolutely unreliable and unpredictable.

After these disappointing experiments I decided that my next relationship must not disturb my well-being, but add something to what I had; and I had a nice apartment, great friends, interesting books, and a well-paying job.

Four months after my last trip to France (I missed it so much!) I realized that I wanted to marry into a foreign country only. I had used a technique before called "forming desirable events using the method of positive thinking." So I came up with a positive affirmation, "I have a great family with a beloved man in a developed warm Western country."

I was repeating this phrase to myself like a mantra or an abraxas. I was repeating it over and over walking to work — just imagine that cold, dirty city snow around. I went to bed repeating it. At that time I couldn't even imagine how that could have happened, I just held onto my belief and hope.

In three months or so, I was talking on the phone with some friend and she told me that she knew a man who for a small charge publishes the ladies' information on the Internet and that several of his clients had already left for America.

I found that man right away and he published my advertisement on fifteen international marriage web-sites. During the next three months, I had received more than 400 letters from single, lonely men from all corners of the earth.

It was like magic. I couldn't believe that it was possible, that it was happening to me. I got letters from Australia, New Zealand, Greenland, Columbia, Venezuela, Canada, Germany, Italy, England, Scandinavia, Middle East, Asia, but most of all from America — because everybody in America has a computer at home.

The gentlemen with serious intentions wrote me, they had houses and gardens, and they were looking for a wife who would help them to run a farm and mow the grass in places like Texas, Australia, and New Zealand.

Sexual weirdoes wrote, too. One English teacher from Thailand made a great impression with his lengthy essays. I had a lot of letters from single men who wanted to have a relationship but didn't want to change anything in their lifestyles — to start regular workouts, for example, in order to shape their less-than-perfect bodies.

One guy from Montreal was very interesting, he was a cartoon producer. He lived in a huge six-room condo in downtown and he wanted me to come there with my two children. But he usually had about fifteen friends living in — he was from a big family, and probably life like that was very comfortable for him. But I didn't understand what I would do there with my children in the midst of that never-ending party, so we didn't go there.

The other "exotic man" was a young diplomat from Venezuela. He constantly called me so he could practice his English.

It was an interesting time. I was continuously receiving calls, letters, and compliments. I spent all my time answering e-mails and consulting the dictionary. In no time I had a huge box file of letters sorted by countries, names, and index numbers, but I had no clue what should I do with all that stuff. Four men were ready to come to Russia to get acquainted with me, so I had to come up with criteria for the candidates.

One night I sat down for a brainstorm and wrote down what I would expect from my future husband. Let him be a tawny, tall blond with blue eyes, tender and attentive, and athletically built... Oh, no — let him be a cute brunet, bright and witty, with a generous and artistic nature — just like that photograph Gilles in Paris... Of course, it would be great if he had tons of money, because otherwise how would I fly back and forth, visiting my mommy? Sure, he must be nice to my children, but who knows, what if he'll torment them? Ouch!

During that time I read a smart self-help book that advised to distinguish what you really need (like everyday bread) and what you want but can survive without (like a pastry that you love).

So I went through all my wishes with a critical eye — what I cannot do without? So many criteria that looked important in the beginning moved to the column "wishes-pastries." Bye-bye, good looks, hypersexuality, blue eyes, charm, hobbies that we would share, and the mandatory everyday flowers for me...

These were my final criteria:

- Our relationship must be comfortable and interesting, not strained;
- He must be well-to-do and have a comfortable lifestyle;
- He must accept my children;

- He has to be ready to take some active steps to develop our relationship — for example, to be ready to come to Russia to meet me.

The last point eliminated all the dreamers, as well as all addicts and loners. Not everybody can afford to buy an expensive ticket to Russia, so it eradicated low-income candidates automatically.

Looking back, I wish I had added to the column "necessary" the point that he had to have his own house, and better yet paid off already. To the point of high income I would add the word "stable" — high stable income. I didn't think about it, so we rent our house, and my husband's income seesaws from high to zero. So I got what I asked for, but I don't complain — anyway, even with of all these instabilities, we live comfortably.

Tom wrote me his first letter in May. From the very beginning everything went smooth. He wrote in detail, seriously, timely answering my questions, and when he saw my photo he said that he had ordered a ticket.

Those photos... I have to admit that I did it well. A good photographer shot two rolls of my portraits, printed the best, and then we doctored the very best a little bit more." [I've seen those photos — there she looks very different, more like a movie star from the 50s, gazing into the distance, dewy-eyed. A sexy jersey dress emphasizes her femininity and the posture is stylish and seductive, coquettish and soft. That Siberian photographer was a real master.]

I was corresponding with one interesting man from Arizona as well, but he could come to visit me only in four months because he didn't want to miss some important golf tournament in Hawaii. So I had to write him that I had reconciled with my ex-husband, sorry! Of course, I felt for him — he even sent me a parcel with a huge English dictionary, several calendars of Arizona scenic splendors and T-shirts for my children.

When I met Tom at the airport he didn't impress me — a short, stocky man, puffy after the flight, and I thought on the spot, Such a pity, he is not my type. He admitted later that I didn't impress him either — he didn't like my grey business suit (and I always thought that that suit looked great on me!). He told me on the spot that I don't look like my pictures. But what could he do if he had come that far already?

But the first moments went smoothly anyway, and everything was even better afterwards. We went on a bus tour to Tomsk to see the old architecture and visited the city festival (Tom liked it a lot because there were plenty of young beautiful girls in mini-skirts). We went to the excursion to the botanical gardens in Academgorodok. Everything was fun with him, even a trip to the grocery store. Right away he put on some incredible shorts since it was hot, hooked his camera onto some weird looking crimson shoulder strap and refused to dress more appropriately, like a typical conservative 40-some year old man would. He looked odd in our city where foreigners were rare birds...

On the tenth day of his visit we decided to get engaged and he went back to obtain a fiancée visa for me. We got it surprisingly fast, in a month; then I had to go to Moscow for the interview at the embassy and in the beginning of October my daughter and I came to America.

I was so stressed out with all the preparations and formalities that I lost ten pounds. I didn't nurture any hopes and expectations about my future life in America — I didn't have time even to think about it, though Tom brought me a nice calendar and photos of his children with a background of blooming rhododendrons. It looked like paradise, but I knew next to nothing about life in the USA.

My dream was to go back to France, frankly speaking, but all the Frenchmen who wrote me for some reason weren't considering marriage. I guess they were just fine, being single in their wonderful Paris.

I was married five months after the first contact with Tom. Counting from the moment when I came up with my "positive affixation," eight months had elapsed. Tom had never called me, it was his personal peculiarity. He didn't care how I sounded over the phone, and this was to my advantage because it was much easier for me to write than to speak. I didn't understand Americans in the beginning at all, and I was afraid to answer the phone. Though Tom always understood my English very well, other people had difficulties. But I spoke better and better since I had to practice every day.

Our wedding day was on December 26th. It was modest but nice, in his parents' house in Texas where we flew for that purpose. Seattle surprised me — there were so few skyscrapers and tall buildings, only in downtown, and the area around looked like a big village, adorned in blooming flowers. I was impressed with the beauty of nature and purity of air — I expected to see something like I saw on TV about New York — skyscrapers, industrial landscape, smog...

For the first nine months we lived on an island, in a huge exotic house that Tom rented for that special romantic time of the beginning of our life together. I remember how I walked alone on the sunny deserted beach for the first time, watching seagulls and gathering seashells — I couldn't believe that I didn't have to go to work and see the boring mean face of my elderly boss, Fillipich...

It was like a dream. Huge supermarkets, full of everything you can only dream about. I didn't even have to wash dishes — we had a dishwashing machine. Though for the first two months I couldn't believe that the machine could do a job better than me, and did the dishes by myself anyway. But once Tom checked the glass against the light and said that it had water streaks, which is inappropriate, and that I had to use the dishwashing machine. In a vengeful mood, I loaded all the glasses into the dishwasher, ready to prove that the machine couldn't possibly do it better than me. But, to my surprise, I unloaded sparkly crystal-clear glasses. Tom was right!

Our first American "romantic house" was really a summer house among the other summer dwellings, abandoned in winter. That house had lots of windows, and the bedroom was just a glassed porch. The ferocious oceanic wintry storms shook the walls, and I was constantly cold. We bought a long pink fleece nightie for me, and Tom playfully called me "my bunny."

It was much colder in that romantic house than in my warm condo in Siberia, yet Tom constantly turned down the temperature if I tried to raise it, so when he didn't see or when he wasn't at home, I raised it. The weather in winter was dreadful, damp and windy. It was raining all the time. I was always cold and wore a warm hat and gloves when outdoors, so I stood out against the locals, who drove cars and didn't wear hats.

For the first five months I was learning to drive, and as it turned out, it was a nightmare for me. Tom purchased for that purpose a fifteen-year-old car that stalled at intersections. All the instructions were given in English, and I couldn't react fast enough when I had to follow them. It irritated Tom — he couldn't understand why I still couldn't drive with confidence after I had learned all the rules and passed the written exam,. It was easy for him to say because he was behind the wheel almost all his life.

After I failed the driving exam for the fourth time, he made such a scene that I could only sob and think how I could get out of here as soon as possible.

I have to say that Tom has a quick temper, and when we had arguments, in the beginning I was upset easily. I understood what he was saying but couldn't find words to answer him in the same manner. Now I argue with him so skillfully that he prefers not to mess with me, so I got it, finally. It was a very valuable lesson for me, for my easy-going nature — finally to gain the ability to stand up for myself.

So after that notorious fourth exam, Tom found for me a driving instructor, a very calm elderly man, very religious and righteous, a father of five and a grandfather of numerous grandchildren. He reassured me that four failures are just nothing — he had clients that failed eight times, but he brought everybody to success.

After five hours of training — for the crazy price of $90 per hour — I passed that ill-fated exam. That was my great victory, the way to freedom from confinement in a house on the island.

That fall I started classes in the local community college, and the next June I started to work and made my own money. We also bought a better car for me. Of course, then I felt better and more optimistic.

In the beginning, we had some disagreements about the cooking. I spent a lot of time trying to surprise and please him with traditional Russian cuisine. He politely tried everything I had to offer, but decided that Russian cuisine is too high in calories and demanded that I cook and serve everything exactly like his mother, a model housewife. He constantly criticized me about what and how I cooked and served. "Here, in America, we remove the skin before frying chicken," or "This dish doesn't look appetizing at all and it doesn't have enough color," or, "What? I can't believe you're offering yesterday's leftover fish for today's breakfast!" He could announce a menu to me, "I would like you to cook eggs benedict with hollandaise sauce for breakfast and chicken cordon bleu for supper." After I made every effort to please him, he would presume to comment that hollandaise sauce from a package doesn't have the same taste as the one that his mother used to make from scratch. It angered me and I hinted that he'd better cut down on eating if he was concerned about his weight.

He didn't like almost any item from my wardrobe that I brought from Russia. He said it was too formal and I had to use a more casual style. I protested inwardly, since I thought it was my business what I wore, but eventually we threw away almost all of my clothes from Russia and changed my hairstyle, letting my hair grow longer and dying it dark chestnut, and instead of glasses I wear contacts now. Long dark hair and no glasses — that was his vision of me. Now and then he looks at me and says how much better I look now, compared with that moment when we first met...

Of course, during all that adaptation period I did feel some discomfort and inner resistance. I felt that I was some kind of substance in a syringe, and under enormous pressure I was being squeezed through a needle.

The transformation was hard, but as a result I can now cook many American, Mexican, and Spanish dishes, and serve them nicely and colorfully. I can drive, and do Internet banking, and do many other things I couldn't do when I was in Russia — for example, to operate all those machines in the house.

During all that adaptation period, I had only a few sad moments, and we can laugh at them now, four years later, still together...

I had many really happy moments. For example, I found out that notwithstanding the fact that Tom works long hours, he wants to spend all his free time with my daughter and me. He has an inexhaustible and very creative ability to invent something interesting, like long or short trips to interesting places, or outdoors adventures. He has good intuition about roadside restaurants and inns — where to eat and where to stay.

We often visited his friends and invited guests to our house, and he always did his share of preparation, deciding how much beer to buy or how much meat to marinate. We shared many interesting adventures, such as trips to nude beaches or to adult clubs.

As it happened, we both like nature. We went white-water rafting and downhill skiing, camping and bicycling, or just hiking in parks or reserves, most of the time in mountains.

I also like gardening, and Tom likes to relax on the porch amid my flowers. Once he helped me make and fertilize a big garden-bed along the fence, and all summer we had our own zucchini, cucumbers, tomatoes and even pumpkins. We got a big aquarium (his idea) and many houseplants, because we both like it.

I met all his friends and he met all mine, old and new. We try to avoid spending our time separately since his philosophy is that families that spend vacations together stay together. So we socialize as a family.

I still keep in touch with my old friends from Russia — many of them live now in other countries, especially my university friends, biochemists. But we communicate over the Internet and by phone, so I have never felt homesick. I read in Russian a lot, too.

When we lived in Seattle, we even had some kind of little Russian club, we met four families where the wives were from Russia. We visited each other, went to picnics. We are still in touch with one couple, they might come to visit us in our new place.

The definite cultural difference in the behavior of "my American," compared to a Russian man, is his desire to spend quality time with his family; he feels his responsibility as a breadwinner and he is a great father — he understands the importance of constant communication with children and fostering the right values. He always looks for feedback from me and wants me to do the same with him.

Of course, here I have compared my Russian and American husbands, so I realize that it might be more about personal experiences than about cultural differences, really.

And Tom also has a traditional view about household roles — that the husband earns money and the wife provides him comfort and helps to spend that money. He doesn't participate in "women's business" and doesn't help me with housework, absolutely. But if something breaks, he finds a repair specialist in no time.

He is extremely neat — he hates a mess. He isn't very romantic and doesn't bring me coffee in bed. He hates, by the way, Valentine's Day, and choosing and giving presents in general. But he takes his time to talk heart-to-heart and he can sometimes buy something for me that he likes, especially clothing items. He buys all his own clothes, from socks to suits, and he hates it when I give him a suggestion or if I give him a present."

* * *

To do her justice, I have to mention that Lena was for some time the bread-winner when Tom decided to quit his well-paid engineering job and go to school to study psychology — after all, she was a well-educated Russian biochemist. Lena e-mailed me a sequel to her story.

* * *

I realized lately that surprisingly many of my problems — for example, the absence of a place that I could call my permanent home and my feelings of helplessness in front of the dominating husband — have their roots in my childhood. I had a very authoritative mother, who often scolded me mercilessly, and for some reasons I often was sick — and usually I came down with bronchitis.

Some time ago, I had a case of acute bronchitis as well. It happened when I started to work on letting go of my old grudges, and I realized that it was especially important to abandon my complaints about my mother. I had read in one book that bronchitis is caused by deep bygones about ruining family ties and about deficiencies of one's "own territory." I started to meditate, feeling the bronchitis pain in my chest, and then I realized that it was a feeling of homelessness, lack of rights, and deep hurt.

Really, so often when my mother scolded me when I was a child, I thought that it would be so good if I could wander out, just such a pity that I had nowhere to go. And I had that feeling so often later on in my life. As one can say, what you have, it possesses you, too. So now I work on remembering those feelings, accepting them, blessing them, and letting them go.

I have to say that I started feeling better, and my bronchitis has eased up, though several days before nothing had helped, even antibiotics — I had felt horrible, with high fever and pain in the chest. I had felt strong antipathy toward the entire world.

Not long ago, using the same method, I got rid of a strong pain in the small of my back that I had for several months — that symptom was probably anger and hurt at the unjust derogation of my material cravings.

I believe that we create the situations that attract the partners that we need, so we'll have to work on some lessons that our soul has to endure in the course of our life.

So often Russian women, who were agonists at home, choose and create the same type of reality that they had in Russia. I witnessed it many times. That feeling of being a victim, just like a magnet, attracts insulting situations, and until she gets rid of that "victim mentality" she won't be able to change anything in her life.

* * *

Lena's 10-year-old Russian daughter Lana looked so much like Lena's American husband that one would think that he was her biological father. While I was talking to her mother, Lana played with Tom and then cozily curled up in his lap.

"Don't they spoil you at home!" I asked her light-heartedly. All of a sudden this soft kitten bristled and harshly answered in Russian, "Home is back in Russia, where my brother still is!"

Lena's ex-husband-programmer had insisted that their son could leave the country only if he went to the US, too, but Tom and Lena couldn't afford to help him out.

But despite all challenges they went through, Tom and Lena at that moment were still together thanks to her flexible nature that paired well with her husband's Pygmalion-type, dominating personality.

Both Lena and her husband pointed out that her perception of a typical Russian man is based on her personal experience. She is not judging Russian men in general.

Lena had a decent income in Russia, but for some reason was wonder-stricken with ordinary household amenities in their rental home in America. Perhaps she needed a strong spouse to overcome her disinclination to deal with all that "machinery." (Generally speaking, if a Soviet woman was an appreciative, starry-eyed consumer who valued even the simplest of material comforts very highly, it worked to her advantage and she was in her element in America. Settling down went smoother and easier, both for her and her American husband — of course, if he was supportive about her shopping joys.)

Lately, Tom has started accepting contracts to work in Europe — they have lived in Spain, where Lena didn't feel comfortable, and in Germany, where she liked the cuisine. Then in Italy — at that time, her daughter had to be sent back to Russia in order "not to grow up as a vagabond." After that, I lost contact with Lena.

BACK ON TRACK

It would be logical to expect that after a failed international marriage an American man would return to well-charted familiar domestic dating. But strangely enough, a good number of them do just the opposite. As if it is some kind of addiction.

A Russian newspaper quoted an American opinion, "In Russia, foreigners open a whole new world, and some of them become so charmed that they don't want to leave it. In that world, women cook breakfast after morning sex, understand that oral sex is obligatory, dress to show what they have, and don't expect you to take care of their careers. They clean and iron your clothes, they cook and buy you small presents. Leave alone the beauty of their bodies and souls. 'My foreign friend explained to me,' wrote a Russian journalist, 'that women from Russia, the Ukraine, and Byelorussia are valuable in the West, 'They are unassuming in meals, housing, and wardrobe.'"[1]

One American had barely sent his young proverbial blonde from Byelorussia packing when he was back on track, flying overseas for new candidates. Candidates seem plentiful, finding a replacement didn't appear to be a problem, and he knew his path to the source. Unfortunately for him, his new find fizzled even faster than the first. He tried to prove to me that all the good American women had already been snapped up, so the only decent possibility for him lies overseas. But it looked more like craving for an easy victory and that pleasant sensation of possessing an exotic trophy, to be a caliph again, even if just for a moment. Probably when an ordinary man all of a sudden discovers that he can be almost a guru for a respectful young woman, he gets used to that sense of stardom.

1 http://gazeta.aif.ru/online/aif/1269/09_01?print

Another American, freshly divorced from his Russian wife, shared this story.

* * *

I guess it's time to go back to an active search of a Russian wife. My marriage with my Beautiful Margo, as I called her, ended yesterday. In reality I made just a first step to a divorce, and before that I went through three months of pain. But I'm starting to feeling better, almost as optimistic as I felt before, though I am a notorious example of a man who became a victim of a female predator.

I spent about $100,000 in four years on Margo and her daughter, but after she got her 'green card' and I helped her to find a well-paid job, she started to talk about divorce. Maybe she started to show her intentions earlier, during her first year here, but I was so charmed that I couldn't even think that I could get into such trap.

When Margo started her confrontation, she told me that I was stupid for not wanting to accept a different way of living — she wanted to have extramarital affairs, telling me that it's not a big thing. But I said that it is against my beliefs and principles, that I couldn't do that. Actually, she was just looking for an excuse to start a divorce.

But now I refuse to keep my fingers crossed anymore — I'm a single man again and I want to find a Russian wife. I remain positive and optimistic and I hope that the majority of the women from the former Soviet Union are more suitable for marriage, especially considering their attitudes towards family values. I would be glad to address this simple message to Russian ladies: I would like to find a decent and loyal wife.

I hope that we'll have some common interests — ballroom dances, walks, weekends in the mountains, back and leg massages, early rising on weekends to attend church — all this is very important to me. The good looks of a woman will bewitch a person only for a month, and after that only the personality will matter, not the skin-deep beauty. I learned my lesson the hard way.

I am 58 years old and I have my own house and business in Washington State; I have a degree in business. I am at the same time short (5'3") and big (250 lb), with brown eyes. I hope somebody will be willing to contact me after all what I have written here.

* * *

There was an expression in Russian media lingo — "the letter called us to hit the road." This one certainly did — it was a perfect chance to check the realities of the story. It helped that the author of the letter had a Russian employee who assured me of my safety. But it was hard to prove to Peter that my interest was solely professional. When I asked for an interview, he sent me his photo and asked for mine. I explained that I didn't have any hidden agenda for our meeting so my looks were irrelevant. I could not believe that illogical hopes could be rooted so deeply in an otherwise smart head — he held a degree from a prestigious university.

At that time, he was already passionately flirting on-line with ladies from the former Soviet Union, sticking tiny red flags on the map where his *amies* lived, alluring those ladies with stories about his fervid desire to start a family, so his wounds could be healed.

"Don't those men see themselves in a mirror?" one Russian immigrant, female, used to say about cases like that. He was unfortunate to have a physical defect that he hid, posing for his Internet pictures, and he was obese.

Maybe he had a heart of gold? But as it turned out, he was short-tempered and moody — he dropped the mask of Mr. Charming when he discovered that I really did not have any matrimonial intentions. Walks in the mountains and the rest of those physical activities he described as very important to him seemed unlikely — the poor man could not walk around the block without panting. But he saw things the way he wanted to see them, or maybe he had just poetically crafted a model of an American family man to attract ladies.

As for money, his Beautiful Margo did not take away any of his property; even an old SUV he had purchased for her was locked in his garage. The home appliances were unbelievably ancient — somebody donated an antique VCR, one of the first models, with top-feed, and his half-broken cooker was born in the 1950s. The "almost $100,000" sum sure must look impressive for his new Russian lady-friends, but it turned out that his Russian family was really inexpensive — he spent, as it turned out, about $10,000 per capita per year, and even that sum is not the gospel-truth.

But as the saying goes, give one a fish, and he'll be fed for a day, teach one to fish, and he'll be fed for the rest of his life. At least he helped her to obtain a profession — in exchange for backrubs and leg massages for four years and her free labor for his company.

His Beautiful Margo definitely went through an ordeal, but I doubt she plunged into it blindly. It made me wonder if he could find yet another one willing to take her place.

RUSSIANS TALK

Russian psychologist Konstantin Surnov branded marriages to foreigners as misalliances, sacrifices, illusions, and mirages, predicting that none of the part-ners would achieve 100% of their goals in those marriages. I wonder how a psy-chologist could imply that such a task is achievable in *any* marriage? Surnov also foresaw unavoidable depression, cultural shock, and repatriation.[1]

Logically, all Russian men should be bitter about their countrywomen's de-sire to seek a partner abroad, but even on this point opinions are divided. One self-proclaimed "former Russian" posted this essay on a web-site that is popular among Russian women abroad, detonating an outburst of controversies.

> According to my observations, a serious male deficiency occurred in Russia. Otherwise why is the Internet so full of advertisements from Russian women of all ages and walks of lives who express their desire to start long-term relation-ships abroad? No wonder, there is always a shortage of something in Russia — this time it is a shortage of men. But where are we? We are in America, Israel, Europe, Australia, somebody drifted even to Africa — and it's not easy to find a Russian girl in Africa, I tell you!
>
> We have made our careers and started thinking about you, our dear ladies who were left behind. Why don't we dream about local beauties? Because we are used to you. You are akin, and frankly, you are more beautiful than all those Europeans and Americans. So we start looking for you, and what do you do? You write in your advertisements that you are fluent not only in Russian, but in Eng-lish, French, Spanish, even Greek. So I look bitterly at all those advertisements and think that you all finished universities and decided to find a job abroad as "personal secretaries" or "personal interpreters." It is good to be in command of a foreign language, of course. But that means that your advertisements are aimed not to us but to the foreigners, though we, your Russian men, are right here, and ready to take you under our wings.

---

1 Konstantin Surnov, "A i B sideli na u.e." *AiF Semeinii sovet*, # 3, 2003

One can study a foreign language in a year, that's not a problem. The problem is that some farmer from Iowa will marry you, and you will bear him five children, and your life will end up there. Americans are less social, they have a different mentality — they are not for you. So please, switch your priority and focus on us, your fellow-Russians, who live now hell knows where and who are ready to share love with you!

Robert.

The response was so emotional that the moderator of the website had to intervene with the explanation that Robert had added that he is happy in his personal life now, that the article was published as a personal opinion, and that everyone who desires to cast stones at Russian men abroad are welcome to the forum.

And so they did cast, since this Robert had hit upon a delicate subject — that is, the fiancée drain — and so the discussion seemed to unravel in surprising twists.

Nadya: "Where have you seen a successful single man, socially active, who would be willing to take a woman under his wing? That type is absent in Russia. We have an abundance of low-paid 'providers,' womanizers, drunkards, and those come in wide varieties. But nobody wants them. The successful, caring men with healthy lifestyles have an enormous choice of women, they don't even need the Internet to find their other halves. So no wonder our women try to find a deserving man abroad. It's out of despair, not because of materialism. And who are you looking for, picky Russian men, if such an abundance of single, beautiful, and deserving women surround you?"

Angela: "What a silly woman would desire to barter away Russia for an American redneck? I don't know any such fools. When have you been in Moscow last? I guess not lately, otherwise you would know that young purposeful girls, who are not spoiled by a Soviet 'spiritual' upbringing, are making meteoric careers. Try to offer them to marry a 'prosperous' Western man — they would take you for an idiot."

Christina: "So why are we seeking foreigners so foolishly, though every woman who married a foreigner knows that they are not compatible with our mentality and it doesn't even have any sense to try? And those Russian men who left us and their country — why are they looking for us? Probably because they realized that foreign women have high standards, so they don't have any choice but to start calling for us. Of course, our Russian men, if they are not drunkards or do not have a sexual fixation, always were and always will be better for us than any foreigner; but aren't they a little bit treacherous towards us?

"Why don't they change our country for the better, so Russian women wouldn't even have a desire to look for happiness somewhere else? Why do they ignore this dangerous tendency as if nothing serious is happening and the abundance of women in Russia is endless? Women of childbearing age are leaving our country in formidable quantities and going someplace else where they are, more often than not, unhappy as well. The demographical situation in Russia is critical already, but it looks like for Robert and others that that doesn't matter. It's sad, gentlemen — the Russian nation is disappearing."

Olga: "There has been a shortage of men in all countries and at all times. I mean men who could support and protect their women. But it doesn't mean that those men who left Russia at times that were critical for the country are the men women would dream about."

Alexander: "Look, they are mad at Russian men! Well, ladies, you'll remember your Russian men once you are abroad, that's for sure!"

Anastasia: "Interesting, why do you think that a Russian woman, given a choice, would prefer a Russian man? I don't think so. Americans, especially the intelligent ones, will give a Russian man a 100-point handicap in the spheres of devotedness, orientation on family values and respect toward a woman."

Svetlana: "Some women have married a foreigner and live in Western countries — we married Russians and live in Europe. To each his own, so to speak. You shouldn't smear Russian men's reputation, it doesn't make you look good. I wish every woman happiness."

Larissa: "Everybody is so different — somebody might be happier with a foreigner than with a fellow countryman, but somebody needs an enigmatic Russian soul nearby. I belong to the second category, and I met my man, whom I loved from the very beginning of our communication, via the Internet. He happened to live in America, but he didn't tell me that right away — he was afraid that I would jump at the bait. But I don't care where we are going to live — in Russia, in America, or somewhere else. The most important thing for me is to live with him. So seek and ye shall find."

Nina: "I suffer with my foreign husband; it is deadly dull here. They don't talk about serious issues, their humor and outlook on life is different; and they are so greedy! No wonder that the tensions and difficulties in the international families rise from misunderstanding. I am looking for a Russian who would be much closer to my soul and body. Once I find him, I'll get the hell out of here, from this artificial life."

Olga: "Why do they jump into marriage abroad, and then cry that everything is so different there? We always act like that: first we do something, then we consider whether we should have done it in the first place."

Oxana: "Our women dream of bringing to the altar of family life abroad their unclaimed capacity for love... And the legend about the exceptional qualities of foreign men and their zest for Russian women work against Russian women's patriotism. So they set out on quest for their soul mates, traveling all around the world."

Alla: "I wonder why some women even bother to look for a supposedly prosperous foreign man? Russian men and their spouses travel abroad often, and there we meet our former compatriots who usually work as servants. When we were in Toronto, I felt at home because the Russian language was spoken all around us at the hotel. Almost all of the maids were from Russia, Moldova, and Ukraine. And they were brimming with happiness and almost wet themselves just because they lived in Canada."

Kira: "Women with higher education, with children, are those who decide to marry a foreigner. For Americans, the fact that you already have a child by another man is not such a huge defect as it is for a Russian man. So we, beautiful and educated, whose first marriage failed, now have a good opportunity to realize ourselves in a new marriage, without fear for the future of our children. Spiteful people may vituperate against us as much as they wish, we simply don't care. Some people are happy in Russia, some people are happy abroad, and why bother with hatred? All the stupid women in crude, sexy clothes are gone, so those who are left behind can enjoy life and relax."

Maria: "A Western woman, more likely, would take the expression 'my husband is my protector' as an abuse — they are used to being independent. But we are not Western, we are Russian, and we are used to be protected by our husbands, so we don't care about opinions of local women. They are all self-sufficient and lonely; they are waiting for their princes and spend their lonely nights doing you know what, while we peacefully sleep with our foreign 'losers,' who are pretty satisfied with their sexual life. If happiness equals soul comfort, than we are happy!"

Rita: "Why blame a woman for longing to see her children happy and for her desire to live a happy, quiet life? I think that the main problem is that our women don't want to do anything upon arrival. If she is successful in her marriage, she doesn't bother to study the language, make friends, find new interests — she is married, and she thinks that's enough. When she finally starts looking for job, she discovers that she has to choose between the careers of a waitress or a cleaning lady. So I would recommend everybody who is preparing to leave for the West: don't dash off sightseeing upon arrival, but study and get to work, because only the work experience that you have abroad is important for your future life."

Natasha: "I wonder why nobody says a word about love? Or do you suppose that it is non-existent in international marriages? I live with him because I love him."

Sergey: "I would call this "Russian Wives" phenomenon a romantic suicide. I know about those situations, both in negative and positive versions. It's very, very sad, and the problem is mostly psychological, much less social. Nobody should be held responsible for the ladies' decisions. I wish each of them a nice new life in a new place, just please, don't renounce your heritage — never ever. The Russian nation is a great nation, and will remain so, no matter what."

Victor: "Why argue about obvious matters? Emigrants, by their nature, are people with weak will. Most often, infantile cream puffs who seek help and support. The real women stayed in Russia and became millionaires, or gained political power. The same is applicable to men. A normal man won't run from his land in trying times, he will turn even the most challenging situation for his benefit, gaining profit. As saying goes, 'put a Russian man in the taiga — he will take a hatchet and make a home for himself.' No wonder we have so many millionaires now.

"The same could be said about women. Even before, not so many women were willing to live in their husband's house, with their mothers-in-law and in-laws. And here the deal is even harder — foreign wives live not just in strange houses, in strange lands, with unfamiliar people, but as dependents on a man who is practically a stranger as well. Normal women would not tolerate that. But immigrants will, since immigrants are not human beings — 'immigrant' is a diagnosis."

Marina: "Everybody has his or her own destiny, but nobody leaves a perfect life and a beloved husband. Those leave who continue to believe in happy endings and love, who are not afraid to start over... We mothers know how difficult that is. I admire those who decide to emigrate."

Nicolay: "In my area, I see many wealthy and decent Western men who appreciate Russian women's mentality and their beauty — including their inner beauty. This is why I am a little bit afraid for my wife and feel pangs of jealousy sometimes."

Sonya: "I chatted with an American on the Net. Then he started to call me. But somehow I didn't like him, and so I decided to scare him away: I told him that all the men here are alcoholics, that I don't have enough money for food and clothes, and I mentioned also my two university diplomas. He started sending me flowers, called me every other day, then came to visit and finally so annoyed me with his love that I had to marry him."

Grigory: "I was very cautious about 'Russian wives.' But when it comes to middle-aged women, I agree that probably they have serious grounds for seeking happiness abroad. I always thought that only 'men with defects' were looking for Russian women, but here I got a surprise: my 40-year-old colleague who doesn't look bad at all, has never been married, has a good job and owns a house, doesn't drink or smoke, announced that he wants to marry a Russian woman.

"I was shocked. As it happened, he posted his ad in the Internet and got an overwhelming number of responses from women of all ages. He chose a 35-year-old nurse from Siberia who had an 11-year-old daughter. He went to meet her in person: he visited Moscow, St. Petersburg, and, of course, her Siberian town. I was surprised when he decided to go to Russia all by himself, and he told me that he didn't want to depend on anybody. And look what it was in reality!

"I asked him why he needs a Russian woman when there are so many available women here, and he just laughed and said that he wants one just like my wife, but unfortunately she is married already, so he decided to go directly to the source.

"His lady-friend is coming here with her daughter to stay for a month and to see how it is here. My friend's mother is absolutely happy, she's even started taking Russian lessons. He is eager, of course, too, though financially it is not easy for him — he has to save every penny since he's paying for everything, including her taxi fare in Russia, and he isn't wealthy at all.

"The woman, by the way, is not a beauty, but seems to be a very nice person as I gathered from our phone conversation (my friend asked me to help to clarify something for her, since she hardly speaks any English). So I asked her what she thinks about all this and she said that he is well-mannered, not bad looking, kind, neat, and non-drinking — how could she not fall in love with such a fine man? She said that she wants to bear a son for him. She thought that she was doomed to spend the rest of her time alone because who would marry her, almost 40 years old, with a child, in her Siberian town? He was a miracle for her, a knight on a white horse. He even likes her daughter — he found out everything about the schooling situation already. She said that hopefully they will be able to afford a decent life because she intends to work, as nurses are always in demand. And she found it so touching that her future mother-in-law is studying Russian words and forcing her son to renovate his house to welcome his fiancée.

"Who knows how it will go. But I think that an average man here, as husband and father, is much better than a Russian. And as far as wealth — that's relative, right?"

* * *

Interesting how all these often antipodal opinions prove that the truth can be conflicting — just like life itself. When black-and-white opinions collide, half-tones and patterns of light and shade emerge, bringing the spectrum more close to the reality. The happy ones are right, the bitter ones have their grains of truth that are harder to digest, and, of course, no one has the right to strip incorrigible optimists of their banner of hope.

RESURRECTION KILLED

"Mail-Order Bride's Dream of a Better Life Ends in Death," the *Seattle Post-Intelligencer* headlined, summarizing Anastasia Solovieva's dire destiny.

Anastasia Solovieva was a teenager, just 18, and lived with her family in Bishkek, capital of Kirghizia, when her mother, Alevtina Solovieva, advertised her daughter on a marriage agency's site. She explained, "Anastasia was an A-student and deserved to see more than just Bishkek."[1]

Anastasia had a relative married to a German, and Anastasia's mother was determined to match her ambitious girl to an American man. The ad stated that Anastasia loved classical music — she graduated from a musical school, just like both her parents — and dreamed about having a family and a baby.

"Anastasia King is white, 5 feet 7 inches tall, 150 pounds, with bleached blond hair and green eyes. She has been known to dye her hair red or black." This was posted two years later, and not on a matchmaking site but on a missing person leaflet.

At that time, Anastasia lived in suburban of Seattle and was indeed married to an American, to 39-year-old Indle King, white, 5 feet 7 inches tall, 270 pounds, bald and obese, and twenty years her senior. But as a Russian journalist pointed out, during his first courtship trip to Bishkek "Indle King had to win not Anastasia's heart but her mother's, who already liked him because of his American

---

1 Mikhail Fainshtein

passport."[1] He seemed to be well-to-do. His father was CEO of a leading industrial-design firm, and his mother, Rosalie, 63, was an art professor."[2]

The man certainly was from a good, wealthy family in a prestigious area of Seattle. He wanted a baby, and though Anastasia's ad mentioned that she was dreaming about having a child, conceiving a baby with King wasn't on her agenda. King needed a baby — he hoped that would improve his relationship with his family and assure his inheritance rights. He announced that he would provide university tuition for Anastasia if only they got married. Practical Anastasia chose the most expensive and highly-regarded courses at the University of Washington Business Management program, and agreed to marry King after living with him and his parents for a month in a spacious house on Mercer Island. Then Indle King's parents bought a large house for the couple in Mountlake Terrace.

"If you are successful, you are respected. Nobody likes losers," Anastasia wrote to her parents. But she married a man who had failed in his professional life and worked as an unskilled labor. At times, he evidently felt desperate — he was caught stealing fruit and soda from a store.

Earlier, when he still held an adjunct professorship, teaching international business and marketing courses at Antioch University, a small college in Yellow Springs, Ohio, he brought his Russian bride to his class one day, evidently proud of his "5-foot 9-inch tall [beauty] with porcelain skin and long, dark hair"[3] — that was his first Russian bride, Ekaterina Kazakova.

> Ekaterina said [that] she went to Ohio as an exchange student, eager to study biology [...]. She had seen a notice in the *Moscow News* announcing an opportunity to study in the United States. She answered it and began [corresponding] with King, who had placed the ad. In September 1993, Kazakova agreed to come to the US as a visiting student [and] King's guest. Within weeks of arriving, King proposed, explaining [that] the only way for her to remain in the United States was to marry him.
>
> After consulting her parents, who lived in the Siberian city of Omsk, and learning [that] they approved of the match, she accepted King's proposal.[4]

Ekaterina Kazakova, just like Anastasia Solovieva, was dreaming of a life in America, and King, after his extensive traveling to Russia in 1990s, developed a passion for Russian culture — and Russian beauties. King's and Kazakova's interests intersected, but their marriage didn't last.

> In December 1995, according to Ohio court records, Kazakova alleged that King "hit her in the head with his fist [...], threw her head against the wall and continuously pounded [her] head against the wall."
>
> She filed for a protection order, alleging that King had warned her [that] "he would find her and kill her if she tried to leave him....The two divorced in

---

1 Ibid.
2 Lewis Kamb and Robert L. Jamieson Jr., "Mail-order bride's dream of a better life ends in death," *Seattle Post-Intelligencer*, February 2, 2001
3 Lewis Kamb and Robert L. Jamieson
4 Anne Koch, "First wife tells of rages, threats," *Seattle Times*

1997, and King... returned to the Northwest.... He later took a warehouse job at Costco.[1]

Anastasia wrote in her diary that King urged her to contact his ex-wife's friend in order to find out the addresses of Ekaterina Kazakova and her parents so he could kill them. He tried to find a hit man, alleged Anastasia. He threatened her with death, also — and with throwing her out of the country. He was already working on a back-up project, corresponding with other women from Russia and the Philippines, looking for a new wife.

Somehow, the Solovievs didn't take the threats seriously, even though they knew very well that King was violent. Alevtina Solovieva stated, "He punched [Anastasia's] face teaching her to drive a car. Perhaps she was doing something wrong, or did it in a way that he found inappropriate, but he punched her jaw, as she wrote us. Then we realized: this is it, this is a tragedy. But anyway I had that dream — to remain in America," said Alevtina, "This is the tragedy, you see."[2]

That was the tragedy, literally — Anastasia's parents knew that her husband abused her physically and sexually, but they harbored the dream anyway, "to hold onto America," as Alevtina put it. To hold on like grim death.

Anastasia wrote in her diary, "On the fourth day after our wedding we had a big fight and he broke the door to our bedroom down. Then I understood that our marriage was a mistake." Several months later, police responded to a domestic violence call from the Kings' house.

Why did he kill Anastasia instead of just divorcing her? This question haunted me, and since I couldn't ask King, I asked Charles Blackman, a deputy prosecutor of Snohomish County, who speaks Russian and who benevolently helped the Solovievs in court as a translator.

"What was the motive of the crime? Did he kill her out of jealousy?"

"A Russian journalist asked me the same question before," said Blackman. That journalist was Mikhail Fainshtein, who reasoned in his documentary that Indle King did not want to divide his property.

"I think King didn't want to be humiliated again," said Blackman. King was extremely angry that Ekaterina Kazakova had divorced him after she obtained her permanent resident status.

When he showed up in Bishkek to bring Anastasia back to the US after her trip home, he told her parents that their daughter was a poor wife. "He also allegedly showed a photograph of Anastasia King with a young man in Las Vegas and demanded an explanation from her father, Anatoliy Soloviev .... King does not speak Russian and Soloviev does not speak English, so the pair used a translation dictionary and hand gestures to communicate."[3]

---

1 Lewis Kamb and Robert L. Jamieson
2 Mikhail Fainshtein
3 Scott North, "Court papers detail Anastasia King's bizarre final days," *The Herald*

But what was King trying to prove — that the Solovievs had failed to keep their word and didn't provide their part of the deal? They couldn't very well inform him that he was just a stepping stone, that "Anastasia told her parents that she planned to get her degree and green card — and then a divorce."[1]

But she also "made comments about having to stay in Bishkek, and how that would not be any worse than her life with Indle King Jr., and that she would rather lose her green card than stay married to and continue suffering with such a man."[2] Unfortunately, the Solovievs decided against it.

On a videotape from Bishkek, she is dancing in her parents' house with King, and when he sings, "I love my wife, she is so beautiful!" Anastasia obediently answers, "I love you too," returning the kiss.

She wrote in her journal that she despised intimate contact with King and confided about secret meetings with other men, which King started to suspect. In her last e-mail to her friend Tatyana Boland, which she sent from Kyrgyzstan on September 19, Anastasia wrote, "[King] knows everything."[3]

Her last day in Bishkek — September 21, 2000 — was bizarre. The situation was so tense that King "allegedly chased his wife down a street after she and her mother climbed into a taxicab to go shopping. [King and Anastasia] had briefly visited a disco. Indle King came home angry, documents indicate. Anastasia explained to her parents that many of the men at the disco were approaching her and asking her to dance. She would respond to them that she was with her husband. Indle did not step up or make it obvious in any way that he and Anastasia were married. Instead, he just looked at her with anger and jealousy, and left the club, forcing her to chase him to get a ride home."[4]

It's hard to imagine a discotheque as a place that King would like to visit, especially right before a long trip, but he videotaped his young wife enjoying herself, dancing in a skin-tight pantsuit on a podium. That night, Anastasia had her last dance. She disappeared upon arrival in the US.

Under oath, King lied to authorities that he had tried unsuccessfully to reach his wife; that he didn't know of Anastasia's whereabouts; that they had an argument and she stayed in Moscow and he flew to the US alone. He claimed that Anastasia must have been hiding because she didn't want to be served with divorce papers which could result in her deportation by immigration officials. He said he couldn't reach her parents in Bishkek, either.

Such easily disproven statements are odd in themselves. Phone records showed that he placed several calls to Bishkek, some quite lengthy. The passenger list proved that they were both aboard the same flight, and customs records stated that they cleared US customs just a minute apart. Very quickly police

---

1 Thomas Fields-Meyer, Keith Raether in Seattle, "Broken Vows," *People* magazine.
2 Scott North
3 Lewis Kamb and Robert L. Jamieson
4 Scott North

found a cab driver who remembered taking the couple from the SeaTac airport to Mountlake Terrace. Obviously, King was lying — but Anastasia was not found.

"Do you know how the missing person case turned into a murder case?" Charlie Blackman asked me. "Mountlake Terrace police, detectives Julie Jamison, Craig McCaul, and their colleagues learned that King was visiting the Snohomish County jail on a regular basis coming to see his former tenant Daniel Larson, who had rented a room in the Kings' home and was arrested for an attempt to have sex with a 16-year-old Ukrainian girl in an Alderwood Mall restroom. Sometimes King even caused disturbances being late to his meetings with Larson but still demanding that he must be given an entire hour."

Daniel Larson became a convicted sex offender at age sixteen for raping his teenage stepbrothers. Larson stated that he and King were lovers and Anastasia had found them out.

The police "used their methods," as Charlie Blackman put it — and Larson disclosed where Anastasia's body was buried, but "he said that it was King who had strangled her. Later Larson changed his story and said that he had to kill Anastasia because King threatened to kill him."[1]

"The news of her death and the manner in which she died was so devastating, her parents couldn't bring themselves to call relatives and tell them."[2]

"Her mother asks God why he took Anastasia away," says a newspaper article, but I don't quite understand why that question should be addressed to God.

Indle King was given the maximum sentence — about 29 years in prison. To Larson's prison time, two concurrent sentences for his attacks on jail guards were also added.

The parents were brought over from Kyrgyzstan to Snohomish County at public expense to assist police and prosecutors investigating Anastasia King's killing. As Blackman clarified, "At that moment, the prosecution thought that they were important witnesses in this case."

"The elderly couple .... [was] angry and bitter over their daughter's slaying.... When we first met them, it was such a stone-cold look of distrust," Deputy Prosecutor Jim Townsend recalled.[3]

But soon they realized that Anastasia was considered not "just a mail-order bride" who was trying to hold onto America at any price but a victim of a terrible crime, and that they, the Solovievs, were being greeted not as parents whose aspirations and calculations had put their daughter in the grave but as a grief-stricken couple who had lost their only child. In January 2001 Alevtina told newspapers that she didn't even want to come to the US — her friends had prompted her to go and "defend our Nastya." But in a few days after the Solovievs' arrival, the

---

1 From "Amerikanskie slezi russkikh zen," police video
2 Anne Koch
3 Scott North, "Indle King Jr.'s alleged accomplice pleads guilty," *The Herald*

Seattle Post-Intelligencer announced, "Parents of slain mail-order bride want to stay here: her grave would be center of their lives, Kyrgyz couple insist[s]."

The Solovievs called a press conference and pleaded with the US government to allow them to remain in the US. And although immigration law does not clearly provide for such relief, the authorities met the Solovievs' demand to "find a way to permit us to live out the remainder of our days here, with our daughter, who perished here, next to her grave."

"In the process of making plans to bury their daughter more than 6,000 miles from where she was born, they now say they want to live where her dreams died," journalists wrote,[1] Anastasia Solovieva was able to bring her parents to the US, now they live in Snohomish County.

Ironically, Anastasia's name means "resurrection."

* * *

When I was writing up this story, not far from Mountlake Terrace where Anastasia was killed, I witnessed a symbolic episode that didn't have much to do with human desires and illusions but spoke volumes about primordial reactions to danger.

In the unfinished outdoor barbeque next to my writing table I discovered a raccoon family — a mother and three pups. The mama-raccoon was not aware that their hiding place had been discovered until once, peaking in, I was not fast enough to back up. Our eyes met. At that instant, I knew that she would relocate the pups, and so she did — immediately, right in the middle of the day.

Being just a raccoon, she couldn't comprehend that she had an expensive designer "burrow" in a prestigious neighborhood. She didn't even consider that these humans had been harmless so far. Her pups might be in danger, and that was the most important thing to her. Her feelings were simple — she was just a raccoon.

"THAT'S LIFE"

Once on a plane to New York I was sitting next to a Russian–American couple. Irina introduced herself as a Muscovite, an artist by trade. She admitted that she misses Old World and assured me that her husband would support her decision to relocate should she choose to do so.

"He'll do what I ask him to do," Irina said proudly.

At the same time, her husband was also talking, quite loudly and slightly drunkenly. "Take your damn purse." He thrust Irina's handbag in her lap, "And forget about all that courtesy shit, you're not in your Russia anymore — don't expect it from me now!" That was a shocking revelation of how reality can collide with desires.

---

1 David Fisher and Robert Jamieson Jr., "Parents of slain mail-order bride want to stay here. Her grave would be center of their lives, Kyrgyz couple insist." *Seattle Post-Intelligencer*, February 9, 2001,

The following snapshots of Russian wives' stories may sound far-fetched, but one has to keep in mind that it is quite possible if you consider that these men took advantage of the naivety of their wives, the women's poor command of English and limited knowledge of the Western world, and their dependency on their husbands for social acclimatization.

A trustworthy man named Paul explained to his neighbors that he was harboring a poor refugee who had worked for the US government in Soviet Russia and had to flee because of fear of retaliation. The neighbors had no idea that she was, actually, his wife. Only when the man suddenly died did the widow discover that the "classified documents" in his computer were nothing but his sexually charged correspondence with women from the Eastern bloc whom he visited on frequent "business trips." The widow even heard from her husband's lover from the neighborhood — the woman was upset that her calls were not returned.

Another alien wife was sitting in an apartment in Alaska, dutifully waiting for her husband to come home after his "secret service duties." Those "duties" left him zonked out on regular basis, but somehow she hadn't come to doubt his legend yet. "And she had [been left with] only ketchup and coke in the fridge when I met her," said a Russian woman-immigrant about that "wife of an emissary."

Nina, a quiet middle-aged woman, became so involved with her long-distance relationship with an American that she was crushed when she received the devastating news of the man's death in a car accident right before their first meeting in person. She wanted to know the details. "I was told that no such person lived at that address, that no such person existed at all, any more than did his "business partner" who had broken the tragic news to me, but that in a small town nearby there was a man who matched the description, though his name is Gary M. Lockman, not Harry M. Lockman. I was also told that no fatal car accidents had been reported at that time at that place. I felt a huge relief — it was better to know that the man had betrayed me than to think that he was dead." Even the fact that "the love of her life" was constantly asking for her nude pictures hadn't put her off.

For a good-looking interpreter from St. Petersburg the "love story" started with an exchange of instant messages with a yachtsman who was traveling through Russia collecting material for his book. The Westerner had an appealing sense of humor, a macho demeanor, the irresistible looks of a romantic pirate, and a villa on an island where his fifteen Shar Pei dogs lived. Those "wrinkled doggies" just melted the woman's heart. Conveniently, the tanned globetrotter happened to be in town and so they met. The very next day, the decisive man asked her to marry him. He was sure that the lady was the love of his life, but at the moment he desperately needed some money to tide him over a rough spot. You can guess how that story ended.

So the traditional image of one-way cons, when Western men are shaken down by Slavic beauties looking for a magic carpet, is not true anymore. Russian women can consult a website that collects information about international marriage racketeers — that macho-pirate was on the list.

The cunning methods that women use, luring overseas princes into matrimonial alliances, might be as old as time: Mark couldn't imagine any alternative to marriage when his lady-friend from a former Soviet republic refused to abort an unexpected — at least for him — pregnancy. "I've made my bed — I have to lie in it," said another gentleman, a devoted Lutheran. Women are quick to discover that this old trick works especially well with religious men, but shotgun marriages do not always end "happily ever after."

The "pregnancy trap" is not a trick exclusive to the female arsenal — Elvira decided to stay in the US illegally, hoping that her boyfriend would finally obtain his divorce, and in a short time she was expecting. The man said he wanted to get a Russian girl to help them with the baby — and so he got a Russian bride. Then he explained that in order to tie down the helper, he'd have to impregnate her as well because "Russians don't leave their children."

Russian girls who come to the US on student visas and later decide to stay illegally often put themselves into situations that evolve from bad to worse. I met a soon-to-be-graduate who was modeling for adult magazines while desperately searching for an American husband. She even offered to pay rent for a family nest and promised a signing bonus.

Often women say that they have to compromise for the sake of their children. A Ukrainian, Ludmila, said that she married an American because she wanted to spare her young daughter a life of hardship in her motherland. But in America, her daughter didn't even have a room and slept in the hallway. She woke her mother up one night with a strange question, "Mom, what are they doing? They sound scary..." As it turned out, Ludmila's stepdaughter and stepson often shared a bed and a shower, but her husband declined to question their behavior, fearing that his college-age children could carry out the threat to move to his ex-wife's home. So Ludmila's young daughter, saved from presumed potential hardships, was exposed to unorthodox sexual habits instead.

A grown-up daughter told another Ukrainian woman she should sit tight and endure an unhappy union with her sloppy American husband in case the daughter herself decided to move to America one day. Meanwhile, juggling two lovers and trying to marry a Westerner, the daughter was living in luxury and idleness in her homeland.

Men's quests for love in Eastern Europe often involve strategies that mercilessly cast out women whose assets fail to match the men's requirements precisely. One hard-core romantic put his prospective fiancées on a comparison chart: he appraised the women's teeth, busts, sexual activity, etc. I wonder how he calculated coefficients — for example, a great bosom and costly bad teeth versus hot sexual temperament and a flat chest?

Another suitor noted that he didn't even want "clouds of physical chemistry to muck up the reasoning." One female candidate survived a campaign trail that included more than twenty checkpoints, and the man said he was happy with the meticulously calculated outcome.

A simpler man discovered that, though he was an exotic foreigner in Russia, in his motherland his appeal went down: "My wife is from the '*intelligenzia* class' (there were three social classes in Soviet Russia: working class, peasantry, and *intelligenzia* — the most sophisticated and educated class, with high cultural traditions, etc.) and I am a simple man with simple needs. She always wants more intellectually, spiritually, materially — and sexually. Today she asked me if I was a gay... I am ashamed that I cannot make a woman happy."

Sometimes those marriages combine individuals with poorly-matched habits and tastes: Lisa was very social, but Dan was a homebody. Once, when they were hosting a party and Lisa was singing a patriotic Russian song — each verse in a different key — Dan brought a recorder and started to tape.

"That's for my colleagues," he explained, "They pester me all the time, asking how it feels to be married to a foreign lady, so I'll show them how lovely my wife sings *before* drinking."

Marina, a young plump Ukrainian, was much younger than Tim. The man was a quiz lover, and sometimes he nonplussed his young wife with difficult questions, such as how many states there are in the US.

"I don't know, I'm si-illy!" Marina chirped playfully. But she wisely learned some encouraging English phases that she rehearsed when meeting with other Russian–American couples, "Tim is good. I love him very much. In the Ukraine, everybody liked Tim."

"Tell them what your mother said about me," Tim suggested.

"What?" Marina didn't understand and asked for help. The Americans hid their smiles behind the cocktail glasses.

"That's life," as Frank Sinatra sang — somebody's life in their new homeland.

STORYBOOK ENDINGS

Never should a man deny simple treats for a Russian lady's children, as Anna's first American husband did. Little wonder that Anna told her Scrooge that she was planning to spend a month in Russia visiting her family. And to Russia she and her daughters went, but just for a week, and when they returned it wasn't her husband but her friend John who met them at the airport. He took a vacation to get to know her and her children better and the four of them plus a parrot plunged right into a trip through California, crammed into his small camper. Since then, they have been together, and blissfully happy but for one moment: an immigration lawyer suggested indicating in Anna's "green card" forms that her ex-husband was the valid one, because "they won't check." As a result, Anna received a deportation warning that the lawyer offered just to toss out.

"How can I leave John?" asked Anna, hugging her tall husband, who looked at his new family of three willowy blonde beauties with the smug smile of a happy tomcat, almost purring with pleasure of being blessed with such loving surroundings.

Ludmila and Craig were pen pals for ten years. In Russia, she taught French in a famous center of learning, "Life there was so suffocating," Ludmila complained, nonetheless. "It was such a backwater!"

In America, she resides in the middle of nowhere in the rural South — and seems to be absolutely happy.

"I didn't have a boyfriend or a family in Russia," she explained, "and here I've got step-grandchildren and absolutely love it. This is my home, I am in the clouds, and my husband provides for us."

Even "computer geeks" can be happy, too. Silicon Valley inhabitant Mike said about his Ukrainian wife, "I expected her to cry with joy when she stepped into my big house, but her first words were, 'Who is going to clean all this space?'"

Olga remembers that moment too, "The rooms were empty except for the computers and wires snaking everywhere."

Now they use all the space: they gave birth to twins, so Olga's daughter got two brothers, and Olga's parents come to visit often. Mike is rightfully proud of his new family.

Almost everything in this world has been seen before. Arina reminds me of Natasha Rostova from *War and Peace* — not Rostova at her first ball but Rostova the married woman who didn't care anymore about her looks. "Maybe my destiny is to get plump and bear children," laughs Arina. She doesn't have a chance to muse about Rostova, guaranteed, since she bore three children in America in the course of five years.

In her Siberian town, she was an accountant at a large bank and a member of a local American Baptist mission. When she came with a church group to the US, a Ukrainian immigrant became her personal guide: he drove her around and finally invited her to spend a week at the beach. The age difference didn't discourage him; she was only five years his senior.

Arina commented, "That's much better than to have a husband who is twenty years older, as many Russian girls here do. At thirty and fifty, interests and energy levels are very different."

She didn't doubt her husband's reliability — otherwise she wouldn't have borne three children — but she was thinking about relocating. "My visiting aunt told me how wealthy people live in Russia now, so I've started thinking about going back." She couldn't adjust to American friendships. "I asked an acquaintance, also a Russian immigrant, an eye doctor, to stop by and check my baby's eye — she didn't promise anything, and of course, never showed up."

Her cleaning lady job earned her ten dollars per hour. "I clean rich houses. They are in good shape since I clean them every week, but still, it doesn't feel right."

NEEDLE IN A HAYSTACK

Alevtina had a very bitter family life experience in Russia. She married her first love at age eighteen, and a year later gave birth to a daughter. Her husband begged for a son, and when she graduated from the university she got pregnant again. However, just a couple of months before her due date her husband announced that he didn't want a son anymore, nor his daughter or wife.

"Everybody felt sorry for me — I was left with two young children, in a post-Soviet country. Our life wasn't easy, to say the least. But I decided to look for my chance in the place where healthy, good-looking children aren't considered a burden but are appreciated. I put my ad on a marriage site and received many letters — too many. The men were old and young, from all corners of the world. But my James was the only one who couldn't have children. I liked that — it meant that my kids will be our only children.

"But in America, I detected familiar symptoms. James said it was because I was exposed to a new climate and food, but I talked him into taking me to a doctor. Certainly, I was pregnant. We had tests together, and it was discovered that we have an ideal physical compatibility — my husband *could* father children, as the doctors finally determined, but only with an ideal partner, and his chances of finding one were slim, almost unreal.

"My husband was very glad to father a boy. He was the only child, and in their family the middle name LeRoy was traditionally transferred from generation to generation. Thanks to me, the family got the chance to keep this tradition.

"In December 1999, Andrew was born, and my in-laws were amazed how much he looked just like James when he was a baby. I was afraid that after the birth of our boy there would be a shift in attitude toward the children, but that didn't happen — James treats all the kids as his own. They are all our children, they are all Larsons, they are all Americans, and they speak unaccented English. Such a pity that they started forgetting Russian and now barely speak it at all.

"My husband and I have a substantial age difference, but it doesn't bother me — though my husband used to say that it would be better if I were at least a decade older than I am. I responded that I didn't make a secret of my age when he married me. Now, when we have lived together for some time, when the children love him as a father and he loves them, when our baby Andrew cemented the family even more — I think James finally realized that my feelings toward him are deep. I think he feels secure now."

Tolstoy was so right — happy families are all alike, and Russian–American unions are no exception.

Bridges and Dividers

Just as an ocean could be considered as a divider by a Bedouin and as a connector by a seafarer, the intercultural differences can divide or connect. Depending on one's personal view, they can be irresistibly attractive or utterly irritating.

Now, when intercultural relations are becoming more challenging, some Americans consider massive immigration not a stirring of the proverbial "melting pot" but a dangerous overflow. But personal likes and dislikes aside, isolation is impossible in the modern world.

Newcomers possess what Bill Moyers described as "'the outsider's impatience, the gritty resolve to storm the barricades and triumph from within.' They bring what I'll call newcomer's zest, an initial drive to succeed that consists of hope, ambition, and trust."[1]

Newcomers have to invest all of their efforts and thoughts in achieving success in their new homeland, without looking back. As Jack London wrote in one of his letters, "When a man journeys into a far country, he must be prepared to forget many things he has learned, he must abandon the old ideals and the old gods and often times he must reverse the very codes by which his conduct has hitherto been shaped."[2]

If newcomers really plan to remain in this country, then sitting on the edge of the chair is dangerous, though understandable — even if life in the native country might have been difficult, it was home, with all feelings, roots, and memories that belong there, and some newcomers' hearts will never follow their relocated bodies.

---

1 Mary Pipher
2 Quoted from Brian Keenan, *Four Quarters of Light*

"I think that in order to establish a normal American life, one has to have a permanent job, speak English, and be open to accepting cultural differences," an alien wife advised her friend in a letter. "This is the other country, with different culture, traditions, and historical roots. In some other countries, like in Japan, for example, the differences will be even more dramatic, so it is impossible to compare one system with another. In order to appreciate the new life, the person has to live — not just to 'survive' — here.

"Relocation to another county is not for everybody. Not everyone can adapt to the new life easy and fast, and before the adaptation takes place, people will have terrible nostalgia about their former lives — the good always is remembered longer than the bad.

"Speaking of differences, Americans are not as wealthy as we traditionally pictured them in Russia, and the structure of expenses here is absolutely different — people pay a lot for housing, medical help, and education. They live very much in a cocoon, without knowing too much about other countries and cultures, thinking that everything in America is so good that it couldn't be any better.

"Life here is more structured and more boring. The values are different. And maybe it seems even more boring in the absence of traditional stresses of daily life in Russia."

Just as one does when making a union with another person, one has to take into consideration both the attractive and the unpleasant features in a new homeland. In that sense, it's really America that alien spouses marry. That alluring, promising, and challenging America.

ACKNOWLEDGEMENTS

I would like to thank my supporters — Kerry and David, Wanda, Blair, Carol, Patrick, Jerry, Jim, Anastasia, Charles, Katrina, Craig... And, of course, my dear Carmen — for everything.

Bibliography

Boccio, Frank Jude, *Mindfulness Yoga*, Pub Group West, 2004

Brzezinski, Zbigniew, *The Choice: Global Domination or Global Leadership*, Basic Books, 2004

Doyle, Laura, *The Surrendered Wife*, Fireside, 2001

Drakulić, Slavenka, *How We Survived Communism and Even Laughed*, HarperPerennial, 1993

Esther Perel, *Mating in Captivity: Reconciling the Erotic and the Domestic*, HarperCollins, 2006

Forward, Dr. Susan and Johan Torres, *Men Who Hate Women & The Women Who Love Them: When Loving Hurts and You Don't Know Why*, Bantam Books, 1987

Gillan, Maria M. and Jennifer Gillan, *Growing Up Ethnic in America*, Penguin Books, 1999

Gonick, Larry, *The Cartoon History of the United States*, Collins, 2005

Gray, John, Ph.D., *Men are From Mars, Women are from Venice A Practical Guide for Improving Communication and Getting What You Want in Your Relationships*, Quill, 2004

Grizzard, Lewis, *It wasn't always easy, but I sure had fun*, Ballantine Books, 1995

Keenan, Brian, *Four Quarters of Light: an Alaskan Journey*, Broadway Books, 2004

King, Florence, *Reflections in a Jaundiced Eye*, St. Martin's Press, 1989

McGraw, Phillip, *Relationship Rescue*, Hyperion Books, 2000

NiCarthy, Ginny and Sue Davidson, *You Can Be Free: An Easy-to-Read Handbook for Abused Women*, Seal Press, 2005

Pipher, Mary, *The Middle of Everywhere*, Harcourt, 2002

Pipher, Mary, *Writing to Change the World*, Riverhead Books, 2006

Romano, Dugan, *Intercultural Marriage: Promises and Pitfalls*, Intercultural Press, 1997

Sykes, Charles J. *A Nation of Victims: The Decay of the American Character*, St. Martin's Press, 1992

Toomre, Joyce, *Classic Russian Cooking, Elena Molokhovets' A Gift to Young Housewives*, Indiana University Press, 1992

Visson, Lynn, *Wedded Strangers*, Hippocrene Books, 1998

Wholey, Dennis, *Are You Happy? Some Answers to the Most Important Questions in Your Life*, Houghton Mifflin, 1986